Infants, Mothers, and Doctors

Infants, Mothers, and Doctors

Eugene B. Gallagher
University of Kentucky

Lexington Books
D.C. Heath and Company
Lexington, Massachusetts
Toronto

Library of Congress Cataloging in Publication Data

Gallagher, Eugene B
    Infants, mothers, and doctors.

    Includes index.
    1. Infant health services—Kentucky—Lexington. 2. Infants—Care and hygiene—Kentucky—Lexington. 3. Maternal health services—Kentucky—Lexington. 4. Family—Kentucky—Lexington. 5. Health surveys—Kentucky—Lexington. 6. Social surveys—Kentucky—Lexington. 7. Lexington, Ky.—Social conditions. I. Title [DNLM: 1. Maternal health services. 2. Infant care. 3. Community health services. 4. Prenatal care. 5. Family. WA310 G162i]
RJ102.5.K4G34   362.8'2   78-2071
ISBN 0-669-02269-1

Published simultaneously in Canada

Printed in the United States of America

International Standard Book Number: 0-669-02269-1

Library of Congress Catalog Card Number: 78-2071

**To my own once-upon-a-time infants—
Susan, Christopher, David, and Robert**

Contents

List of Figure and Tables

Acknowledgments

Many persons helped me in many ways to bring this book to realization.

My interviewers were Billy Allen, Charles Allen, Theodore Beck, Richard Bibb, James Roy Biggs, Mallory Harling, John Lang, Carl Marling, and William Moore. They spent a hot summer of hard work on this project.

The late Helen Fraser, of the Department of Health, Commonwealth of Kentucky, greatly facilitated access for interviews with mothers and physicians in the community. Robert Chamberlin gave wise pediatric advice on interviewing mothers. Garth Olde, with the assistance of Marion Ball, performed many, many data analyses, in the course of which I gradually refined the empirical findings to those that appear here. I was further assisted in data organization and interpretation by Richard Bibb, Beverly Favre, David Novak, and Pat Sims. John Haley gave useful, clear statistical consultation.

For editorial suggestions and bibliographic assistance, I thank Carolyn Bacdayan, Ed Emery, Hugh Fulmer, Carol Gallagher, Ian Shine, and Charlotte Zerof. The following persons typed major portions of successive manuscript drafts: Deborah Cooke, Martha Lancaster, Rita Levitan, Dorothy Manon, Donna Meier, Elaine Meyer, and Tamara Yancey. Ruth Stanton has my special gratitude for her sustained, concentrated typing of the entire final draft. Joanne Ries gave skillful editorial assistance throughout the prolonged closing phases of manuscript preparation. Sharon Accardo assisted in preparing the index. Margaret Zusky, editor at Lexington Books, made excellent suggestions leading to a simpler, more cogent book.

I wish to acknowledge Milo Leavitt, Jr. and Joseph Quinn for enabling me to work on this book during 1975-1976 in the stimulating ambience of the Fogarty International Center at the National Institutes of Health.

My intellectual debt is strong to Michael Banton, Sam Bloom, Ray Elling, Thomas Ford, Renée Fox, Eliot Freidson, Derek Gill, George Godber, August Hollingshead, Douglas Hooper, Sol Levine, Daniel Levinson, David Mechanic, Jerome Myers, Richard Olmstead, Evan Pattishall, Marion Pearsall, Lois Pratt, David Robinson, Margaret Stacey, Robert Straus, and Andrew Twaddle. These mentors helped me through discussion and through their writings on family roles, human development, health services, and community structure. From their work I gained strategic and analytic impetus for the tasks of assembling empirical information and organizing it into a coherent framework.

Many thanks to my wife, Marilyn Milne, for her nourishing encouragement, common sense, keen reading eye, and quick allergic reaction to sociologese masquerading as English. I appreciate her efforts—largely successful—to enlighten an innocent, hapless male investigator on arcane matters such as pregnancy, breast-feeding, and the gainful employment of females, all of great import in these pages.

Infants, Mothers, and Doctors

1 Introduction

This is a sociological study with four focuses. Its first focus is health care, particularly health care of the expectant mother and the infant. Its second focus is the care of young infants. Its third focus is family roles, particularly those of mother, father, and infant. Its fourth focus is the community context of health care, infant care, and the family.

The scene of the study is Lexington, Kentucky, a metropolitan area of 206,000 lying between the South and Midwest. Lexington has many features typical of communities in the United States within the population range 100,000 to 500,000. We believe that the picture of behavior and attitudes to be developed within the covers of this book has sociological value for representing a broad spectrum of contemporary American communities and families.

Society changes over time, as do communities and the values of the people who comprise them. Social changes are real, though perhaps less rapid in their progression and impact than the daily blare of television, newspapers, and magazines would have us believe. The four focuses of the study are at the center of major historical trends and contemporary social forces. We will briefly examine each focus in these terms. This examination will convey the background of interests, ideas, and issues in which the study took root.

1. *Health care.* Health care before the latter part of the nineteenth century was mostly a matter of luck and guesswork, though it may have provided succor and support to those people who obtained it. Its cure rate was unimpressive and it had no rational preventive practice. Because of ignorance and the desire to "do something," it frequently damaged the ill person. A reliable scientific basis, starting around 1880, has given medicine a far greater effectiveness. Adequate health care is now an essential part of modern life.

The institutions and professions that provide formal health care are, however, becoming ever more specialized and complex. Health care is also becoming very expensive in aggregate terms, regardless of how the cost is partitioned among direct family income, insurance, taxes, and Social Security funds. The public seeks, expects, and demands medical care that is competent, convenient, not too expensive, and delivered with compassion. It resists tradeoffs that offer efficiency at the price of depersonalization, or accessibility at the price of lowered competence. Public overexpectation of medicine succumbs quickly to disappointment and estrangement. This cycle has done much to generate the present ambivalent relationship between the public and the health professions.

1

Medical surveillance and health maintenance for adults and children who are in essentially good health pose a set of difficult problems. The accumulation and implementation of biomedical knowledge have generated a series of specialties in the health professions. It is virtually axiomatic that the specialist is not trained in the art and skill of relating to patients, but must rely upon whatever native resources he or she may possess for communication and empathy. The situation is perhaps even worse than that. The specializing health professional who happens to have some talent for relating to the patient may suppress it, on the theory that his highly trained technical expertise is misused if he devotes much time or energy in that direction. Current concepts of rational utilization of health manpower would have it so.

2. *Infant care.* Statistics tell us that the average infant born in the United States today is on a far more secure track for survival into adulthood than was the infant born a century ago. As the challenge of sheer biological survival is surmounted, social and family expectations shift toward an increasing desire that the infant have a favorable development of his or her various potentials. The gradual decline in the birthrate goes hand in hand with a growing parental interest in the quality of infant care. Contemporary parents seek to individualize and perfect the treatment of each child. Precepts from folk wisdom are being displaced by guidance from professional infant-care and child-rearing experts.

The routines of infant care—feeding and clothing the baby, maintaining a comfortable physical environment and a stimulating, supportive socioemotional environment, responding to its developing range of needs and expression—are basically no different now from what they have been through the history of the human species. Mothers and fathers care for their babies, love them, and play with them. Modern technology, however, creates new possibilities and alternatives for carrying out the routines. The sway of cultural values and tastes is also strong, affecting the popularity of alternative ways of meeting infant needs, such as breast or bottle for feeding, permissiveness versus strictness in scheduling of activities, unisex or sex-typed clothing. Modern parents are increasingly knowledgeable about alternatives and they feel responsibility in making choices. We do not yet have an objective science of human development that provides unequivocal answers to the many questions and problems that parents have, but few would dispute the widespread parental interest in acquiring sound orientations and techniques for the tasks of infant care.

The deep concern with good infant care can broadly be seen as part of a growing concern with the quality of life. The biologically dependent, culturally plastic human infant is today's "resource" which, if properly nurtured, will embody and enact desired values in the future, when it is no longer a resource but an autonomous adult carrying out his or her own family and social responsibilities. As industrial societies move toward a plateau in their economic and population growth, there will be an increasing concern with the ways in which infant and child care fit into a model that interrelates the human being and his or her society and physical environment.

This study will contribute to the stock of social information on contemporary infant-care practices. It will also show how patterns of care have changed over time, and it will examine the current context of expert advice on infant care.

3. *Family roles.* Everyone is aware that the contemporary family is undergoing profound changes in its internal dynamics and its anchoring in society. Perhaps it has ever been thus. One can imagine the proto-sociological pundits of medieval times gravely prophesying that the trend away from marriage as a prudent disposition of property and status and toward marriage based upon love and personal commitment would spell the doom of the family "as we know it."

Whatever the changes of the past, great changes are clearly under way at present. The employment of wives and mothers outside the home is significant. This trend affects everything from infant care, one of the most shielded and vital aspects of family life, to the family's economic position and its relation to the external community. The employment of married women can happen only in a commercial, industrial, and service economy which absorbs their skills and energies. It can happen only if women are motivated toward gainful employment and if the cultural repertoire of acceptable female roles includes that of working wife. For his part, the husband has little choice but to continue on as the major family provider. However, his pattern of activities within the family is built up from diverse new possibilities. The Victorian pattern of sex-stereotyped family relationships, dominant in the last century and the early part of this one, is yielding to a more modulated and flexible patterning of relationships and activities.

Infant and child care, as one of the most essential tasks of the family, least able to be shouldered by other institutions, is obviously affected by these trends. Further, the ultimate consolidation of the family unit into the small nuclear family of parents and dependent children, and the concomitant decline of the extended family, have thrust the modern family more than ever upon its own resources of energy, emotional vitality, time, household space, and material supplies in caring for the young.

4. *Community context.* Infant care, health care, and family functioning occur within a local community in which people live and toward which they feel loyalty. As the setting of this study, Lexington well exemplifies this concept. It has been aptly characterized as an "overgrown small town." It has experienced substantial industrial expansion and population growth over the past twenty-five years. Its health-care resources have also increased tremendously, particularly with the establishment of the University of Kentucky Medical Center. Despite the bustle of growth, it is still a community with which its inhabitants, both native and immigrant, identify themselves.

At a basic conceptual level, a community has a physical aspect and a social aspect. In its physical aspect, the community is a deployment of residences economic and cultural facilities, and a transportation-communication network. The social aspect of a community refers to the solidarities and divisions of social groups within it. Personal social characteristics such as socioeconomic level, religious affiliation, and racial status give rise to identified subcommunities or groups which coexist with varying degrees of tension and accommodation.

Health care and family functioning are private, intimate processes which are secluded from the public life of the community. Yet there is a significant interdependence between the private and the public. Many of the forces affecting community structure have consequences that impinge directly upon individuals and families. Compelling historic ideals of the total society, such as human dignity and equality of opportunity, must, if they are ever to be realized, find realization in local communities. With the increasing importance attached to health care in modern society, the access of disadvantaged people to health facilities becomes a civic goal which takes its place alongside improved access to adequate education, housing, and legal protection. Under the general concept that the health of children is an investment in the future, community interest should focus especially upon the health supervision of lower-class infants and children, who may be exposed to greater health hazards and receive less health care than others.

Another set of forces affecting community life is generated by the continuing growth of suburban residential populations at the expense of blighted downtown areas. Lexington has not yet reached a point on the scale of urban growth at which there is a renaissance of apartment-dwellers in the central city. Many families own their own homes. Private home ownership increases the physical separation between place of residence and place of work; it also separates residential location from needed family services such as professional health care. Private family housing also tends to be extravagant of material resources. Much commuting consumes much fuel. The impending need for resource and energy conservation may have implications not only for housing but also for the community distribution of health services. Some health-service organizations, such as hospitals, are highly concentrated in space; physicians' offices, in contrast, tend to be decentralized, though often clumped near middle-class areas. Mounting consumer pressures for more convenient and more equal access to health services point toward the reduction of geographical barriers, economic obstacles, and other restricting factors.

The foregoing delineation of the four focuses of this book gives a general picture of what the reader may expect. We do not intend to startle with astounding new facts, perplex with high-sounding neologisms, or bore with endless statistics. Rather, we intend this study to provide a sound contemporary view of infant care and health care in smaller metropolitan areas of the United States. It may objectify and confirm the personal experience of many readers who have lived in communities like Lexington. We believe that there is a great, increasing need for social documentation of the way we live, for our collective understanding of where we have been and are going, and for the more macroscopic purposes of planning and policy decisions which affect our lives in a centralized, organized manner.

2

Getting the Data: Study Design, Field Procedures, Interviewing

The scientific study of human behavior is no stronger than its methodology. The growth of the contemporary behavioral sciences has occurred through the development of research methodology—the questionnaire, the interview, observational techniques, experimental design, and statistical analysis of data. Strong methodology increases the reliability of research findings and affords a secure basis for interpretation.

The methodology of central interest here is that of the field survey. The data for our study arise from interviews conducted in a sample of households in a community. The study is thus a field survey. If the investigator in a field survey changes the wording of questions, selects respondents in a different way, or uses a different kind of interviewer, the findings of the study may be materially altered.

These considerations have special appositeness to the investigation of health phenomena. Recent decades have seen an increasing popular awareness of health conditions and problems in our society. Attention has focused on the high costs of medical care, on the lack of health resources and personnel in many parts of the nation, on the persistence of preventable diseases such as tuberculosis, on the health needs of the aged, and on many other issues. Although these issues fall within the purview of medicine, the laboratory techniques of the biomedical scientist and the clinical skills of the practicing physician are insufficient to investigate them. Wider efforts are necessary to identify and comprehend these problematic health phenomena. Not infrequently, the requisite research skills and methods fall within the scope of the behavioral sciences. Any systematic investigation requires a uniform framework for the elicitation of data from human beings who may experience ill health and who use (or fail to use) health services. The behavioral sciences can provide tools and strategies in such matters as questionnaire construction, sample selection, interviewer training, statistical analysis of data, and conceptual interpretation of the human behavior delineated by the research findings.

This study will develop an accurate and meaningful picture of prenatal, infant, and family health care in a particular geographic area. This is not an essentially methodological study intended to refine investigatory techniques. Methodology is a means to the end of obtaining data that illuminate our primary domain of

5

inquiry. Nevertheless, in social research as in other human endeavors, results acquire something of the flavor of the means used to obtain them. Our results rest upon a foundation of data-gathering procedures, which we will set forth here.

Setting and Sample

The study was conducted in three Kentucky counties: Fayette, Woodford, and Jessamine. They lie in the east central portion of the state, 80 miles south of Cincinnati, Ohio, 70 miles east of Louisville, Kentucky, and 110 miles west of Huntington, West Virginia. They form the center of the "bluegrass" area of Kentucky, renowned for its lush pastures, white rail fences, and horses. Lexington, the largest city of the area and the base of this study, has long been a trade and service center for the contiguous geographic area and for a much larger region extending deep into eastern Kentucky. Prior to the Second World War, the backbone of the local economy was horse breeding and the raising of burley tobacco. Subsequently, there has been substantial industrialization.

The 1970 Census population of the three counties was 206,187; Woodford County had 14,434 inhabitants, Jessamine had 17,430, and Fayette had 174,323. Woodford and Jessamine counties are rural, with most of the population living on farms and in small nonfarm settlements. Fayette County is highly urbanized, with 93 percent of the population living in Lexington and its environs. The 1970 population of Greater Lexington, comprising the urban part of Fayette County, was 161,711. The rapid population growth of the three-county area can be seen from these figures: the 1960 three-county population total was 157,444; the 1970 figure of 206,187 represents a 31 percent increase over the 1960 figure. The Greater Lexington population increased by 44 percent over the same decade.

The data for the study come from completed household interviews with a 10 percent representative sample of all the live, legitimate births occurring during a ten-month period in the three-county area. Names and addresses of the infant and parents were provided by the Kentucky Division of Vital Statistics. There were 321 infants listed on the roster of births for the sample. The mother of the infant served as the interview respondent. Of possible family respondents, the mother seemed the most uniformly available and also the best-informed respondent for the subject matter of the study.

The Interview Schedule

The interview schedule was designed to provide an orderly elicitation of relevant data bearing upon the major areas of interest in the study. The major categories of information, arranged in sequence of coverage within the interview, were the following:

1. Household composition and residence
2. Social characteristics of mother and father
3. Family economic status
4. Pregnancy
5. Delivery
6. Early development and health problems of the infant
7. Infant and family health care
8. Household facilities

Much of the information asked of the mother was objective or factual, e.g., husband's occupation, source of prenatal care, place of delivery. Some questions were less objective, e.g., whether the infant was a predominantly quiet and undemanding baby, or a crying, demanding baby. Questions concerning the occurrence of various infant health problems—diarrhea, constipation, major illess—also permitted the mother some latitude of response. Other questions were subjective in character, e.g., the mother's predominant emotional affect, positive or negative, during pregnancy.

A paramount consideration in framing the interview schedule was simplicity; the questions should be such that the mothers would be able to answer easily, accurately, and without great conflict or deliberation. Moreover, it was desirable to make the interview process reasonably simple for the interviewers, many of whom lacked previous interviewing experience. Much of the interview direction and process was built into the schedule itself; the interviewer could check off, step by step, the interviewee's responses on the schedule as the interview proceeded.

Another important consideration in designing an interview is that, while obtaining the requisite statement of information, attitudes, and opinions from the interviewee, it should not provoke anxiety. This condition can only be approximated. The interview stiuation is inherently a confrontation of strangers. It is anxiety-arousing in some measure, depending upon the interviewee's degree of security and confidence in strange situations; in this respect, much depends upon the interviewer's skill in creating a relaxed interpersonal atmosphere. The subject matter of the interview may be threatening. It may touch upon topics that are sensitive in society at large or in particular subcultural groups. Perhaps the ideal would be an interviewee who fully grasps the essential impersonality of the interview: his responses, individual and personal to him, will be statistically mingled with those of many others to form a composite, generalized picture of the subject matter under study. On this basis, he could disengage from his anxiety and respond freely. Obviously, interviewees are too human and too involved to assume this detached stance. Interviewers too are subject to their own constraints. It behooves the investigator, then, to keep sensitive questions to a minimum, and, in his role as situation manager, to make as painless as possible those inquiries that pose a threat.

Health is a serious human concern; implicit in it is the basic human fear of pain, disability, and death. Our interview could scarcely find out about the health problems of the infants and mothers without raising anxieties in these directions. Other sensitive areas were touched upon, such as the mother's attitude toward her pregnancy. In the course of the study, we learned that some middle-class mothers had been made quite anxious by questions concerning bathing the baby, for example, how often is it bathed? At the time of framing the questions, few topics seemed more innocuous. In regard to the touchy topic of amount of family income, an expedient way of neutralizing reluctance was employed. The interviewer posed the question about income and then requested the interviewee to check off on a card handed her the income category which fitted her family. This tactic impersonalized the question and placed it under the mother's objective behavioral control.

The Interviewers and Their Training

The interviewing was done by eight male medical students. Seven were University of Kentucky students; of these, two had completed one year of the four-year curriculum, three had completed two years, and two had completed three years. The eighth had recently completed college and entered another medical school when this study was over. The interviewing team was thus composed of young males in the 22 to 25-year age range.

The role of medical students as interviewers in this research can be seen as one instance of a growing trend in medical education toward increased opportunity for learning about health care in a community setting, away from the bureaucratic atmosphere of the teaching hospital and clinics. Through structured curricular programs in fields such as behavioral science and community medicine, and through summer research experiences, medical students currently are learning more about the social context and content of health care than did their counterparts a generation ago.

Work on this study constituted gainful summer employment for these students. The fact that this was a job provided reasonable assurance that they would be motivated to perform their assignments conscientiously. In addition, we supposed, on the strength of their vocational choice, that they had some intrinsic interest in interviewing mothers about infants. The seven University of Kentucky students had completed courses (Human Growth and Development, Society and Health, and Communications and Interviewing) that provided didactic content and case demonstrations of interpersonal relationships, including mother–child relationships. This academic background provided preparation for the interview task and perhaps stimulated the interviewers' personal interest in gathering data on infant care. Further, three of the students were looking ahead to the pediatric clerkship in their third year, while two had recently completed it. One of the latter students remarked that his interviewing experience, which took him into the homes of a cross section of the community, including very poor homes, was "practical pediatrics" in comparison with the clerkship, which occurred entirely in the antiseptic premises of the hospital wards and clinics.

The interviewer team possessed other characteristics that qualified them for their work. The sheer fact of college graduation and medical-school admission guarantees a high level of intelligence. Many of the interviewers had previous experience in selling, both door-to-door and in retail stores; one had worked with many kinds of patients as a hospital orderly; another had been a personnel interviewer in the army. Almost all the interviewers said that they liked to meet people and had little difficulty in relating to strangers.

An intensive, two-week training program prepared the interviewers for field interviewing. During this period they read materials on interview technique, infant health and development, mother–infant relationships, and the social demography and ecology of the three-county area. Medical Center faculty discussed interviewing technique from various disciplinary standpoints: the students met with a social anthropologist, a sociologist, a social psychologist, a child psychiatrist, a pediatrician, and a social demographer. Each student also did a practice interview, using the interview schedule, with a young mother (from among the secretaries in the University of Kentucky Medical Center) in an interaction laboratory. His interviewing performance was observed by the other students in another room through one-way glass; each practice interview was then analyzed and criticized in a group discussion.

During the second week of training, each interviewer conducted six interviews in the field with mothers whose names were on a supplementary list provided by the vital statistics division. These interviews were treated as practice material, the most realistic simulation possible of the interviews upon which the study would be based. The field-practice week also provided opportunity for a final pretesting of the interview schedule.

Starting with the third week and continuing for the next six weeks the interviews for the study were conducted. Throughout this period we closely supervised interviewing progress. Each completed schedule was checked over the same day to be sure that the interview material was fully usable for subsequent coding and data analysis.

Field Procedures

Sending out eight interviewers over a three-county area to interview mothers in 321 households is not a task that can be accomplished by happenstance. Planning is necessary; resources for locating the households must be mobilized; ways of identifying the study to the mothers must be devised. Although the interview process inevitably depends heavily upon the initiative and personal style of the interviewer himself, he needs guidelines to facilitate his ease and effectiveness in relating to the interviewee.

It is a truism to say that the foundation of a study such as this is the interview. But this emphasizes the point that ways must be devised so that interviews may take place and produce valid data. An interview creates a social relationship, but not a natural or spontaneous social relationship. Interviewing as a means of obtaining social data is unknown in many societies. When strangers meet in peasant and preliterate societies, their interaction is directed toward establishing common threads of life experience; the concept of a directed interaction in which one party gives information and the other receives it is absent from the cultural repertoire of relationships. Interviewing in our own society is a relatively recent phenomenon, roughly coincident with the rise of the social sciences. It is the butt of cartoons and criticism in the mass media, particularly insofar as it treads upon the privacy of the individual and the home. This means that an interview study must establish itself on the basis of an appeal to a larger social value with which the interviewee can identify. Here, the mother was appealed to on the basis that her time and effort would be spent in a reasonably satisfying manner, in the service of the worthwhile goal of establishing reliable information on prenatal and infant health care.

Beyond the bare securing of cooperation, it is desirable for the interviewer to convey an intelligible picture of the scope and purpose of the interview; an informed cooperation on the part of the interviewee reduces the likelihood of careless, inaccurate, biased responses. Further, as a matter of good faith, the interviewer should leave the interviewee with a favorable feeling toward the experience as a whole. Seen in these terms, questions concerning the identification of the interviewer, the explanation of the purpose of the interview, and the sponsorship of the study assume critical importance. The approach for creating the optimal interview situation involves many considerations—strategic, tactical, and ethical.

We decided upon a letter as the best way of initially informing the mothers about the study. A letter was sent from the state department of health on official stationery bearing the seal of the Commonwealth of Kentucky and the signature of the medical director of the division of maternal and child health. The letter presented the sponsorship, purpose, and the scope of the study; it stated that a medical student would conduct the interview, and requested the mothers' cooperation. The letters were not sent all at once; rather, each interviewer selected names from his own list at such a pace that he could count upon visiting each household two or three days after the mother received the letter.

The decision to mail an introductory letter was important. The interviewers might have simply appeared on the doorstep, or, for the many households with phones, could have made an advance phone call. This decision was more tactical than strategic: we were strongly disposed to select the general approach that promised to yield the highest rate of interviewee cooperation. We thought that to schedule an interview by phone would run a high risk of rejection; it is easy to say no to a strange voice making a request by phone. If a mother once declined to be interviewed, it seemed unlikely that she would later consent, and any subsequent attempt to win her consent would seem presumptuous and intrusive. Similar considerations applied to a cold-turkey, knock-at-the-door approach. Closing the door on a stranger is not much more difficult than hanging up the phone. On the other hand, we thought an advance letter would serve to prepare the mother and accustom her to the expectation without creating an anticipatory resistance. The letter lent a planned, predictable aspect to the interview. We thought that sponsorship by the state health department, as stated in the letter, would be weighed positively in the balance by most mothers. With this introduction, the arrival of the interviewer in person a day or two after receipt of the letter would be favorably regarded as the timely fulfillment of a projected event.

It was necessary also to devise an initial stance which the interviewer could use for that critical moment when he greeted the prospective interviewee. The interviewers were instructed to identify themselves immediately as medical students and to show employee identification cards issued to them by the state health department. They were to refer to the letter, and if it appeared useful in the situation, to produce their own copy. Then the interviewers were to speak about the general purpose of the study and to provide assurance of the confidentiality of the interview material. We told the interviewers to draw upon the langugage of the letter in explaining the interview. We presumed that most mothers would by then be familiar with its contents. To remind them of it and draw upon it anew would convert the encounter into less of a terra incognita for the mother.

Intuition and sensitivity are important in creating the interview situation. Research is basically a rational process, but many types of social investigation have important adaptive features. On occasion, most of the foregoing procedures were violated. We did at times approach a mother without previous mail notification. This was necessary in those instances when she had no operative mailing address. In some cases, the initial contact was by phone; this was done to reach mothers who were never home during daylight hours. We never interviewed after dark. For a few families who had moved a considerable distance from the three-county area, we phoned or corresponded with the mother and got her cooperation in filling out the interview schedule in that manner.

We sent letters describing the study to postmasters, police chiefs, health departments, local government officials, and the medical societies in the three counties. This was done partly to clear the way for the interviewers; if an anxious mother contacted the police, our letter would provide explanation and legitimacy to the study. Also, local officials helped to locate families. Contact with the medical societies was important because some interview questions dealt with specific sources of health care; in their locally organized capacity, medical practitioners have a strong proprietary interest in investigations touching upon the conduct of medical practice.

Locating the Families

By the time of interview, the infants' ages ranged from 3 to 14 months. We anticipated that many families would have moved during this interim, and that tracking their current addresses would be difficult. National patterns of residential mobility show that approximately one person in every five changes his address during a twelve-month period (U.S. Census Bureau, 1971: 51). The rate is higher among young adults than among older people. In addition to the ordinary high volume of moving among young adults, we had to contend with the circumstance that the arrival of a baby crowds living space and frequently leads to a change of address.

We found that 79 of the 321 families on our list had moved. Families who had moved were sometimes impossible to locate. Moving was a major obstacle to obtaining interviews. In the end, we interviewed 279 of the 321 families; various obstacles, to be discussed below, prevented interviews with the remaining 42 families. Of the 279 interviewed families, 61 (22 percent) had moved; of the 42 noninterviewed, 18 families (43 percent) had moved. This difference in proportions has a chance probability of less than .001.

Differential moving rates for families of different sizes also provide a glimpse into the dynamics of moving as a decision reflecting family circumstances. The tendency to move is appreciably higher for "infant-only" families (those families for which the infant is the first child) than for families where the infant already has older siblings. There were 71 infant-only families; of these, 31 (44 percent) moved. Of the 208 multi-child families, only 30 (14 percent) moved. This difference in percentages has a chance probability of less than .001. Many of the infant-only families were young couples who had recently married and commenced domestic life in small quarters. Some lived in the residence of the wife's or husband's parents. With the advent of a baby, the living space became cramped, physically and psychologically, and the young family moved out. The move was not always immediate; we found that about two thirds (38 of 61) of the moving families moved after the infant was nine months old. (The other third of the families moved when the infant was younger.) This tendency is perhaps due to well-known features of child development: during the second half of the first year, the infant becomes a crawler and an avid space-consumer, adding further to the family feeling of being cramped.

Some families had moved not once but several times since the infant's birth. Every move made more difficult the problem of locating the family. In this task we were immeasurably helped by postal procedures. The initial letter was marked "Do Not Forward—Return to Sender." Obviously, it would do us no good for a letter to be forwarded (to those families who moved and left forwarding addresses) unless we knew the new address. Under the usual postal procedure, the letter would routinely be delivered to the forwarding address. The mother would then be expecting our visit, but we would not know that she had moved. Instead, the letter was returned to us; this told us that a move had occurred. Then a new letter was sent, this time to be fowarded by certified mail; by this procedure, once the letter was delivered at the correct address, a card was sent us designating that address. Thus the mother was informed of the imminent visit, and we knew where to visit her.

Postal procedures were of no avail for families who left no forwarding address. In such an event the letter was delivered, neither the post office nor ourselves realizing that the family had left. Only when the interviewer appeared at the former address did he learn of the move. At this point, his ingenuity and resourcefulness came into play. This part of the study was the "bloodhound" aspect; some of the interviewers were keen trackers. To these specialists went the toughest cases.

There were other reasons than residential mobility for the lost trails and dead ends. Sometimes the address as given on the original listing was incorrect; no such family had ever lived at the address. Sometimes the address did not exist, there was no dwelling unit at the given street number or else it had existed but was subsequently demolished, or the street itself never, or no longer, existed. Whatever the difficulties in locating urban addresses, rural addresses were on the whole harder to find. Fifteen percent of the households were rural. The residence was identified only by a road name or mail delivery route, which might be ten to twenty miles long through open countryside. Here again the post office was helpful; the rural carrier could in most instances identify the mother's name and give the interviewer explicit instructions by reference to bridges, cemeteries, and other landmarks for locating the residence, which in the more difficult instances lay far back from the road.

The Interview Process

The interviewers sometimes approach their task diffidently, apprehensive lest they impose upon the interviewee's time, privacy, or goodwill. This tendency has been enhanced by recent concern in professional journals, in the mass media, and in legal forums about the ethical aspects of social-psychological experiments that employ deception, the use of anthropologists as intelligence agents in underdeveloped countries, and the more exploitive features of public-opinion interviewing. There are serious issues at stake, such as the proper way to seek consent for participation, how to maintain privacy for the participants, and how to safeguard the rights of institutionalized and dependent participants. The behavioral sciences have for far too long ignored these issues. At the same time, we suggest that being interviewed can be a benign and pleasurable process for the interviewee, an interpersonal transaction that, negatively, imposes little strain, and positively, affords emotional satisfactions.

The overall impact of the interview obviously depends upon many factors, some unique to the style of the interviewer, others stemming more generally from the content of the interview and the structure of the situation. Common to all interview situations is the opportunity it affords the interviewee to be listened to. In our case, the mother could legitimately claim the interviewer's attention. While the interviewer oriented the mother to the areas of interview interest and posed specific questions, his activity was merely the staging of the interview. The essential purpose of the interview was to create a flow of information and attitudes on infant care from mother to interviewer. In this process, she received and he provided attention. Another positive feature of the interview was that, unlike public-opinion and market-research interviews, it solicited the mother's knowledge concerning a subject on which she was a unique and indisputable expert—her baby. All mothers are experts on their own babies; to most, the occasion for serving as expert witness is gratifying. While she might trade notes with other mothers on the development and management of babies, here was an occasion unconstrained by the ordinary social disciplines and reciprocities; she need not pay attention in order to gain attention. Indeed, given the interview subject and situation, some mothers tended to unbend and discourse at length, pressing the content beyond the limits of the schedule.

Every mother knew that her interview was part of a larger study, that it was one interview among many. This fact, if sufficiently absorbed by the mother, might have created a sense of detachment or distance vis-à-vis the interview; instead of deriving stimulus for the interview from her involvement with the baby, she might disconnect on account of it. Yet the predominant tendency was for the mother to enter fully and responsively into the interview. As a counterpoint to concern about exploiting the interviewee, it may be observed that the mothers were to an extent able to use the situation for their own satisfaction. The word "plight" frequently crops up in public and mass-media discussions of the life situation of the contemporary mother of young children: the mother is harassed by the manifold tasks of infant care, by the demands of older children, and by household chores. It is not too farfetched to suggest that however brief and circumscribed the encounter, many mothers assimilated the presence of the interviewer to their own unmet daily needs for expression to another adult.

The identification of the interviewer as a medical student posed another set of considerations which affected the give-and-take of the interview. Education and learning are highly valued in our society; the student or learner is favorably regarded. At the same time, he is recognized as a novice, an inexperienced, incomplete version of the seasoned practitioner. The perceptual accent varies with the beholder. Lower-class persons, whose educational background is limited, may regard students as possessing considerable skill and knowledge; they are probably inclined to minimize the difference between the student and the mature professional. Middle-class persons, by contrast, are more knowing concerning professional qualifications and less likely to perceive the student as highly competent. These several considerations take on additional meanings in relation to the medical label. Medicine has high prestige in the public eye; to maximize public acceptance of the interviewers, a household survey could scarcely employ a better social category than medical students. But the obvious problem posed for the conduct of the interview was that mothers might solicit advice about infant or family health problems. We viewed this as an undesirable contingency, not only because it might easily lead to the students' being confronted with requests far beyond their professional depth, but also because it might by degrees distort and reverse the interpersonal situation from one in which the mother, with her knowledge and attitudes concerning the care of her infant, was the main resource–provider, into a very different schema in which the interviewer, as student physician, was expected to provide advice or service.

During the training period, the interviewers anticipated and discussed various difficulties that might arise in this direction and the reasonable responses the interviewer might make to the mothers' requests. In regard to the deliberate assumption of an authority role by the interviewers, we felt that the formidable nature of medical-school training would exert a strong inhibition upon any inappropriate posture vis-à-vis the mothers. Few kinds of professional students are made so thoroughly aware of their lack of expertise as are undergraduate medical students. At the same time, the students expected that they would be regarded as authorities by many mothers. Most of the interviewers reported that some mothers did seek advice or help. They usually dealt with these requests in a mild and nonfrustrating manner, by suggesting that the mother ask a physician (or public health nurse) for professional advice.

The mothers received a small reward for serving as interviewees: each was given a copy of the U.S. Children's Bureau publication *Infant Care,* a widely distributed booklet containing practical advice on many aspects of infant care. Also, the interviewers told the mothers that a summary report of the study would be prepared and mailed to those interested. A large majority indicated interest. Subsequently, under auspices of the state department of health, a five-page report was mailed to all the mothers, whether or not they had expressed interest. It presented in simple terms some of the major findings of the study. The report was intended by us as an appropriate courtesy that gave each mother the sense that she was an essential piece in an overall picture.

The Incompletes

As noted earlier, interviews were completed in 279, or 87 percent, of the 321 target households. The remaining 42 were the "incompletes" which appear in any such field study. We categorized the incompletes into seven groups by cause of occurrence. They are as follows:

Cause	Number
1. Infant deceased	1
2. Address as stated on birth certificate did not exist	2
3. Family unknown at stated address	9
4. Family moved and left no address	18
5. Address correct but no one home (on repeated attempts)	4
6. Interview completed, but interviewer lost the data	3
7. Mother refused interview	5
Total	42

From this it may be seen that the majority of incompletes were due in one way or another to failure to locate the family. The whole array of tracing devices described above was employed, but ultimately to no avail.

Did these incompletes, in the aggregate, bias the sample obtained or prejudice the major findings or conclusions of the study? This question cannot be answered definitely, because so little information was available on the incompletes. With regard to family characteristics, the incompletes and completed interviews both had approximately the same proportion of only-child and multi-child families. Even though, as we have seen, the only-child families were more likely to have moved, their migration did not reduce the chance of an eventual interview. There was no difference between the proportion of completes and incompletes residing in urban, as compared with rural, areas. However, one trend was apparent regarding those families residing in the Lexington metropolitan area, who were much the greater part of the whole study. A map plot of current (or last known) addresses for both completes and incompletes in Lexington revealed that the incompletes included a higher proportion who lived in or near the center of the city. Most residences in the downtown area were in poorer condition and in less desirable neighborhoods than residences in the peripheral and suburban areas. We suppose that the 42 incomplete interviews contained a higher proportion of socioeconomically disadvantaged families than did the 279 completed interviews. Such a skewing is the general tendency of field surveys. The U.S. Census, which attempts to make a complete population enumeration, finds many obstacles in poor neighborhoods.

The main implication for the interpretation of our findings is this: Insofar as the study is a descriptive, fact-finding study, it may underestimate the frequency of those health conditions, infant-care patterns, and family constellations that have particular association with low socioeconomic status. However, the descriptive aim of the study is subsidiary to the aim of analyzing various features of infant and family health care in relation to their social context. Considered in the light of this main purpose, bias in the distribution of incomplete interviews would not seriously affect the validity of our findings.

3 Social Class, Family, and Household

A major aim throughout this study will be to investigate the relationship of social status to health behavior, infant care, and family functioning. Social status is a basic phenomenon which has long engaged the attention of social scientists. The division of society into social strata and the consequent determination of the economic chances of individuals have stimulated much sociological inquiry and many sociopolitical reform programs to reduce or eliminate social inequality. As knowledge of the nature of social status accumulates, it becomes increasingly clear that one's status in society has many consequences in addition to direct economic effects. High-status individuals not only eat better and live in nicer houses than lower-status individuals, but they also talk differently and have different sexual styles, different religious beliefs, and different child-rearing practices. A high-status man is not simply a low-status man with money added. Some differences among the classes, such as housing quality, are directly related to wealth and economic level; others have no direct connection with economic level.

We will in this study pursue the differences that high and low status make in many aspects of individual and family functioning. For example, who participates more in the daily routines of infant care, higher-class fathers or lower-class fathers? How does social status affect the medical care of the mother during pregnancy? In subsequent chapters, our substantive interest in pregnancy, daily care of the infant, and health care will be identified more fully and then related to social status. Preliminary to that, we will set forth in this chapter the way in which we conceptualize and measure status, and then describe the sample in terms of social status. We will also describe the sample in terms of family and household characteristics as a background for later findings and interpretations concerning infant care. A major portion of the interview was devoted to information on the infant's family: its size and composition, its income level, its housing and household facilities, and social characteristics of the infant's mother and father.

The question of the influence of social class on infant care falls within the larger questions of how the infant is socialized and how the family brings emotional, material, and social resources to bear upon its care. The human being at birth is a physical organism, but not a social person. For biological survival and personal development, it depends upon a favorable socioenvironmental matrix. During the early years, this matrix is constituted almost entirely by the family. The infant's earliest needs for nourishment, protection, and love are fulfilled

17

entirely within the family setting, with the mother typically playing the most important part. The household, as the physical environment of the family, provides living space and essential material facilities.

The influence of the family is manifest in other significant ways. As the growing child ventures into a wider, extra-familial community, he is at first identified as a member of his family rather than in terms of his personal qualities. He is viewed in the light of the social status, or standing, of his family. Sociologists speak of "status ascription" as a primary function of the family. From the start, the infant's life-chances are given direction and limits by the status of his family.

The Concept of Social Status

Social status is an ubiquitous force in society, and social scientists have devoted much attention to it. Yet there are many features of status that are ambiguous and subtle. Since the analysis of the effects of status will be a major task in this study, we will consider in detail the notion of status used here.

The force of social status perhaps derives ultimately from the circumstance, familiar in all societies and communities, that people evaluate each other in terms of personal qualities, material possessions, achievements, and many other attributes that are commonly regarded as desirable or undesirable. In assessing a person's social status, we take into account a wide variety of such attributes, and from this arrive at an overall sense of his position on a scale of social value. Societies vary in the weight they accord to various attributes. In a farming community, amount of land owned is critical, as is one's connection with powerful kin groups; in urban, industrial societies, educational and occupational attainment are important; in religiously oriented societies, such as medieval Europe and India, piety and spiritual devotion receive recognition. It is a fundamental feature of status that individuals in the same society tend to rank others in a similar fashion—to give prominence to the same criteria and to show substantial agreement in placing others on a social scale.

We have discussed status thus far in purely individual terms: In a given society, which emphasizes certain qualities, individual A has a status that is higher than, lower than, or equal to that of individual B. This formulation must, however, be qualified to take into account the biological organization of the sexes and generations into family groups. The family is a basic social unit with ties of descent and marriage. In the eyes of the community, it is a homogenous social unit, its members having equal status. For members of the same family to have unequal status would be a disruptive state of affairs; unequal intra-family status would create a set of centrifugal forces subversive of interpersonal solidarity within the family. Significantly, none of the current models for liberalization of marital and family relationships seizes upon this basic feature as a point for reform.

A further extension of the status concept is the notion of social class. The unit element of a social class is a family, rather than an individual. A social class is composed of families of equivalent social status in the community. In this study, we shall characterize the families of the infants in terms of social-class position. The composition of the family so characterized is, in most instances, mother, father, infant, and older siblings of the infant. This is the so-called nuclear family of parents and immature children sharing a common residence, which has come to be the predominant family type in the United States. There are in our sample some exceptions to this norm. Some households contain three generations, and some contain adult aunts and uncles of the infant. For purposes of social-class analysis, we treat the nuclear family as the social unit to be categorized by class.

The social status of the families is assessed according to the methodology of the Hollingshead "Two Factor Index of Social Position" (1957). This scheme, a familiar instrument in social research, was devised by Hollingshead and associates at Yale University for use in studies of mental illness and social class in metropolitan New Haven (Hollingshead and Redlich, 1958; Myers and Bean, 1968). The index bases social status upon characteristics of the head of the family, which in the usual case is the husband-father. This is consonant with the fact that in urban, industrial societies family status is determined chiefly by the occupational activities of the husband, usually conducted outside the home.

The index uses the level of social prestige accorded his occupation and his level of educational attainment. Occupation is assigned a numerical score of 1 to 7, determined by reference to a comprehensive list of occupations at all status levels. The most prestigious occupations receive a score of 1, the least prestigious a score of 7. Major professionals such as lawyers, professors, and physicians are scored 1, as are owners of large businesses and major business executives. Lesser professionals, proprietors of smaller businesses, and lower executives, administrative personnel, and other white-collar workers receive an occupational score of 2 to 4. Skilled manual employees such as electricians and machinists are scored 5; semiskilled workers are scored 6; and unskilled or transient workers are scored 7. Educational attainment is similarly scored 1 to 7. A family head with less than seven years of school is scored 7; a high-school graduate is scored 4; a college graduate is scored 2, and a person with a post graduate degree is scored 1.

After these two scores are determined, education is weighted by a factor of 4 and occupation by 7. These weighted scores are combined to give the family's placement on the Index of Social Position. The weighting of 4:7 was determined, in the original derivation of the two-factor index, by a multiple correlation procedure so as to produce a quantitative score for a series of families which would most closely match qualitative social judgments made by residents of metropolitan New Haven concerning the social status of those families. The Index of Social Position (ISP) ranges from 11, the position of highest status, to 77, the position of lowest status.

The family's ISP score is then used to assign it to a social class. Five social classes are represented in the Hollingshead system. The index scores associated with the social classes are as follows:

Social Class	Range of Index Scores
I	11–17
II	18–27
III	28–43
IV	44–60
V	61–77

Hollingshead (1957) interprets the assignment of families to classes as follows: "When the *Two Factor Index of Social Position* is relied upon to determine class status, differences in individual scores within a specified range are ignored, and the scores within the range are treated as a unit. This procedure assumes there are meaningful differences between the score groups. Individuals and nuclear families with scores that fall into a segment of the range of scores assigned to a particular class are presumed to belong to the class the *Two Factor Index of Social Position* score predicts for it."

Social class within a community is a strong and pervasive factor affecting family and personal behavior in many ways. While systematic measurement undeniably has artificial aspects, these can be accepted for the sake of delineating the larger phenomenon of class and its effects.

How do we conceptualize the effect of social class or status? This question will be dealt with primarily in the context of specific findings. Here a few preliminary comments are appropriate. First, for our purposes, social class is always an independent variable and never a dependent variable. Many of the findings concern aspects of infant care. The infant's social status is purely derivative from that of his family, the infant itself obviously having done nothing to raise or lower it. Other findings deal with health behavior of the family and with the household; there is little basis for believing that the family's class position is created or altered by the behavior set forth in the findings.

Our second comment deals with the mode of class action: If families at a given class level possess a certain distinctive characteristic, why is this so? What in the nature of class position disposes families to behave or feel in this manner? These questions remind us of the pervasiveness and many-sidedness of social-class influence. In part, a social class is a reference group. Friendships and cliques tend to be intra-class. One's aspirations and standards of comparison derive from, and extend to, others of similar status level. What a person thinks and does in regard to style of dress, educational goals, use of health resources, housing, and many other aspects of life depends upon class-related notions of appropriate behavior. Social class is a major source of values that regulate behavior and attitudes.

Another mode of class influence comes from the differential wealth and income of social classes. With greater buying power, upper-class and upper-middle-class families can purchase goods and services that would strain the resources of lower-class families. Financial pressure is obviously greatest when a lower-class family's values dispose it to want something it cannot afford. But families with limited resources may adapt to their circumstances without an acute sense of deprivation. Many poor families do not avail themselves of services and benefits that are available to the general public through legislative provision and tax moneys; for example, some eligible poor people do not attempt to qualify for federal food stamps or assistance in residential relocation, whether from pride, lack of information, or for some other reason.

The contemporary sweep of health consciousness through all segments of society has made poor people more desirous of receiving good health care. When we examine the infant-care patterns and health practices at various class levels, we shall consider the question of how far different values, and how far differential resources, can account for class differences.

Social Class and Residential Location of the Families

The 279 families in the sample have the social-class distribution set forth in Table 3-1. These class levels can be described in relation to major economic and social features of the metropolitan Lexington area, and in relation to locally prevailing conceptions of status and strata.

We observe that Class I, 10 percent of the sample, includes upper-class elements plus much of the upper middle class. The traditional upper class of the bluegrass area—the wealthy, landowning, "horse" families—has few representatives in the sample. Most Class I families in the sample base their status not on agricultural holdings but upon the high occupational status of the breadwinner. The sample includes, for example, eight families where the father is a physician.

Class II covers the lesser professionals and medium-level business positions, going to the lower ranges of the upper middle class. The Lexington area has been the scene within the past decade of a large influx of technical and professional personnel, especially in the health and electronics fields. Many of the families participating in this general trend are relatively young, in the child-bearing phase, and thus appear in the sample. Many of them are in Class II.

Classes III and IV together are the "common man" stratum in urban populations—clerical employees, skilled and semiskilled factory workers, firemen, police, and postal employees. This stratum comprises 50 percent of the sample. Considered in relation to other urban areas, this figure is probably too low, largely because Lexington is relatively deficient in mass-production industry for an urban area of its size. Its occupational structure has a gap, rather than a bulge, at the level of factory operatives.

Table 3-1
Distribution of Families by Social Class

Social Class	Number of Families	Percentage of Total
I	28	10
II	32	11
III	64	23
IV	75	27
V	80	29
Total	279	100

Finally, Class V, the lower class, includes 29 percent of the sample. This component is relatively high. It includes many of the rural families in the sample, whose breadwinners are employed in menial positions as grooms on the horse farms, or as tenant farmers.

By residence, 85 percent of the families live in Fayette County, which is highly urbanized. Seven percent reside in Jessamine County, and the remaining 8 percent in Woodford County. As we shall subsequently see, the fact of urban or rural residence is in general a more important distinction than the actual county of residence. Nevertheless, the political or county jurisdiction is relevant to the use of certain health services, such as tax-subsidized hospitals.

Income

Another important family characteristic, closely related to class position, is income. The income figures obtained for this study include all sources of income—wages and salaries received by all family members, interest and dividends, Social Security and welfare sources, and other forms of income. The interviewers were trained to help the mother to compile an annual income figure, if she could not readily supply it.

Table 3-2 shows class-income relationships that will bear importantly upon later analyses of family health behavior. The obvious pattern, scarcely unexpected, is that class and income are covariant: higher-status families have, to a statistically significant degree, higher incomes. But we cannot read off a family's status simply from knowledge of its income position. Sociologists frequently regard occupational status, educational attainment, and housing quality as better predictors of status than income. In its influence upon behavior, money facilitates, but does not demand or determine. Kahl and Davis (1955) state: "Observation suggests that the core of status is a culturally defined, group-shared style of life, and income is a necessary but not a sufficient condition thereof. Values intervene between the receipt of a paycheck and its expenditure in conspicuous consumption." These considerations apply with special force in

Table 3–2
Mean Annual Family Income by Social Class (1971 Dollars)

Social Class	Mean Annual Income	Standard Deviation	N
I	$17,337	$9,331	28
II	12,008	8,860	32
III	7,155	3,153	64
IV	6,882	2,686	75
V	4,150	2,080	80
Total	$ 7,799	$6,162	279

Analysis of variance: F-Ratio = 46.52
Degrees of Freedom = 4,274
$p < .001$

the very populous Class III and IV zone of the sample. The income differential between Classes III and IV is not large, but the variation in income within each class is appreciable, as indicated by the standard deviations. Thus many Class IV families enjoy a somewhat higher standard of living than many Class III families. In accounting for findings that differentiate these classes, we shall rely upon values and attitudes, as well as purchasing power.

How is the family income obtained? Ninety-one percent of the families depend primarily upon the husband's occupational earnings. Although one sixth of the wives work, in only 6 percent of the families is the wife's income equal to or greater than the husband's. Many of these families are student families, wherein the husband-student holds either a part-time job or none at all. A small number of families, again primarily student families, receive most of their income from outside sources, such as in-laws or federal programs for veterans.

Race

In thirty-two families—11 percent of the sample—the mother is black; in every such family, the father is also black. There are no other nonwhite families. In comparison, the three-county population is 13 percent nonwhite. Since blacks comprise 97 percent of the nonwhite population in the area, there is substantial equivalence between the two categories, black and nonwhite.

Racial characteristics of the sample are important for gross descriptive purposes, and as a potential factor influencing infant care, family roles, and health behavior. We will see below that the black families as a group differed from the white families in several aspects of health care. Any analysis of differences between blacks and whites must reckon with the fact that blacks as a segment of the population suffer from low social status and general socio-economic disadvantage. Not surprisingly, the social-class position of the blacks in our sample was well below that of the whites. (Detailed data is presented in Table 4-13.)

Family Size and Composition

Sociologists call the typical family form in modern society the "nuclear" family. It consists of mother, father, and dependent children ("dependent" in the context of our research refers to the normal material, social, and psychological attachment of the young to their parents and home environment until they are roughly 18 years of age). The nuclear family is a minimal intact, marriage and reproduction unit; it is highly compatible with the demands of urban, industrial society. Its economic support comes from gainful employment of the husband-breadwinner in a nonfamily occupation, supplemented increasingly by the wife's work. It has no stake in land or productive capital. It is geographically mobile. Nuclear families are the most common form in the urban areas of highly industrialized societies. They are less common in nonindustrial societies and in rural areas.

The family form that contrasts with the nuclear family is the extended family. There is no single type of extended family, but rather a complex series of types, documented and analyzed in detail by social anthropologists. Different forms of kinship recognition give rise to widely varying kinds of extended-family composition. Always, however, the extended family includes kinsmen in addition to those of the nuclear family. The three-generation family, one of the more common forms of extended family, brings together into one household grandparents, one (or more) of their children and that child's spouse, and that couple's children.

In speaking of the nuclear family, or the extended family, as being the typical form for a given society, we mean not only that it numerically predominates, but also that in the values and sentiments of people concerning human relationships, it is the "right," or most desirable, family form. In our society, many young people who live with their parents until marriage soon establish a new household physically separate from their parental homes. The effort and expense expended in this endeavor reveal the value placed upon it; the independence, privacy, and convenience of the young couple are paramount considerations. Societies such as the classical Chinese stressed filial piety and idealized the large extended family headed by a patriarch. But most preindustrial societies had relatively few families that actually exemplified this cultural ideal.

Many factors combine to determine the composition of families included in any empirical study. There are many variations around the predominant type. Nuclear families may be broken by death or divorce. A nuclear family may be enlarged by the addition of an elderly parent who would otherwise live alone or in a nursing home; to the participants, such an arrangement might not be ideal, but under the circumstances it is acceptable and preferable to the alternatives. In the light of these considerations, what kind of family does the sample depict?

Every household includes, at the minimum, the infant and its mother. In ten families, the father is absent. One father is deceased, two are on military duty, and seven are separated from their wives. No Class I, II, or III fathers are absent; of the ten, three are from Class IV (comprising 4 percent of Class IV) and seven are from Class V (9 percent of Class V).

The average infant age at the time of interview was nine months. Given the general rates of divorce and separation in our society, any longer-term follow-up study of this sample would, we expect, reveal a number of divorces and additional separations.

Household size ranges from 3 to 14, with the distribution as given in Table 3-3. The median size is 4.3; the mean size is 5.1, with a standard deviation of 1.9. The three-person households are composed for the most part of mother, father, and infant. Most of the larger households include older children in addition to the study-infant.

Table 3-4 shows the distribution of household size by social class. It shows that in Class I, 21 percent of the households contain three persons, 25 percent of the households contain four persons, and so on. Lower-class households are, to a statistically significant degree, larger than higher-class households. Particularly noteworthy is the relatively high proportion of large households in the lowest class; 34 percent of the Class V households have seven or more members. If we compare Class V with all other classes combined, it stands in statistically significant contrast. In other words, much of the class variation in household size is due to the special contribution of the lowest class.

Variation in total household size, for purposes of this analysis, may be regarded as having two components: (1) differing numbers of children, and

Table 3-3
Distribution of Household Size: Number of Persons in the Household

Household Size	N	Percentage
3	54	19
4	65	23
5	68	24
6	38	14
7-9	48	17
10-14	6	2
Total	279	99

Table 3–4
Percentage of Households of Given Size, by Social Class

	Number in Household					
Social Class	3	4	5	6	7–14	Total N
I	21	25	43	4	7	28 (100%)
II	28	28	16	12	16	32 (100%)
III	33	22	19	14	12	64 (100%)
IV	12	35	27	11	16	75 (101%)
V	11	11	24	20	34	80 (100%)
Total	19	23	24	14	19	279 (99%)

Chi^2: Household size by Social class = 45.59
D.F. = 16, $p < .001$
Chi^2: Household size by social class
    Classes I–IV combined versus Class V = 26.17
D.F. = 4, $p < .001$

(b) differing numbers of adults. These sources of variation are closely connected with the notion of nuclear and extended families. The only way in which a nuclear family can vary in size is in terms of number of children, since by definition it consists of mother, father, and their offspring. Extended families may also vary in the number of adults; that is, parents of either the infant's mother or father are present, plus possible collateral relatives and in-laws. To understand the variation in household size, we must examine household composition in the foregoing terms.

First, we shall look at the number of children in each family. To obtain this data, we found out how many children are "associated with" each mother. The term "associated with" covers all children in the household who were under the mother's care. The usual case, of course, is limited to those children who are biologically the mother's own. In addition, "associated with" covers the occasional adopted or foster child, and several children who entered a family from an earlier marriage of the father. The 279 mothers have a total of 770 children associated with them—an average of 2.8 per mother.

Approaching the question of number of children from a different direction, we may ask how many siblings the study-infants have. The 279 study-infants must be subtracted from the 770 total, leaving 491 siblings. At the time of birth, 71 of the study-infants were the first and only children in their family; during the interim between birth and the interview with the mother, two of these infants acquired younger siblings. If we address our question to the situation at time of birth, we can then say that of the 279 infants, 71 are first births and only children; the other 208 infants have a total of 489 siblings (491 minus the two born subsequently), or an average of 2.4 per infant.

Table 3-5 shows the relationship between social class and number of children in the household—the same as the number of children associated with the mother. It includes the 279 study-infants (plus the two younger siblings mentioned above). The first column contains all the infants (N=69) with no siblings. The second column contains all the infants with one sibling, and so on for the remaining columns.

It can be seen that Class III has the highest proportion—38 percent—of "infant-only" families. Class I has a very low proportion (11 percent) of families with four or more children; Class V stands out clearly as having the highest proportion of these families. Also, only 41 percent of Class V families have one or two children. The statistical analysis of this table shows first that the overall association between class and number of children is statistically significant. Although Class V occupies a unique position, as seen in Table 3-4, in terms of total household size, it appears to be less different in terms of number of children. Comparing Class V with the combined other classes in Table 3-5 does not produce a significant chi-square value.

The mean number of associated children per household in each class is: Class 1, 2.6 children per household; Class II, 2.6; Class III, 2.4; Class IV, 2.8; Class V, 3.2. Class V has the highest number and proportion of households containing a child who is not the offspring of either the mother or the father. Sixteen families have one or more such children; of these sixteen, twelve are Class V families. These children are, in the main, younger brothers and sisters of the mother. That is, the mother and her husband and infant live in her parents' household; and these "unassociated" children are the children of her own parents. In a few instances, however, the unassociated children are nieces and

Table 3-5
Percentage of Households With Given Number of Children, by Social Class

Social Class	Number of Children				
	1	2	3	4-12	Total (N)
I	21	29	39	11	28 (100%)
II	31	31	13	25	32 (100%)
III	38	23	16	23	64 (100%)
IV	16	33	28	23	75 (100%)
V	21	20	23	36	80 (100%)
Total	25	27	23	26	279 (101%)

Chi^2: Children in household by social class = 24.09
D.F. = 12, $p < .05$
Chi^2: Children in household by social class
     Classes I–IV combined versus class V = 7.10
D.F. = 3, $p \not< .05$

nephews of the mother, the children of the mother's or father's sibling, whose family also shares the household.

Three-Generation Families

Let us now consider the household in terms of the adults present. The phenomenon of the three-generation family is significant in this regard. The three-generation family includes an older generation of grandparents, an intermediate generation of parents, and a new generation of grandchildren. The study-infant belongs to the latter generation. The sample contains 26 such families.

We may inquire further into the composition of the three-generation families, with a focus upon the tie between the generation of parents and grandparents. The kinship structure of our society favors neither the patrilineal nor the matrilineal line of descent. Although surnames pass along the male line, virtually all other practices associated with kinship are symmetrically bilateral. Our kinship terminology does not distinguish cousins, aunts, uncles, in-laws, or grandparents on the mother's side from those on the father's side. Likewise, no such distinction appears in family law dealing with minors, incest, inheritance, intestacy, and the like.

Students of the American family note, however, that along with a formal bilateral symmetry of kinship, there are empirical tendencies toward informal matrilineal ties between the generations. Sweetser (1966) believes that industrial society favors ties between a mother and her grown daughters. With the decline of rural society, the basis for father-son cooperation, in farming and other economic enterprises, dwindles. In the wake of this, a kindredness of mothers and daughters persists. Parsons (1954: 185) notes a similar tendency, though he sees it primarily as a deviant tendency found in lower-class families: "There is evidence that in lower class situations, in different ways both rural and urban, there is another type of deviance from this main kinship pattern. This type is connected with a strong tendency to instability of marriage and a 'mother-centered' type of family structure—found both in Negro and white population elements."

Parsons' invocation of social class as a factor affecting family structure finds support in contemporary discussion of poverty phenomena. Moynihan (1965) and Weller (1965), writing on poverty groups as diverse as urban blacks and rural Appalachian whites, both emphasize the "mother-centered" feature of the family structure. For a variety of reasons, the father tends to be absent or uninfluential, and those intergenerational ties that survive between adults and their grown children tend to be mainly on the mother's side.

In the light of these perspectives, we investigated the composition of the three-generation families in our sample. We found that at least one maternal grandparent is present in 17 of these families and at least one paternal grandparent in the other nine. On a null hypothesis that 13 of the 26 families would have maternal grandparents present, and 13 paternal, the data have a chi-square value of 1.88, with a chance probability of less than .20. While this is not a high significance level, it indicates a trend consistent with other family studies.

Table 3-6 presents data on the class distribution of these families. The lower-class bias is immediately apparent. Class V's share is so large that compared with Classes I to IV combined, it alone is statistically significant. Table 3-6 also examines the composition of those three-generation families found at each class level. It shows that a matrilineal bias is especially strong in Class V. In that class, there are 15 three-generation families. We may subtract from this number one family where the study-infant has a nephew, rather than a grandparent, present. This family appears as one of the 15 three-generation families which together constitute 18.8 percent of all Class V families, shown in the left side of the table; it is not, however, represented in the portions of the table that extend to the right, because as previously noted, this study-infant does not have a grandparent present in the household.

Among the remaining 14 Class V families, eight have both maternal grandparents present. Three others have a maternal grandmother present without her spouse; one other has a maternal grandfather present without his spouse. On the paternal side, two grandmothers are present without spouses. Thus, among these fourteen families maternal grandparents are represented in twelve cases, and paternal in only two.

Further study of Table 3-6 reveals that a more even balance exists between the maternal and paternal sides at the class levels above Class V. Of the five Class IV families, two have maternal grandparents and three have paternal grandparents present. Of the five Class III families, three contain maternal grandparents, and two contain paternal grandparents. In Class II, there are no maternal grandparents; one of the two three-generation families in this class contains a paternal grandparent couple, and the other contains the paternal grandmother without her spouse.

Three-generation families can arise from three distinct situations. First, a young couple after marriage may reside in the home of the parents of either the wife or the husband. In this situation, one member of the couple moves in to an established household, as an outsider entering the family of procreation of his or her spouse. Such an arrangement is culturally prescribed and relatively permanent. The extended-family system of traditional China is a good example; it provided a family home through many generations and an enhancement of the family line as a strong cultural principle. In the second situation, a young couple, too poor or too inexperienced to establish an independent household, resides in the household of the husband's or wife's parents. While this situation is structurally similar to the first, its meaning is quite different: the joint residence is viewed not as a valid family principle but as a temporary expedient, to be ended whenever the young couple can establish itself independently. In the third

Table 3-6
Three-Generation Household Composition and Social Class

Social Class (N)	Three-Generation Household		Maternal Side						Paternal Side					
			Grandmother Present		Grandfather Present		Both Present		Grandmother Present		Grandfather Present		Both Present	
	N	% of Class	N	% in Class	N	% in Class	N	% in Class	N	% in Class	N	% in Class	N	% in Class
I (28)	0	0.0	0	0.0	0	0.0	0	0.0	0	0.0	0	0.0	0	0.0
II (32)	2	6.3	0	0.0	0	0.0	0	0.0	2	22.2	1	16.7	1	16.7
III (64)	5	7.8	3	18.8	1	8.3	1	9.1	2	22.2	2	33.3	2	33.3
IV (75)	5	6.7	2	12.5	2	16.7	2	18.2	3	33.3	3	50.0	3	50.0
V (80)	15	18.8	11	68.7	9	75.0	8	72.7	2	22.2	0	0.0	0	0.0
Total (279)	27	9.7	16	100.0	12	100.0	11	100.0	9	99.9	6	100.0	6	100.0

Chi^2: Three-generation household by social class = 12.01
D.F. = 4, $p < .05$
Chi^2: Classes I–IV combined versus Class V = 10.56
D.F. = 1, $p < .01$

situation, an elderly couple or a widow or widower comes to live in the home of a married child. This situation typically arises when the elderly persons become increasingly dependent or widowed. Like the second situation, it is a variant adaptation of the nuclear family, rather than a cultural commitment to an extended family. There is no built-in intergenerational residential continuity; without altering nuclear-family structure, this arrangement simply expands the household to include dependent older persons.

Lacking direct evidence on the situations that created the three-generation families in our study, we can nonetheless make inferences. Only 15 percent (4) of the 26 three-generation families that include the infant's grandparent have their own residence (whether owned or rented): the remaining 22 live in residences maintained by the grandparents. By comparison, 60 percent (152) of the 252 two-generational families have their own residence (we omit the case of the family where the infant has a nephew present, so that the total in the groups compared is 278, not 279). The difference between these two proportions is significant at the .001 level. Also, 50 percent (13) of the three-generation families have no children except the study-infant, compared with only 22 percent (55) of the two-generation families; this difference is significant at the .10 level. These facts suggest that most of the three-generation families fit the second situation above—a younger couple living with parents of husband or wife, usually the latter.

Two other revealing facts about the three-generation families are these. In 23 percent, or 6, of these families, the infant's father is absent (five separated from the mother, one in the military), compared with only 2 percent, or 4, of the two-generation families (two separated, one deceased, one in the military). Nineteen percent (5) of these families are black, compared with only 11 percent (28) of the two-generation families.

Housing

The establishment of an independent residential household is an important part of the values concerning the nuclear family. Recent decades have seen a gradual decline, for the United States as a whole, in the percent of married couples who live in a household that is not their own. Joined with this is the trend toward home ownership: while the nuclear family could well remain the dominant family form as independent home ownership decreased, the broad inclination in the United States has been toward home ownership. Though many young married couples rent a residence, often an apartment, as their first home, there has been a strong tendency to purchase a residence with the addition of children to the family, though the rising costs of home ownership and energy may eventually reverse it.

Of the 279 study families, 40.1 percent, or 112, own their residence. The home-owner category combines those families, numerically predominant, in which the infant's parents own the home with the smaller number of families in which the infant's parents live in a home owned by grandparents. Similar considerations apply to the other 60 percent of families, who live in rented quarters.

The extent of home ownership varies considerably by social-class level. As Table 3-7 shows, the percent of home ownership ranges from 86 in Class I down to 14 in Class V. These differences are statistically signficant. The very low extent of Class V ownership is a finding that we believe is directly attributable to limited financial capacity, and less to differential class values. The purchase of a home is the largest single financial obligation ever contracted by most families. A down payment must be accumulated, which is difficult for many families and an insuperable obstacle for most poor families. Further, good credit standing is necessary to secure a mortgage loan. While it is conceivable that the traditional societal ideal of family home ownership is not fully shared in Class V, these other considerations weigh heavily. Notable also in this connection is the earlier finding (Table 3-4) that Class V families are larger; thus the greater use of rented quarters among these families cannot easily be regarded as simply a transitional step, to be succeeded by the purchase of a home when the first or second child arrives. Chronic financial stress prevents them from acquiring the family residence that many families in Class IV and higher have acquired.

Overall housing quality was assessed by each interviewer, who rated the house on the following seven-point scale:

Table 3-7
Housing Characteristics by Social Class

Social Class (N)	Percentage of Class Owning Residence	Housing Quality Index		Number of Rooms		Crowding Index	
		Mean	S.D.	Mean	S.D.	Mean	S.D.
I (28)	85.7	2.93	.90	8.54	2.91	.59	.19
II (32)	50.0	3.19	.93	7.06	2.46	.69	.20
III (64)	50.0	3.53	.69	6.56	2.13	.73	.21
IV (75)	38.7	4.17	.92	5.85	1.63	.90	.34
V (80)	13.7	4.89	.92	5.10	1.71	1.29	.66
Total (279)	40.1	3.99	1.12	6.21	2.26	.92	.49

$Chi^2 = 51.34$
D.F. = 4
$p < .001$

Classes I–IV combined
versus Class V: $Chi^2 = 32.52$
D.F. = 1
$p < .001$

Analysis of variance:	Analysis of variance:	Analysis of variance:
F-Ratio = 42.56	F-Ratio = 17.64	F-Ratio = 2.15
D.F. = 4,274	D.F. = 4,274	D.F. = 4,274
$p < .001$	$p < .001$	$p \not< .05$

Excellent. Large houses in top repair with ostentatious, landscaped grounds. Housing quality index (HQI), 1.

Very Good. Houses and grounds slightly smaller than above but larger than utility. Exclusive apartment buildings, large flats. HQI, 2.

Good. Medium to large single-family houses in good repair, but little ostentation in house or grounds. Apartment houses with medium to large flats, well kept, but no fancy display. HQI, 3.

Average. Small and neat single-family houses, six rooms or less. The best quality two-family houses with adequate yard space. Small apartments in clean but plain buildings—strictly utility. HQI, 4.

Fair. Small houses in poor condition. Average two-family houses, not much yard space. Apartments in deteriorated buildings, often converted from homes. HQI, 5.

Poor. Run-down buildings but repairable. Semislum. HQI, 6.

Very Poor. Buildings beyond repair, unhealthy and unsafe. Areas very unattractive—broken windows, trash about. HQI, 7.

The interviewers based their rating upon the physical structure of the house, its state of maintenance, the attractiveness of the immediate grounds, and the general quality of the neighborhood. We obtained the following frequency distribution of ratings:

Rating	N
1	3
2	18
3	68
4	109
5	55
6	22
7	4
	279

Table 3-7 shows the relationship between social class and housing quality. The mean rating for the sample is 3.99. Class I has a mean of 2.93. The class means decrease monotonically, reaching 4.89 for Class V (this latter mean, it may be noted, is higher than the fair index rating of 5). Within each class there is appreciable variation, as the standard deviations show. One quarter of the

Class I houses are rated as only average or fair. Class IV has houses in every category except excellent. One third of the Class V houses are rated good or average.

Inquiry was also made as to the number of rooms in the residence. The number of rooms ranges from one to eighteen. The one-room residence is rented by a father who works irregularly in auto shops. The household includes himself, his wife, and their infant of eleven months. Their one room is a combination bedroom, living room, kitchen, and dining room, located in a rooming house. This family shares a corridor bathroom with other residents of the house. In marked contrast, the 18-room mansion is located on a picturesque country road in the horse-farm area north of Lexington. It belongs to a Class I physician and is occupied by him, his wife, and their three children. Table 3–7 shows the mean number of rooms in the residences by social class, with the standard deviation in each class. An analysis of variance shows that the class variation is statistically significant.

Of greater functional importance than the sheer number of rooms is the density of occupancy. A small family—father, mother, and one child—in a three-room apartment might be less crowded, in terms of privacy, freedom of movement, and noise insulation, than a large family in a seven-room house. The presence of an infant in the household imposes extra demands upon living space. The density factor is given quantitative expression by the crowding index, or number of persons per room. In the total sample, the index ranges from .33 (one person for three rooms) to 4.5 (nine persons for two rooms). The crowding index shows a consistent relationship to social class. Class I has .59 persons per room—the lowest index value—and each class below it has a higher value. Class V has 1.29 persons per room. The sample mean is .92, slightly less than one person per room. While the class trend is clear, it fails to achieve statistical significance at the 5 percent level.

4 Pregnancy and Delivery

The 279 families that constitute the final study sample share the common features of the mother's pregnancy and the subsequent birth of an infant. These features are the focus of investigation in this chapter.

Pregnancy as a process and childbirth as its culminating event have acquired a strongly medical cast in modern society. When a woman believes she is pregnant, she visits a physician. She depends upon that physician to render the definitive diagnosis of her condition. Once the fact of pregnancy is established, contemporary standards of health care require the mother-to-be to place herself under continuing medical surveillance. If the pregnancy proceeds to term, then delivery occurs in a hospital at the hands of the physician. (The medical profession has communicated the need for hospitalization to the lay public, and the latter has accepted it: public acceptance of such changes from earlier practice is likely to be rapid and uncritical because the physician initiates it within the doctor-patient relationship, which has a strong aura of trust and solidarity.) An important side effect of this "medicalization" of delivery is the isolation of the woman not only from her family and accustomed domestic environment but also from the outside world in general.

Anything less than full prenatal supervision followed by hospital delivery under auspices of a qualified physician is viewed as deficient care. The medical specialty of obstetrics has developed and focused its expertise precisely around the management of pregnancy and childbirth. The application of scientific knowledge concerning pregnancy and labor has been largely responsible for the great reduction in maternal and perinatal mortality over the past century. Many anomalies of conception, complications of pregnancy, and rigors of labor that were once common can now be averted or eased. Many biomedical fields—pharmacology, anesthesiology, immunology, hematology, and surgery—have contributed, yet for all the biomedical advances that make the reproductive experience more secure and comfortable, much remains that stamps it as an extramedical phenomenon with irreducible human and social features. Despite the increased security of the process, it provokes apprehension on the part of many mothers-to-be. The denouement in the labor and delivery suites of the hospital is not infrequently experience by mothers as an ordeal over which they have no control and in which they are ignored, or insensitively handled at unpredictable intervals.

Many women feel that their psychological needs during pregnancy are not adequately recognized and dealt with by physicians. There is a tendency for physicians to regard women as emotionally labile and irrational during pregnancy; hormonal change is invoked as a single-factor explanation, which has a finality to it because of its biological character. On that account the physician perhaps implicitly permits himself to pay less attention to the patient's psychological status than he does to that of patients who have no basis comparable to pregnancy for the manifestation of emotionality.

Indeed, one may question whether the hormonal changes during pregnancy, which are in themselves well-established, are sufficiently understood in their behavioral and emotional effects. It may be that physicians, through extra-scientific modalities, have simply absorbed traditional lore regarding pregnancy from Western culture. As an extreme yet representative element of this cultural tradition, pregnant women in medieval Europe were expressly permitted to steal certain fruits and vegetables at market, as a concession to their supposedly over-powering passion for specific food items. Perhaps similar prejudices, in diluted form, have passed into modern culture and coexist alongside scientific knowledge in the praxis of contemporary medicine. Under the sway of such half-conscious beliefs, the doctor may come to hold a patronizing attitude toward his or her patient.

Professional coping with the human-relations aspect of pregnancy has yet to achieve the great gains that obstetric medicine has made in understanding and reducing the biological hazards. In this respect, pregnancy is little different from many more serious conditions and diseases that have yielded to biomedical advance: the psychosocial problems persist in the face of considerable scientific knowledge for effective handling of the patient's clinical situation.

In this chapter we present findings from our study which reveal the mothers' attitudes toward their pregnancy, and how they regarded their state of health during this period. We also look at their employment status: were they employed during pregnancy, and how long into pregnancy did they continue to work? These findings will give us perspective on the following questions. Is pregnancy a normal biological function of the female, or is it an illness? If it is an illness, then does it, like other illnesses, impose a "sick role" upon the gravid woman?

In Chapter 3 we located the families in a community context by examining social class, race, and housing. This line of inquiry will be furthered in Chapter 4 by focusing upon the community hospitals which were used by the mothers at time of delivery. Hospitals are the most salient medical institutions in most communities, and an important feature in community history and geography. In terms of contemporary function, they are typically regarded by physicians as a resource in the treatment of patients who require the application of equipment and personnel not available in the doctor's office. Though the major portion of hospital capacity goes to the diagnosis and treatment of severe pathology, the maternity service is a familiar, often sizable, feature of contemporary hospitals. It is the hospital's major link to the healthy portion of the community, that is, to families headed by young adults who are in the reproductive phase of the life cycle and who are, by virtue of their age, relatively free from physical disorders.

Hospitals have their distinctive niches in community lore and reputation. In a multihospital community, which segments of the community use which hospital? This is an important question in the sociology of medical care. We shall answer it for the families of our sample in terms of their social status, race, and religious identification.

Attitudes Toward the Pregnancy

The interviewer set the stage for questioning about the mother's attitudes toward her recent pregnancy by asking her to think back to the time when she realized she was pregnant: "How did you feel about it when you first knew a baby was on the way?" Given this question, almost all the mothers responded in terms of a favorable-unfavorable dimension. While the specific responses varied widely, most could be arrayed along this axis.

Many reported attitudes that were favorable, as indicated by brief positive responses such as "happy," "thrilled," "excited," and "delighted." Some mothers went on at greater length: "We had been trying for a long time. We wanted a companion for the other child. We were very elated about it." And, "I was tickled to death. Me and my husband were divorced a year and then we remarried. Then Debbie came along. We joined the church and got saved and everything." Other responses revealed a more reluctant or negative attitude: "I guess I was glad. But you can't get as excited about the sixth as the first"; "I wasn't happy. It's expensive, and we were hard-pressed for cash"; "I didn't like it too well. It was too soon after the last baby," or "I wasn't too pleased at first, but then I began to accept it. I realized that nothing could be done about it, so I changed my attitude."

Not all the mothers attempted strictly to recapture the first feelings associated with the pregnancy. Pregnancy is a process which eventuates in the "product," an infant. Some mothers seized upon the product and then extrapolated backward to evaluate the pregnancy process. One of the outstanding characteristics of the product is its gender, male or female. Some mothers expressed positive feeling about having borne a second child whose gender was opposite to that of their first child. Other mothers said they were not pleased at first but came over time to accept the pregnancy. Presumably there were other reluctant mothers who also made the best of the inevitable, but who had by the time of the interview completely forgotten that their initial reaction had been negative.

Inspection of the diversity of responses, from favorable to unfavorable, revealed another axis around which many responses revolved: Was the pregnancy planned or not? The accomplishment of a planned pregnancy seemed to enhance the sense of satisfaction in many mothers. Correspondingly, where the pregnancy came as a surprise, it frequently was an unwelcome surprise; several mothers said they had wanted another baby, but "not then."

We followed the open-ended question about the mother's general attitude toward the pregnancy with another which focused more sharply upon the issue of whether the mother had wanted to become pregnant: "Did this pregnancy come at a time when you were especially hoping to be pregnant—or not?" One factor to be reckoned with in studying attitudes toward pregnancy is the general "social desirability" tendency toward affirmation of the worth of babies, especially one's own. Some mothers may have shaded their responses so as not to seem rejecting, or unmotherly. To minimize this, we phrased the question in an extreme form ("especially hoping"), which would make it relatively easy for the mother to say, "No, I had not been especially hoping." Then, for those mothers who said they had not been especially hoping, a further question was asked: "Did you feel that you would be able to manage everything all right or did it seem to you that this pregnancy would interfere with other important things?" The mother could indicate that the pregnancy, though not hoped for, was nonetheless manageable, or, if there had been stronger fears or other negative feelings, she could indicate a greater degree of reluctance. The interviewers were instructed to probe gently in determining the strength and basis of her reluctance.

The categories we employed resemble those used by Miller (1975) in a study of how women acquire the pregnancy identity. From her interviews with pregnant women, she developed three categories based on pregnancy decision which she called true-planners, sort-of-planners, and non-planners. Using our scheme to classify attitudes, we find that 38 percent of the mothers were in the positive, "especially hoping" category; 47 percent were in the neutral, "manage all right" category, and 15 percent were in the negative, "interfere" category.

These figures can be compared to those from a national sample study by Bumpass and Westoff (1970) of the extent to which parents of births occurring between 1960 and 1965 wanted the births. They estimated that 17 percent of the white births and 36 percent of black births were unwanted. Moreover, the percentage of unwanted births showed a marked social-class gradient, rising to 27 percent for whites and 42 percent for blacks with family incomes under $3,000.

We will next examine pregnancy attitudes in our sample in relation to social class and family size. Table 4-1 portrays the relation between the mother's social class and her attitude toward the pregnancy. Class I, the highest class, has the highest proportion who were positively oriented. Class V, the lowest class, has the smallest proportion in this category, and Classes II, III, and IV are intermediate. The proportion of mothers with a "manage all right" attitude shows a general increase as status decreases, although Class IV has a lower percentage than Class III. An uneven picture emerges in regard to the negative attitude which sees pregnancy as an interference; approximately one fifth of mothers in both Classes II and V have this view, and every other class holds it with less frequency. In general, Table 4-1 shows that higher-class mothers have a more

Table 4–1
Mother's Attitude Toward the Pregnancy, by Social Class

Social Class	Number in Class	Percent in Class Who Were "Especially Hoping"	Percent in Class Who Felt They Would "Manage All Right"	Percent in Class Who Felt That "Pregnancy Would Interfere"
I	28	57	32	11
II	32	37	41	22
III	64	39	52	9
IV	75	43	45	12
V	80	27	53	20
Total	279	38	47	15

$Chi^2 = 11.34$
D.F. = 8
$p \not< .05$

Note: The percentages add to 100 across each row.

positive attitude toward their pregnancy, although the class differences are not statistically significant.

A second possible determinant of attitude was investigated, namely, the number of children in the family. We expected that women with no children would have more positive attitudes toward the pregnancy than those who had children. Table 4–2 supports this expectation. Of the mothers with no previous children, 49 percent say that they hoped to be pregnant; 40 percent of the one-child mothers express this positive attitude, as do only 32 percent of the mothers with two or more children. Twenty-one percent of the latter group express a negative view, compared with only 8 percent in the other groups.

Table 4–2 suggests this question: Why is a positive attitude not more common among women with no children? The desire for progeny is a deep social and personal value, but only 49 percent of those with no children said they had hoped to be pregnant. Though increasing, voluntary childlessness in marriage is still relatively exceptional and could scarcely account for the remaining 51 percent. We suppose that many of the latter wanted children but were unenthusiastic because the pregnancy was untimely. Further, some may have had fears about the course of pregnancy and the travail of childbirth, although they desired the baby.

It appears, in summary, that the pregnancy attitudes expressed by the mothers in this study vary in content along a positive-negative axis of personal feeling and along another axis reflecting the extent to which the pregnancy was wanted. The attitudes were influenced by social class and family size. Our findings provide only a tentative assessment of a complex attitudinal area. The interview responses did not permit a finer discrimination among the various emotional

Table 4–2

Mother's Attitude Toward the Pregnancy in Relation to Number of Children

Number of Children	Number in Category	Percent in Category Who Were "Especially Hoping"	Percent in Category Who Felt They Would "Manage All Right"	Percent in Category Who Felt That "Pregnancy Would Interfere"
No Children	71	49	42	8
One Child	72	40	51	8
Two or More Children	136	32	47	21
Total	279	39	47	15

Chi^2 = 11.97
D.F. = 4
$p \nless .05$

Note: The percentages add to 100 across each row, except for rounding discrepancies.

bases that underlie a given attitude. Certainly a mother's response reflects a number of factors other than her social class and existing family size. It is also based upon her ideas about family life, her aspirations for herself, and her orientation toward family planning.

A major social influence comes from the growing popular awareness of the disadvantages of population growth. Through the mass media, people are becoming sensitized to the adverse effects of large populations upon the natural and manmade environment, upon the supply of scarce natural resources, and upon the general quality of life. It is, of course, one thing to identify this trend in social awareness and another to say that such awareness directly and significantly affects the concrete and intimate behavior of couples in regard to family size. Nevertheless, we suggest that in conjunction with more tangible considerations, such as the cost of rearing children, the population issue has some independent effect.

We suggest further that the newer methods of contraception—the relatively precise, effective, and comfortable control afforded by the pill and the coil—raise to a more acute level the question of whether or not a pregnancy is wanted (Gallagher, 1972). In societies and social groups where contraception is less understood, less accepted, or less available, attitudes may be more broadly impassive, viewing pregnancy as a natural contingency like the seasons or the weather.

Another major influence comes from changes in abortion practice. A 1973 U.S. Supreme Court decision invalidated state laws that virtually prohibited abortions. This decision gave support to widespread public sentiment for abortion reform (Sarvis and Rodman, 1974). Abortion is a more potent option for terminating unwanted pregnancies than it was two or three decades ago. Perhaps women who proceed with their pregnancies have in general a more positive attitude than formerly, since the opportunities for prevention or interruption of pregnancy are now greater. But it would be a mistake to suppose that even with the fertility options available nowadays, most families follow a strictly rational course which yields for them the number of children they desire or plan (Kiesler, 1977).

Physical Health and Emotional Status During Pregnancy

The mother's physical health was assessed by simply asking her how she felt during the pregnancy and then asking for a brief description of any health problems she had encountered. Seventy-nine percent of the mothers reported good health throughout pregnancy. The remainder reported a variety of problems, such as high blood pressure, varicose veins, kidney infection, backache, and fatigue. Several said the first trimester had been difficult, with nausea, dizziness, and headaches that cleared up thereafter. A few mothers reported that the pregnancy had been difficult throughout.

The mother's emotional status was also investigated. Because feelings of depression are frequently experienced during pregnancy, we assessed this by asking, "Were there many times when you felt low or blue?" Forty-two percent replied in the positive. It thus appears that "blueness" is fairly common and considerably more prevalent than physical health problems. But there was a connection: 31 percent of the mothers who had often felt blue also reported health problems, compared with only 12 percent of the mothers who had not felt blue.

We expected to find variations in physical and emotional status. An important factor related to these variations is the ambiguous definition of pregnancy in our society (McKinlay, 1972). It may be regarded as a "sick role" in the sociological sense of Talcott Parsons (1951: 433–439; 1975: 257–278): A pregnant woman is expected to place herself under medical care; she acquires a social status that entitles her to special rights, such as maternity benefits at her place of employment, and to exemptions from usual responsibilities. On the other hand, by biological design pregnancy is a potential phase of the female life cycle; virtually all females are equipped to conceive and to bear children. The cultural ambiguity regarding the sick or well quality of pregnancy gives large scope for a woman's conception of it to be influenced, from childhood on, by contact with women of her own and her parents' generation. Whether pregnancy is experienced by the mother-to-be as a stressful illness or as a normal phase of life depends in part upon what she anticipates.

Pain is a much narrower category of experience than pregnancy, but studies of pain are suggestive on this point. Beecher (1961) found that individuals vary considerably in their subjective evaluation of the same objective pain source. The implications of such studies for a process so extended and ramified as pregnancy suggest the importance of social and psychological influences in the woman's overall evaluation of her pregnancy experience. The role of social influence was examined by Rosengren (1961), who in a study of 76 pregnant women of differing social status found that the lower-class women tended to assume a stronger sick-role posture than did women of higher status.

The discussion of pregnancy in terms of the sick-well dimension runs the risk of oversimplification. Medical supervision during pregnancy is the norm in our society. The physician cares for the sick; yet this does not necessarily mean that most women regard themselves as sick when pregnant. Medical contact is often initiated because of the suspicion of pregnancy, rather than because of physical distress. The first symptom is commonly a negative one, namely the absence of a menstrual period. A more modest and perhaps more accurate view of the role of medical supervision is simply that most women desire authoritative assurance that events are proceeding normally, and they wish to establish a relationship with the professional person who will later assist the delivery.

The Pregnancy Difficulty Index

We have discussed several components of the pregnancy process that influence its place as a generally positive or negative experience in the mother's life. From the standpoint of systematic examination of pregnancy in relation to subsequent infant care, it seemed desirable to construct a composite measure which could then be studied in relationship to other measures and indices. For this purpose, the Pregnancy Difficulty (PD index) was devised.

The PD index has eight components, each equally weighted and scored one point, thus giving a possible range of zero to eight (score adjustments are discussed below). A mother whose pregnancy had none of the difficulties would thus have a PD score of zero, the most favorable possible score. At the other extreme, a mother with a maximally unfavorable pregnancy would have a PD score of eight.

The eight components are as follows:

1. Poor health during pregnancy, or presence of a health problem, as previously discussed.
2. Frequent feelings of being low or blue, as previously discussed.
3. Negative or unenthusiastic attitude toward being pregnant; those mothers in the "pregnancy would interfere" or "manage all right" categories of Table 4-1.
4. Birth weight of less than five pounds. This is based on the fact that low birth weight is frequently associated with premature birth and with minor or major aberrations of pregnancy.

5. Mother married more than three years before the infant was born, no other children in family. It was hypothesized that this kind of pregnancy tended to reflect difficulty in achieving conception or a planned delay, and that the pregnancy would for either reason be accompanied by considerable anxiety.

6. Previous miscarriage or stillbirth in families where the study-infant was the only child. As in component 5, it was hypothesized that this reproductive history would generate an anxious emotional state on the mother's part during pregnancy.

7. In families with an older child, the next oldest child was more than five years older than the study-infant. It was hypothesized that in such cases the study-infant could be the product of a conception that was either difficult to achieve or unintentional. In the former instance, the pregnancy would be marked by unusual anxiety; in the latter, by an indifferent-to-negative attitude. Further, it seems likely that many mothers in this situation would have somewhat unfavorable anticipations of resuming the burden of care for a small infant. These circumstances would count as adverse on the PD index.

8. Birth prior to marriage, or conception more than two months prior to marriage. It was hypothesized that pregnancy commencing prior to marriage would carry with it an extra degree of anxiety or involuntariness. (Seven infants were conceived earlier than two months prior to marriage. Three were born prior to marriage, though their birth certificates were reclassified as legitimate upon subsequent marriage of parents, and thus came to be included in the roster for this study).

It was necessary to equalize raw scores in terms of the above components, since not every pregnancy was eligible to be scored on all eight elements. For example, an infant with no older siblings could not be counted on component 7, as having a sibling more than five years older than himself. Likewise, any infant who has an older sibling could not be counted on the sixth component as the sole child and product of a pregnancy preceded by a miscarriage or stillbirth. Components 1, 2, 3, 4, and 8 were potentially present for all pregnancies. Adjustments were necessary on components 5, 6, and 7 to give every pregnancy a possible-score range of zero through eight.

The Pregnancy Difficulty index is open to methodological criticism on the basis that it combines a number of logically disparate characteristics of the pregnancy, and because it bases itself upon several suppositions, such as the mother's state of mind when there is a long interval between the birth of successive siblings and the connection between low birth weight and abnormalities of pregnancy. Balanced against these shortcomings are its assets as a convenient measure for analysis and as a composite tool that gives empirical breadth to the analysis of pregnancy in relation to other maternal and infant parameters.

The PD index, constructed, weighted, and adjusted as described above, has a mean of 1.2 among the 279 respondents, and a standard deviation of 1.1. The maximum score obtained by any mother is under six; the minimum is zero, signifying that none of the indicated problematic features of pregnancy are present. The score distribution is as follows:

Score	Frequency
0– .9	102
1–1.9	92
2–2.9	62
3–3.9	5
4–4.9	17
5–5.9	1
	279

It can be seen from the foregoing that the PD values cluster strongly toward the low end of the index; more than one third of the scores are less than one. Nevertheless, there is appreciable variation within the total sample. This prompts us to explore the sources of variation and identify some of the factors that make pregnancy an easy or difficult process.

Intercorrelations: Pregnancy Attitude, Index of Social Position, Emotional Status, Physical Health, Family Size, and Pregnancy Difficulty Index

To obtain a broader view of the pregnancy, we looked at the interrelationships of the several kinds of data obtained. Table 4-3 presents the intercorrelations between the mother's attitude toward pregnancy, physical health, emotional status, and the Pregnancy Difficulty index. Two additional variables are included because of their potential importance as independent background influences upon the pregnancy variables: these are family size and Index of Social Position (ISP) (both were discussed in Chapter 3).

Table 4-3 shows that attitude toward the pregnancy is significantly correlated with the Index of Social Position (–.12), family size (–.25), and emotional status (.28). Those mothers with a positive attitude toward the pregnancy have higher social status (lower ISP score), fewer children, and less frequent depressive feelings. (Tables 4-1 and 4-2 present in more complete form the data that lie behind the first two of these three correlations.) Social status and family size are preexisting conditions that influence the mother's attitude toward pregnancy; the direction of influence—that is, the negative correlation—is what we might expect. The correlation between attitude toward the pregnancy and feeling of depression is more difficult to interpret. It might be argued that the woman who wants to be pregnant is less likely to feel low or blue than the woman who does not want to be. But since both orders of data were obtained retrospectively, it

Table 4–3

Intercorrelations: Pregnancy Attitude, Emotional Status, Physical Health, Family Size, Index of Social Position, and Pregnancy Difficulty Index[a]

	(6) PD Index	(5) ISP	(4) Family Size	(3) Physical Health	(2) Emotional Status	(1) Pregnancy Attitude
(1) Attitude toward Pregnancy (high score: "hoping")	$-.38^b$	$-.12$	$-.25$	.05	.28	1.00
(2) Emotional Status (high score: not often "low or blue")	$-.68$	$-.10$	$-.14$	.26	1.00	
(3) Physical Health (high score: good health reported)	$-.62$	$-.13$	$-.02$	1.00		
(4) Family Size (score equals number of children associated with mother)	.11	.14	1.00			
(5) Index of Social Position (high score: lower social status)	.13	1.00				
(6) Pregnancy Difficulty Index (score equals number of difficulties)	1.00					

[a]Table contains Pearson r between pairs of variables, with the following scoring.

(1) Attitude toward pregnancy: "hoping to be pregnant"–3; "manage all right"–2; "pregnancy interferes with plans"–1.
(2) Emotional status: not often "low or blue"–2; often "low or blue"–1.
(3) Physical health: good health–2; not good health–1.
(4) Family size: number of children associated with mother, ranging from 1 to 12.
(5) Index of Social Position: scores range from 11 to 77, with Class 1 having lowest scores and Class V having highest scores, as discussed in Chapter 3.
(6) Pregnancy Difficulty Index: scores range from 0 to 5.9. Scoring discussed in Chapter 4.

[b]For N of 279, the standard error of r is .06. Correlations with greater absolute magnitude than .12 deviate more than two standard deviations from zero and would occur by chance less often than one time in twenty.

might also be reasoned that those mothers who experienced frequent blue periods subsequently recast their attitudes so as to make the pregnancy seem less desired. Therefore, we prefer to regard neither the attitude toward pregnancy nor the emotional status as having an antecedent causal status; it suffices to note their strong interdependence.

The PD index correlation with the Index of Social Position is significant, indicating a strong tendency for lower-status mothers to have more problems during the pregnancy. The high correlations of PD with pregnancy attitude, emotional status, and physical health are simply part-whole correlations. It will be recalled that each of these three variables is a component of the PD index.

Several other relationships stand out strongly. Physical health and emotional status correlate .26, which suggests an appreciable degree of unity in somatic and emotional function during pregnancy. Family size and social position appear as generally influential background variables, except that the former had no relationship to physical health.

Prenatal Care

Prenatal care is a crucial element in the framework of child and maternal health. In connection with a study of prenatal care in metropolitan Boston, Donabedian and Rosenfeld (1961: 1) write:

> There are relatively few areas of medical practice in which clearly formulated minimum standards are available concerning time for initiation of medical care, frequency of patient visits, and content of professional care. . . . Care during pregnancy is one of the conditions for which standards that are widely accepted among medical practitioners and health agencies have been developed. . . . The health status of the mother and the genetic constitution of the mother and the fetus have an important bearing on the outcome of pregnancy for both. To an ever-increasing degree, adequate medical care can affect the outcome.

The first visit comes early in the first trimester, when the mother-to-be first suspects that she is pregnant. At this point, the doctor is likely to give a thorough workup covering medical and reproductive history, general physical exam, pelvic exam, and blood and urine tests. Once pregnancy is confirmed, the physician can become alerted to any complicating health problems the patient may have. For example, diabetes is associated with a higher risk of premature delivery, stillbirth, and other obstetrical complications. The risk can be reduced with proper medical management.

Following the initial workup, prenatal care involves ongoing medical supervision and self-management. Aside from medical help with special health problems, the pregnant woman can benefit from counseling in regard to weight gain, diet, sex activity, employment, exercise, and rest. While the value of a regular regimen of prenatal care is not to be minimized in the case of the experienced, multigravida, it is perhaps more critical for the primagravida. Medical recommendations regarding ongoing, routine supervision are usually framed in terms of frequency of visits, with the visits spaced further apart early in pregnancy and closer as the projected delivery date approaches. The details of such recommended programs vary, but a typical plan would be one visit monthly until the thirty-fourth week, and weekly visits thereafter until delivery.

Before presenting data on prenatal care, it should be emphasized that the foregoing enunciates an ideal program of medical care during pregnancy. Many women make a safe passage and have a normal delivery and healthy infant with less care. Certain segments of medical opinion believe that prenatal care as extensive as that sketched above is a middle-class luxury, available to those who can afford it but wasteful of obstetrical manpower. This argument emphasizes also that pregnancy is a normal biological potentiality and expression of femininity, not an illness requiring close supervision, and that after hazards such as diabetes and RH incompatibility between mother and embryo have been ruled out little need exists for routine supervision. While recognizing the force of such thinking, most opinion favors an adequate regime of prenatal care as a source of support for the patient. Further, complications—toxemia, anemia, urinary infection—do occasionally develop during the course of pregnancy.

The interview covered the question as to whether or not the mother had had any amount of prenatal care at all, with a particular focus upon absence of care. The interviewer asked, "Did you go somewhere for care and checkups during this pregnancy?" This basic question was then followed by questions about the source of care. A limited assessment of the quality or comprehensiveness of prenatal care was thus made.

Nine (3.2 percent) of the 279 mothers lacked prenatal care. Another Lexington study of prenatal care among 186 recently delivered mothers in four low-income census tracts revealed that eight (4.3 percent) lacked such care (Kennedy, 1967). Comparable studies in other areas indicate somewhat lower levels of deficiency: Schonfield (1962) and colleagues, in a study of 163 mothers in Cambridge, Massachusetts, found that 1.2 percent of these mothers had fewer than three visits throughout pregnancy; Yankauer (1958) and colleagues, in a study of 1,433 mothers in 15 upstate New York localities, found that fewer than 1 percent had had no prenatal care. There are, however, other regions where sizable numbers of pregnant women have little or no prenatal care. Gibbs and his colleagues studied reproductive health care among 1,500 poor Mexican-American women in San Antonio, Texas (Gibbs et al., 1974). They found that 44 percent lacked prenatal care, and that this group had a higher rate of obstetrical complications and perinatal mortality than the groups that received delayed care or early care.

In our study, lack of prenatal care is closely related to social class. Seven of the nine mothers lacking prenatal care are in Class V, one is in Class IV, and one in Class II. To gain insight into the personal factors underlying lack of prenatal care, we asked these mothers why they had not had such care. The following responses were obtained:

"I was busy. I felt all right, so I just didn't go. I guess I am a little stoic about this, but I believe what will be, will be. I feel prenatal care is important but not really necessary if you eat good food and are feeling well." (Class II mother of six children prior to infant.)

"We didn't have the money and my husband would have refused to pay for any help. I did go to Dr. __ once at seven months because of a kidney infection." (Class V mother of two children prior to infant.)

"It was difficult to go because of my two small children. I had no baby-sitter and couldn't afford to pay one. I would like to have been able to go." (Class V mother of six children prior to infant.)

"I had three small children and my husband was on the road driving a truck." (Class V mother of 11 children prior to infant.)

"It's too expensive for one thing. I didn't have anyone to stay with the children. . . . I did go to the county health department but the lady there talked to me so hateful. My feelings aren't easily hurt, but I just didn't go back. I was four and one-half months along then." (Class V mother of three children prior to infant.)

"We didn't have the money and we were moving after a few months of pregnancy anyway." (Class IV mother of four children prior to infant.)

"I just didn't care. I just didn't want to go." (Class V mother of two children prior to infant.)

"I just didn't feel like I had the time. I felt I could get along all right but I know I should have gone. . . . Didn't nothing really bother me or I would have went. . . . I took proper care of myself." (Class V mother of five children prior to infant.)

"It was just I was scared of doctors. I just ain't been to doctors hardly at all in my life. Did go to see a doctor once and he said James would be born any day. That was on January 31st." (Class V mother with no previous children. The infant was born February 6.)

As these responses indicate, the second, fifth, and last mothers each made one visit for health care during pregnancy. We nevertheless counted them in the "no care" group because the first's visit was made only under the duress of a health problem, number five's visit was not sustained, and the ninth's visit was extremely belated.

The forgoing reasons for lack of prenatal care offer clues to the attitudinal and situational barriers that must be surmounted if prenatal coverage is to become universal. The main barriers were expense, inconvenience, and a doubt that prenatal care is really essential. The most frequently mentioned factor—expense—cannot be fully credited because free public care was available; this does not, however, deny the expense of baby-sitters and transportation. Furthermore, some of the mothers may not have known or believed that free care was available. Health departments are sometimes reluctant to advertise too widely the services they offer "for free," through tax and volunteer support. Fear of the doctor was cited only once, and that by the only first-time mother, or primapara, of the group. It is of interest that all of the other mothers had at least two children prior to the infant, and the average (excluding the primapara) was five children. The difficulty of getting to the doctor or clinic was probably very salient to them. Gibbs and associates (1974) report a similar range of deterrents to obtaining prenatal care among the San Antonio mothers.

Does increased parity experience foster a casual attitude toward pregnancy? In the responses of some of the mothers above, there is a hint that it does—especially in the first and the eighth. The Donabedian-Rosenfeld study (1961) found that increasing parity led to greater delay in seeking prenatal care; also, that more experienced mothers tended to regard care during the first trimester as not essential. For physicians and public health personnel, this question is posed: How can a woman with previous normal pregnancies be convinced, without diminishing her sense of reproductive security and competence, that prenatal care is still important? In raising this question, we must recognize that medical opinion is not unanimous. A segment of obstetrical opinion takes the mother's prior experience as a guide to the amount of prenatal care needed; if a multigravida woman has had routine pregnancies and deliveries in the past, she has "proven herself" obstetrically; she may then, according to this opinion, be regarded as a safe, reliable childbearer. This opinion of course fits in with contemporary emphasis upon channeling medical manpower into areas of greatest need. In this connection, a study by Kane (1964) found that the greatest need does not necessarily lie where it is most expected. His study of full-term births showed a correlation between prenatal visits and decreasing perinatal mortality— but only among primagravida, and *not* among multigravida. It showed further that with or without prenatal care perinatal mortality hit a low point for the second pregnancy and then rose with the third. By the third pregnancy, if not earlier, many physicians and mothers start to have the unwarranted, secure feeling that there is no risk. The lack of correlation between prenatal care and perinatal mortality is not an indictment of the value of such care; it means, rather, that such care might well be more intensively focused upon the specific trouble potentials in the pregnancy and delivery.

The interview included questions about the source of prenatal care—whether private care under a physician or free care at public expense. Fayette County provided for free indigent maternity care through a clinic maintained by the board of health; in Jessamine and Woodford counties, free care was provided in the offices of private physicians who received a stipend from the county health department. Fifteen mothers reported using public clinics for prenatal care. All were Fayette County residents. Of the 15, 4 were in Class IV and 11 were in Class V.

Employment During Pregnancy

Employment during pregnancy is one facet of the complex phenomenon of female employment. In our study 83 (29.7 percent) of the 279 mothers worked outside the home during pregnancy. A brief survey of historical trends will place our data in perspective.

Female participation in the labor force has increased markedly in recent decades, concurrent with the urbanization of the population and with changes in the structure of the economy, family, and household. While household management remains a time-consuming and predominantly female activity, the modern household, even with children present, can be managed with less effort than was required before the era of prepared foods, manufactured clothing, and vacuum cleaners. Housewives have been freed to some extent for other pursuits. The economic system has developed in directions that absorb great amounts of female labor—in light manufacturing fields, in commerce and communciations, and in service fields such as teaching and nursing. The trend toward increasing female, and wifely, employment received extra impetus during World War II, when the demands of the civilian war effort conferred a new legitimacy upon women's work outside the home.

In 1890, 18 percent of all women 16 and over were gainfully employed; in 1940, 29 percent; and in 1970, 43 percent (Blau, 1975: 217). The proportion of married women among all employed women has also increased, from 13 percent in 1890 to 30 percent in 1940, and to 58 percent in 1971; there has been a corresponding decrease in the proportion of employed women comprised of single, divorced, and widowed women. A closely related question is, How likely is a wife to be a wife who works? In 1890, 4.5 percent of all married women were employed; in 1940, 14.0 percent; and in 1960, 32.0 percent.

Along with wifely employment, maternal employment has also increased. In 1940, only 9 percent of all married women with children under 18 years of age worked outside the home, but by 1964, this proportion had increased to 35 percent. Even a substantial proportion of mothers of preschool children are employed. The U.S. Department of Labor estimated that in 1964, 22 percent of mothers with children under three years of age were employed.

Why do wives and mothers work? Money is no doubt the chief incentive; a wife's earnings can considerably increase family income. Many families with high total family income stand high not only because the husband earns a good deal but also because the wife works (Kuznets, 1962: 34). Equally, in many poor families the wife's income contributes substantially to total family income (Blau, 1975: 224). Work can also provide an opportunity to exercise and develop personal professional skills, an avenue for social contact, and a release from domestic routines. It does have negative features as well. It carries the disadvantage of reduced availability for the needs of household and family. It adds a burden of occupational responsibility with little concomitant reduction in domestic responsibility; even where husbands and children pitch in on household tasks, the amount of help rendered is as a rule not commensurate with the working mother's outside involvement.

The motivations for work of married women and mothers have changed markedly as the overall employment figures have changed. Fifty years ago, work outside the home had the same range of meanings as now, but the accent has shifted. Nye and Hoffman (1963: 9-10) give a succinct statement of the changes in female motivations for work: "In general, the employed mother prior to World War II . . . had several children and was forced into an unskilled, physically tiring, low-paying job by direct economic necessity. . . . Now married women living with husbands are not usually forced into employment because of a need for their income as the principal support for their families. The large majority live with husbands who are employed, and this factor allows them to enter employment selectively." That is to say, the money incentive remains important but is not so frequently a matter of survival as it once was.

We may inquire more specifically about the effect of pregnancy upon female employment. In one sense, as a biological event, pregnancy exerts no direct impact upon behavioral categories such as employment—at least, not initially. The first question to consider here is whether a woman was already employed when the pregnancy occurred. In turn, whether she was already employed depends upon the various aspects of her life situation that led her toward or deterred her from employment.

Of the 4,096 women in a national sample study of employment during pregnancy, for pregnancies terminating in legitimate live births (National Center for Health Statistics, 1968a) in 1963, 31 percent were employed, close to the 29.7 percent of our sample. Table 4-4 shows from the national study that a woman's likelihood of working was related strongly to her maternal parity and her educational status.

From this table it can be seen that the better-educated woman is more likely to be employed during pregnancy if it is her first pregnancy; otherwise, educational status makes little difference. By parity, first-time mothers are more likely to be employed than those with children.

In our sample, there is a marked difference between the first-time mothers, or primaparas, and the multiparas in terms of their employment during pregnancy. Of the 71 primaparas, 35 (49.3 percent) worked, as compared with 48 (23.1 percent) of the 208 multiparas. A primapara thus has twice the chance

Table 4-4
Percent of Women Working During Pregnancy in Each Educational and Parity Category

| Parity | Educational Status | | | |
	Elementary School	Part or All of High School	More than High School	Total
First Birth	27.9	55.9	71.2	57.5
Later Birth	24.4	21.3	22.5	21.7
Total	24.7	30.6	39.1	31.0

Source: National Center for Health Statistics, 1968: 18

of being employed than a multipara has; this difference is statistically significant (critical ratio of difference between proportions employed is 7.44, $p < .001$). This finding agrees with that of the national study and accords with the common-sense expectation that the woman with children is more likely to be primarily engaged in the housewife-mother role and less likely to hold a job outside the home. The primapara, lacking these domestic responsibilities, is more likely to be employed prior to pregnancy and to continue working for a portion of it. Another factor that enhances the contrast is that most of the multiparas have young children in their care at home. Such mothers are less likely than mothers of older children to hold outside employment. While recent decades have seen a general expansion of participation by mothers in the labor force, it remains true that the level of participation is lower for mothers of preschool children than for mothers whose youngest child has entered school. (We shall deal further with the topic of working mothers in Chapter 5 when we discuss work after the birth of the infant.)

Table 4-5 relates employment during pregnancy to social class. It shows that there is a significant overall relationship between social class and employment. In general, a larger proportion of higher-class mothers than of lower-class mothers worked; Class I-II (combined here because of small numbers in the two separate classes on the parity columns) had the highest proportion working and Class V had the lowest proportion. Table 4-5 also shows the joint effect of social class and parity (primapara or multipara). We see that among the primaparas, descending class is associated to a significant degree with a lower proportion working. This trend is less evident among the multiparas. The level of employment is, as we would expect, lower for the multiparas than for the primaparas within each class, but the difference is not large within Class IV (35.7 percent primapara, compared with 31.1 percent multipara). Among the multiparas, Class IV has the highest proportion employed—almost one third.

An important aspect of employment during pregnancy is its duration: How far into pregnancy does an expectant woman continue to work? Advice on this subject is usually framed in terms of the type of work performed and the extent of responsibilities at home. The U.S. Children's Bureau pamphlet *Prenatal Care* (1967: 27) says, "If your work is strenuous and cannot be lightened in any way, give it up after the fourth or fifth month. If it is not too heavy, you can probably go on working much longer than that, possibly into the eighth month, provided you get enough rest, eat the right kinds of food, and are reasonably satisfied with the way things are going at home." Still other factors, such as the economic need for the wife's income and the meaning of her work to her, play an important role.

Other things being equal, the woman whose work provides a major source of family income would, we expect, want to remain on the job as long as possible. Those women for whom work means self-expression, social contact, or a professional career, with income as a less important consideration, have more

Table 4-5
Employment During Pregnancy, by Social Class and Parity

Social Class	All Women		Parity			
			Primapara		Multipara	
	Total N	Percent of N Who Worked	Total N	Percent of N Who Worked	Total N	Percent of N Who Worked
I-II	60	45.0(27)[a]	17	88.2(15)	43	27.9(12)
III	64	26.6(17)	24	41.7(10)	40	17.5(7)
IV	75	32.0(24)	14	35.7(5)	61	31.1(19)
V	80	18.8(15)	16	31.2(5)	64	15.6(10)
Total	279	29.7(83)	71	49.3(35)	208	23.1(48)
	Chi² = 11.80 D.F. = 3 p < .01		Chi² = 13.99 D.F. = 3 p < .01		Chi² = 5.51 D.F. = 3 p ≮ .05	

[a]The numbers in parentheses are the actual number in each category who worked. Thus, of the 43 multiparas in Classes I-II, 12, or 27.9 percent, worked.

freedom to retire early in the pregnancy and to make the state of expectancy into something of a vocation. However, the various noneconomic satisfactions from work can exert an attraction of their own that equally serves to keep a woman working well into pregnancy. Personnel policies at the place of work provide another set of influences that bear upon work during pregnancy. With the general increase of married women in the labor force, a growing number of employers offer maternity benefits. Such plans may stipulate a period of time before and after the projected due date, during which the worker receives paid leave. Alternatively, she may receive unpaid leave, with her job being held for her until her return (U.S. Women's Bureau, 1972).

Of the 83 working women in this study, 7 percent (6) worked into the last week of pregnancy. Twenty-four percent discontinued work during the last month, but before the last week; 23 percent discontinued during the second month before delivery. The remainder, 46 percent, stopped work still earlier (the earliest to stop working were three women who stopped in the seventh and eighth weeks of pregnancy). For the entire group of employed women, the average time for the termination of work was 11.7 weeks before delivery, with a standard deviation of 9.5 weeks. As the previous figures indicate, many women work until the last month, while smaller numbers stop at varying earlier points.

Table 4-6 shows the relationship of duration of work to social class and parity. Its figures represent the number of weeks prior to the infant's birth when the mother stopped working. No strong connection with social class is evident: the Class 1 mothers were the earliest to stop working, while the Class II mothers worked further into pregnancy than any other class. Again, no connection between social class and duration of work is apparent when we hold constant maternal status. It is of interest to note, however, that the 35 primaparas worked until 9.3 weeks before delivery whereas the 48 multiparas stopped at 13.5 weeks before delivery. This difference is significant at the 5 percent level. Within classes, the difference between the primaparas and the multiparas is most extreme for Classes IV and V.

Advice concerning work during pregnancy is usually framed in terms of the potential physical and mental strain involved, and not in terms of the parity of the woman. For the multipara, pregnancy may come to be a burden superimposed upon ordinary responsibilities for her household and children. Maintaining her work into pregnancy may be more difficult than for the primapara, and, as our findings indicate, she stops earlier. The situation of the lower-class or working-class multipara is additionally complicated. There may be a high need for her contribution to the family income. Her work is likely, however, to be physically demanding, requiring manual exertion or standing, which leads her to stop relatively early in the pregnancy.

Table 4-6
Interval Between Termination of Employment and Birth of Infant For Women Employed During Pregnancy, by Social Class and Parity

| | All Employed Women | | | Parity | | | |
| | | | | Primapara | | Multipara | |
Social Class	N	Mean No. of Weeks	Standard Deviation	N	Mean No. of Weeks	N	Mean No. of Weeks
I	9	17.6	11.0	15	12.0 (I-II combined)	12	9.6 (I-II combined)
II	18	7.7	6.4	10	11.1	7	8.0
III	17	9.8	8.1	5	2.8	19	17.0
IV	24	14.0	10.2	5	4.0	10	15.3
V	15	11.5	10.4				
Total	83	11.7	9.5	35	9.3	48	13.5

Analysis of variance:
F-Ratio = 2.32
D.F. = 4, 78
$p \not< .05$

Standard Deviation for All Employed Primaparas = 8.8 Weeks

Standard Deviation for All Employed Multiparas = 9.6 Weeks

Critical Ratio of Difference between Means for all Primaparas and all Multiparas = 2.07, $p < .05$

Site of Delivery: Home or Hospital?

In our study, 98.2 percent (all but 5) of the infants were delivered in a hospital. The national average is 99.2 percent. These figures demonstrate the extent to which standard obstetric practice for childbirth has been accepted and implemented in our society. Like prenatal care, hospital delivery is regarded as essential for adequate health care. This has come to be the professional opinion in virtually all advanced societies, and in all, each decade sees a rising proportion of births in hospitals. Only Holland maintains a principled commitment in its health system to home delivery, with 90 percent of births occurring at home (Cohen, 1964: 86). England, with 50 percent home deliveries, cannot be said to have adopted the principle of home confinement; rather, it tries to accommodate maternity demand to a short supply of hospital beds.

In 1940, the figure for home deliveries in the United States was 56 percent (U.S. Public Health Service, 1960). The critical decades for the shift from home births to hospital births were the 1930s and 1940s. This shift not only affected the position of the hospital as a social institution, but it also marked an important social change for the individual and the family. Many women who themselves had been delivered by their mothers at home and who, enjoying good health, had never been hospitalized for illness entered the hospital for the first time to give birth. Home delivery has declined drastically in importance. Likewise, its accompanying practitioner, the lay midwife, has declined numerically as a profession from 14.3 lay midwives per 100,000 population in 1948 to 1.4 per 100,000 in 1970 (U.S. Department of Health, Education and Welfare, 1974: 194).

The experience of "going to the hospital to have a baby" is a major component in the vast increase in the utilization of hospitals in recent decades. The fact that almost all women, from all socioeconomic levels, now use hospitals for this purpose provides an important reason that general hospitals have become a community resource and a focus of general community concern, and are no longer the preserve of the infirm elderly or the sick poor, as they were at one time. Hospitals nevertheless have disadvantages. Occasional episodes of cross-infection create alarm about the safety of the hospital as a site for patients in general. The neonate, with no immune system except what it absorbed from its mother, is especially vulnerable. There is concern also about the crowdedness of hospitals and their depersonalizing routines.

From time to time there is a home delivery on the part of an urban middle-class mother who has ample financial and geographic access to medical care and hospitals, but who desires to demonstrate the privacy and security of the home for critical events of the life cycle (Younger, 1960). (Intentional home delivery may in the future become more widespread than it is currently. One national organization, the Association of Mothers for Educated Childbirth, specifically promotes home delivery and educates expectant mothers for it.) This must however be regarded as highly atypical, and it remains true that hospital delivery, even in the most uneventful of pregnancies, is preferred to home delivery. The primary rationale is that only the hospital has the array of resources potentially necessary for safe delivery and immediate postnatal care of mother and infant. Even medical care programs that are geared to home delivery provide for the use of hospitals when a difficult or complicated delivery is expected. Health departments in many metropolitan areas have now developed a corps of obstetrical technicians to provide routine prenatal care and home delivery in their neighborhoods; but an integral feature of these programs is the availability of reserve hospital beds and obstetrical expertise in emergencies.

The preceding discussion has been based on the assumption that a woman has only two alternatives: home delivery or hospital delivery. In some other countries there are special institutional settings other than general hospitals for delivery of infants. France and England have maternity hospitals where many women go to have their babies (The Boston Women's Health Book Collective, 1973: 157). The United States has very few such institutions, though the Boston and Chicago Lying-In Hospitals are well-known examples.

In relation to home deliveries in our study, information on Kentucky as a whole is pertinent. Ford (1964: 117), in his study of demographic aspects of health in Kentucky, wrote: "As recently as 1940 only one Kentucky infant in five was delivered in a hospital, only slightly more than the number delivered by physicians. By 1960 nearly 94 percent of all Kentucky births occurred in hospitals. Only 3 percent of the white births and 4 percent of the nonwhite births were delivered by midwives."

In our study, five infants (1.8 percent) were born at home. All five were intentional home deliveries, that is, none occurred at home because of precipitous labor or other exigencies. The connection of home delivery with class position is quite evident; four of the mothers are in Class V, and the other is in Class IV. Other descriptive particulars on these families are given in Table 4-7. Although the numbers are too small for reliable inference, it may be surmised that rural residence also plays a part in home delivery—rural residence not as a

Table 4-7
Descriptive Particulars of Five Infants Born at Home

Case	Residence	Father's Occupation	No. of Children (excluding) infant)	Race
1	Lexington	Auto-body repairman	2	White
2	Lexington	Road construction laborer	12	Black
3	Nicholasville	Plumber	3	White
4	Outside Nicholasville	Spreader in garment factory	5	White
5	Outside Versailles	Farm worker	1	White

geographical fact but as a condition predisposing toward old-fashioned health care. Of the five families, two live on farms and one lives in Nicholasville, which in 1970 had a population of 5,829. Of course, within the whole sample by far the greater number of rural mothers had hospital confinement.

Selective Utilization of Hospitals

Inquiry into the question of home versus hospital delivery can be framed in relation to quality of health care. It is generally presumed that hospital delivery entails less risk to mother and infant and gives a higher quality of care. When the question shifts to the selection of one hospital among several in a given area, a different interest arises, namely, the relation of the hospital to community.

The provision of medical care represents an application of biological science and professional expertise which is in theory directed toward the patient's needs regardless of her particular connections and status in the community. Whether or not the medical care rendered to patients is in fact similar in different hospitals, the care function of the hospital—its role in providing "hotel" services and a daily routine for the patient—serves as a basis upon which hospitals generate different images in a community. When an urban area has several general hospitals, sociological studies as a rule reveal that each has a characteristic patient clientele (Elling, 1963). Although so-called community hospitals endeavor to serve all sectors of the population, and in fact achieve some success in this objective, the force of traditional images among their potential publics and the power of what Freidson (1970) calls the "lay referral system" remain strong. Instead of serving a representative cross section of the patient population base, each community hospital has a selective constituency.

When we speak of hospital utilization, it should be understood that the hospital a mother used was not selected by her through an explicit decision. The medical-care system does not operate like that. It would be more correct to say that the mother selected a physician, rather than a hospital. The physician was affiliated with a particular hospital and accordingly admitted her to that hospital. Only a few physicians had staff privileges at more than one hospital. Even then, the mother need not necessarily have been given an explicit choice between hospitals by the physician. With these qualifications, the social significance of utilization of hospitals can be explored.

The mothers in our study went to four hospitals: in Lexington, to St. Joseph, Good Samaritan, and Central Baptist; and in Versailles, to Woodford Memorial. (Versailles is the county seat and largest city of Woodford County, with a 1970 population of 5,679. Jessamine County has no hospital.) St. Joseph is a Roman Catholic hospital, Good Samaritan is United Methodist, and Central Baptist is operated under affiliation with the Kentucky Baptist Convention. Woodford Memorial has no religious affiliation. Each of these hospitals functions as a general hospital, with medical and surgical services in addition to obstetrical care, and with predominantly short-stay patients.

As a preface to considering the distribution of the mothers among these hospitals, we note those characteristics of each hospital—location, sponsorship, community relationship—that might selectively affect admissions.

Woodford Memorial Hospital, as a small, general hospital in the county seat of a rural county, is primarily oriented to the hospitalization needs of its own area. It has, however, no officially delineated population area and, as we shall see, a few nonresident mothers in fact used it.

One notable fact about Lexington health resources is the lack of a tax-supported municipal hospital. Such hospitals, serving the needs of the urban poor on a charity basis, are commonly found in all the large metropolitan areas of the United States, and they are not uncommon in smaller urban areas the size of Lexington. Of the three hospitals in Lexington, Good Samaritan comes closest, in community reputation, to filling such a role by receiving a large share of poor patients. Support for this characterization can be found in the fact that subsequent to the study, the city of Lexington floated a sizable bond issue for enlarging the bed capacity of Good Samaritan, with the bonds to be repaid from the anticipated increase in hospital receipts. Location also supports such a role for Good Samaritan. Geographically, Lexington is bisected by an east-west Main Street. Half the population—the poorer half—resides north of Main Street; the wealthier half resides south of Main, in which area all three hospitals are located. Of the three, however, Good Samaritan lies considerably closer than the other two to the poorer, northern half.

St. Joseph Hospital is maintained by a Roman Catholic religious order which operates four other hospitals in Kentucky and West Virginia. Although it is administered by nuns residing on the hospital grounds, all professional patient care is carried out by lay personnel. Catholic religious symbolism and ritual are evident in the corridor furnishings and heard over the public-address system. However, St. Joseph serves a broader segment of the Lexington metropolitan population than the Catholic portion alone. That portion comprises approximately one sixth of the Greater Lexington population, making it one of the largest religious groups, but nevertheless, distinctly a minority in the total community.

The community base of Central Baptist can be portrayed by comparing it with Good Samaritan. Both are voluntary community hospitals with historical ties to Protestant denominations. (In both cases, the religious ties have ceased to exert any strong effect upon internal hospital policy or routine; by contrast, St. Joseph is Catholic not only from the standpoint of ownership and control by a regional Catholic order but also by virtue of a more expressive religious atmosphere within the hospital itself.) Central Baptist was built in 1954. Its governing board strongly emphasizes its local autonomy and community orientation and opposes outside influence upon hospital affairs by state or federal government. It has made evident its opposition by declining to seek government loans or support for modernization and enlargement. Its community orientation is mainly toward the white middle-class and working-class sectors of the community, and away from the lower-class sector. Further, almost half its total admissions are from outside Fayette County. At the time of the study, it was a lily-white hospital, maintaining an unstated policy against the admission of black patients. This policy is now liberalized.

As indicated above, Good Samaritan, while receiving many white middle-class patients, is oriented as well to lower-class and black patients. Despite the financial and administrative burdens, Good Samaritan maintains a relatively open policy toward indigent patients.

Having discussed in general terms the community position of the four hospitals, we next examine the pattern of obstetrical admissions in our study. This pattern will be expressed in terms of four social characteristics of the mothers: (1) county of residence, (2) religious identification (Catholic versus non-Catholic), (3) social class, and (4) race.

By county of residence, the overall distribution of the 274 hospital deliveries is as appears in Table 4-8. Woodford Memorial had 8 percent of the total deliveries. For reasons that appear shortly, we may regard the three Lexington hospitals as constituting a system, ignoring Woodford. Half the Lexington deliveries occurred at Central Baptist and one quarter each at Good Samaritan and St. Joseph.

To what extent does Woodford Memorial serve residents from its own county base? Table 4-9 provides the answer. Nineteen of the 22 Woodford County residents (86.4 percent) with hospital deliveries used Woodford Memorial Hospital; only three used Lexington facilities. Also, a few Lexingtonians, some of whom had a past or current connection with Woodford County, used it. Obviously, Woodford Memorial met the obstetrical needs of most women in its own geographical base. This finding may reassure those health planners who, projecting a rationally graded series of satellite and central hospitals, worry that some patients will use remote medical centers in preference to nearby local hospitals. Good highways facilitate this behavior, and the greater prestige of metropolitan medical centers provides a motivating impetus. In this instance, there is no significant tendency for the Woodford County women to use Lexington hospitals.

Table 4-8
Distribution of Hospital Deliveries by County of Residence

Hospital	N	Percent of Total	Percent of Total (Lexington Hospitals Only)
Woodford Memorial	22	8.0	—
St. Joseph	63	23.0	25.0
Good Samaritan	64	23.4	25.4
Central Baptist	125	45.6	49.6
Total	274	100.0	100.0

Table 4–9
Utilization of Woodford Memorial Hospital, by County of Residence

Hospital	Woodford County Residents		Non-Woodford Residents		Total	
	N	%	N	%	N	%
Woodford Memorial Hospital	19	86.4	3[a]	1.2	22	8.0
Non-Woodford (Lexington hospitals)	3	13.6	249	98.8	252	92.0
Total	22	100.0	252	100.0	274[b]	100.0

Chi^2 = 187.41
D.F. = 1
$p < .001$

[a]Two of these mothers had previously lived in Woodford County.

[b]This table excludes the five home deliveries; of these, one was a Woodford County infant and four were non-Woodford infants.

It thus appears that the three Lexington hospitals, situated in close proximity to each other, providing modern obstetric care, and making comparable charges for their services, can be examined in terms of their selective utilization by mothers in the sample. The three hospitals constitute a closed system of community hospitals in the sense that a mother who uses one of the three does not use the others; there are no other hospitals in the community. Further, only three of the Lexington-area mothers went out of their county; as noted above, they went to Woodford Memorial Hospital, situated ten miles from downtown Lexington. Obstetric care, with its unschedulable final event following periodic prenatal visits, does not lend itself to a great geographic separation between mother's residence and hospital.

The role of religious identification in promoting distinctive patterns of hospital utilization will be examined by comparing Catholic with non-Catholic mothers. This is in effect a comparison of Catholic and Protestant mothers. The sample contained no mothers who identified themselves as Jewish. Thirty-one (11 percent) of the mothers identified themselves as Roman Catholic, 245 (88 percent) as Protestant, and 3 (1 percent) as having no religious affiliation. No systematic data were gathered on Protestant denominational identification. While it is conceivable that Baptist and Methodist identifications (both are strong churches in the area) influence admissions to Central Baptist Hospital and Good Samaritan Hospital, we confined our scrutiny to the effect of the single religious distinction, Catholic-Protestant. The question is, to what extent is Catholic identification related to use of St. Joseph Hospital?

To answer the question, we established three religious categories: Catholic couples, mixed Catholic—non-Catholic couples, and non-Catholic couples. The mixed category is included to assess the effect of religiously mixed marriages on hospital utilization. To classify couples thus, we also drew upon data on husbands' religious identification. The overall distribution for husbands is 32 (11 percent) Roman Catholic, 237 (85 percent) Protestant, and 10 (4 percent) with no religious identification.

Table 4-10 shows hospital utilization in relation to religious identification. The Catholic hospital was used by 70.8 percent of the mothers in the Catholic couples, by 43.8 percent of the mothers in the mixed couples, and by 16.7 percent of the mothers in the non-Catholic couples. These differences are statistically significant. Catholic religious identification plays an important role in hospital choice; the more religiously homogeneous the couple, the stronger the role.

We stated above that the particular hospital used by a mother was not necessarily deliberately chosen by her from among several hospitals equally available to her. We argued that the mother's choice falls upon a particular physician, who in turn arranges for her admission to the particular hospital with which he or she is affiliated. Having made that argument, we would like to point out that the foregoing findings on hospital utilization in terms of mother's religious identification are consistent with the alternative argument, namely, that the mother directly chose her hospital with religious criteria in mind, because she would feel more comfortable and secure in "her own" type of institution. The argument makes more sense, we believe, for the independent variable of religious identification than for the other independent variables examined here—county of residence, social class, and race. Even so, the paramount fact remains that the mother directly chose the doctor and not the hospital. Of course, nonmedical considerations such as religion and ethnicity may regulate

Table 4-10
Hospital Utilization by Religious Identification (Catholic and Non-Catholic)

	Religious Identification of Parents							
Hospital	Both Catholic		Mixed		Both Non-Catholic		Total	
	N	%	N	%	N	%	N	%
St. Joseph	17	70.8	7	43.8	39	16.7	63	23.0
Other hospitals	7	29.2	9	56.2	195	83.3	211	77.0
Total	24	100.0	16	100.0	234	100.0	274[a]	100.0

Chi^2 = 40.21
D.F. = 3
$p < .001$

[a]This table excludes the five home deliveries.

the choice of doctor. We shall look into this general issue in Chapter 6, where we examine choice of specialist–nonspecialist doctor in relation to mother's social class, and race of mother in relation to race of doctor.

Table 4-10 may be studied from another standpoint. Instead of inquiring about the strength of religious influence upon hospital utilization, we may ask, To what extent does St. Joseph Hospital serve the Catholic obstetrical patients of the sample, and to what extent does it serve non-Catholic patients? Of the 63 St. Joseph patients, 24 (26 percent) came from partly or wholly Catholic couples. While by far the larger proportion of Catholic families used the Catholic hospital, the Catholic hospital also served a very large proportion of non-Catholics. Almost three quarters of its patients were non-Catholic. If all the Catholic and mixed couples had used St. Joseph Hospital and none had used the other hospitals, this would have added 16 Catholic patients to the St. Joseph roster, increasing its Catholic utilization rate to 62.5 percent. Even with utilization by all Catholic and mixed couples, the hospital would still have to depend upon 37.5 percent non-Catholic utilization. This fact corresponds well with the generally open orientation of St. Joseph and signifies also an important set of environmental contingencies.

In many major metrpolitan areas of the nation, the Roman Catholic component of the population is large enough to require the full capacity of existing Catholic hospitals, and utilization by non-Catholic patients is minimal; such hospitals are as religiously homogeneous as Catholic parochial schools. Further, many of the patients are elderly, first- or second-generation American citizens in modest economic circumstances, and the medical care provided invokes the force of charitable religious tradition. By contrast, the Catholic component of the Lexington community, and of many other smaller metropolitan areas, is a minority of insufficient size to provide the basis for an exclusively Catholic hospital. In addition, perhaps more unique to Lexington, the Catholic component is substantially middle-class, able to purchase its full hospital care and not requiring charitable provision. Having a predominantly paying, heterogeneous Catholic and non-Catholic clientele gives St. Joseph a stronger orientation to the whole urban area. By contrast, Catholic hospitals in larger metropolitan areas have a more closed and parochial atmosphere.

The passage of the federal Medicare and Medicaid programs has substantially reduced economic barriers to hospital care. Poor people need not place such heavy reliance upon purely charitable hospital care, though there is still need for it (Lyons, 1972). While economic considerations remain important, our study suggests that cultural and religious factors are also a viable force in hospital utilization.

What effect has the mother's social class upon her hospital utilization? It was suggested above that in multihospital communities, hospitals tend to develop different social-class profiles even when all are community hospitals and maintain a receptive posture toward various population segments.

Table 4-11 shows the influence of social class. Let us consider Woodford Memorial Hospital first. Since this hospital is county based, the question of social-class composition of the Woodford Memorial mothers becomes in part a question about the class composition of Woodford County, particularly that portion of the population in the childbearing phase of life. Census figures show that the Woodford County adult population had a median education of 8.8 school years, a 15 percent illiteracy rate (less than five grades of school), and a labor force that was 43 percent unskilled labor. The general population base thus tended to be lower-middle and lower class, as were the mothers who delivered at Woodford Memorial Hospital.

The figures for the Lexington hospitals support the general concept of differential utilization by social class. The greatest contrast occurred between Good Samaritan and Central Baptist. Half the Good Samaritan mothers are in Class V. Some Class V mothers are indigent; of these, the ones who are residents of the city have their hospitalization costs paid partly by city welfare funds. It is to be noted, however, that Good Samaritan is not simply a lower-class hospital; 20 percent of its patients are from Class I-II. Its traditional good reputation in the community for medical expertise and humane care probably makes it a favored hospital for many old-line, upper-class Lexingtonians. It has, however, a marked deficit of utilization by Class III and IV patients. By contrast, Central Baptist Hospital has much stronger utilization by the "common woman"—the Class III or IV mother—with over 60 percent coming from these strata. Many Class I-II mothers also use Central Baptist. However, this hospital lacks a complete community profile because of its relative lack of Class V mothers. Of the three hospitals, St. Joseph has the most uniform distribution of patients by social class. Almost half its patients come from Classes III and IV, with the other half coming equally from Class I-II and Class V.

The final patient characteristic that remains to be examined for its impact upon hospital utilization is race. In raising the question of the effects of racial status upon hospital utilization, we do not propose that such effects flow from race as a biological characteristic. Whatever the biological effects and concomitants of race may be, they are heavily overlaid by the preponderant sociocultural influences that bear upon so highly complex and symbolic a behavior as a woman's entry into a hospital. For our purposes, race is a purely social category which may hold varying consequences and life-chances for the individual.

We said in Chapter 3 that the sample contained 247 whites and 32 blacks. One of the blacks and four of the whites delivered at home. Excluding these, the distribution of deliveries is that presented in Table 4-12. The most striking fact is that no blacks entered Central Baptist Hospital. This finding is in accord with the previously noted admission policy prevailing there. The effect of this policy is seen all the more clearly from the fact that Central Baptist had the largest number of mothers in the sample. In St. Joseph and Good Samaritan hospitals, approximately one quarter of the patients are black; at Woodford Hospital, only

Table 4-11
Hospital Utilization by Social Class

| Social Class | Hospital | | | | | | | | | |
| | St. Joseph | | Good Samaritan | | Central Baptist | | Woodford Memorial | | Total | |
	N	%	N	%	N	%	N	%	N	%
I-II	16	25.4	13	20.3	30	24.0	1	4.5	60	21.9
III	18	28.6	5	7.8	39	31.2	2	9.1	64	23.4
IV	13	20.6	14	21.9	37	29.6	10	45.5	74	27.0
V	16	25.4	32	50.0	19	15.2	9	40.9	76	27.7
Total	63	100.0	64	100.0	125	100.0	22	100.0	274[a]	100.0

$Chi^2 = 39.87$
D.F. = 9
$p < .001$

Chi^2 excluding
Woodford Memorial = 24.10
D.F. = 6
$p < .001$

Chi^2: St. Joseph
versus Good Samaritan = 13.01
D.F. = 3
$p < .01$

Chi^2: St. Joseph
versus Central Baptist = 3.73
D.F. = 3
$p \not< .05$

Chi^2: Good Samaritan
versus Central Baptist = 30.13
D.F. = 3
$p < .001$

[a]The five home deliveries are not included.

Table 4-12
Hospital Utilization by Race

Race	St. Joseph		Good Samaritan		Hospital Central Baptist		Woodford Memorial		Total	
	N	%	N	%	N	%	N	%	N	%
Black	14	22.2	16	25.0	0	0.0	1	4.5	31	11.3
White	49	77.8	48	75.0	125	100.0	21	95.5	243	88.7
Total	63	100.0	64	100.0	125	100.0	22	100.0	274	100.0

$Chi^2 = 35.37$
D.F. = 3
$p < .001$

one patient of the 22 is black. The overall distribution of patients is significantly different from chance expectation, and this difference is largely due to the Central Baptist component.

An overall comparison, as presented in Table 4-12, between all whites and all blacks ignores one important parameter—the comparative social status of the two groups. In the geographical area of this study, as in most other parts of the United States, to be black is to bear many disadvantages, in social status, housing, employment, and education. As Table 4-13 shows, the black families in the sample have lower social status than the whites. The 32 black families comprise 11.5 percent of the whole sample, but the 22 black families in Class V comprise 27.5 percent of that stratum. Only in Class V are blacks overrepresented. Even in the relatively low-status level of Class IV they are underrepresented, comprising 8 percent (6 of 75) of that class. Toward the higher end of the class ladder, there are only four black families in Class III (17.4 percent) and none in Classes I and II.

To permit a more definitive comparison of blacks and whites on hospital utilization (as well as other variables), we constructed a matched black-white comparison group. We took the black mothers in the sample and then, regarding the white mothers as a pool of potential matches, we selected one by one a series of white mothers whose characteristics closely resembled those of the black mothers. The mothers are individually paired on the characteristics of social class, age, and number of children. In an additional step designed to maximize the comparability of the two sets of mothers, we limited the groups to mothers who were residents of Fayette County. This was done in order to exclude rural and small-town participants and to confine the comparison to persons who shared the predominantly urban environment of the county. This latter provision was important in relation to choice of hospital and also in

Table 4-13
Social Class and Race

Social Class	Race					
	White		Black		Total	
	N	%	N	%	N	%
I–II	60	24.3	0	0.0	60	21.5
III	60	24.3	4	12.5	64	23.0
IV	69	28.0	6	18.8	75	26.9
V	58	23.4	22	68.8	80	28.6
Total	247	100.0	32	100.1	279	100.0

Chi^2 = 30.62
D.F. = 3
$p < .001$

relation to other items of health behavior still to be examined. Excluding the non-Fayette families led to the exclusion of two black families; accordingly, the matched comparison group consists of 30 black and 30 white families.

Table 4-14 presents hospital utilization by race, using the 30 matched pairs of black and white mothers. It affords a precise examination of race and hospital utilization with several other important variables controlled. As it happened, one black mother used Woodford Memorial Hospital although she was a Fayette County resident; and, as previously noted, another black mother delivered at home. Table 4-14 shows that half the remaining black mothers went to St. Joseph and half went to Good Samaritan. Of the 30 matching white mothers, 15 (50 percent) went to Central Baptist, 9 (30 percent) to Good Samaritan, and 6 (20 percent) to St. Joseph. This distribution is significantly nonchance; as in Table 4-12, the factor that most significantly structures the distribution is the absence of blacks at Central Baptist, rather than a disparity in black-white admissions at the other two hospitals.

The latter observation suggests three further considerations. First, when a hospital restricts the admission of black patients it effectively places a greater lower-class burden upon other community hospitals. Second, since poor patients tend to present more medical complications and risks in maternity care as in other branches of medical care, the burden may also make added demands upon other hospital services, such as the emergency room, blood bank, and clinical lab. Third, the distinct financial difficulties of dealing with poor patients are avoided and transferred to other institutional shoulders. These difficulties include trouble in collecting unpaid bills from the patient and meager payments by public agencies which do not cover the full cost of expensive services.

A question may be raised about the relative quality of care in the three hospitals: By their absence from Central Baptist and dependence upon Good Samaritan and St. Joseph, do the black mothers receive second-rate maternity services? This question is naturally suggested, since so often racially segregated facilities and institutions, even though policies are premised on the concept of "separate but equal," offer an inferior grade of service to nonwhites. When racial attitudes crystallize into patterns of exclusion and discrimination, the majority or excluding group may, however, perpetuate demand for segregated institutions that do not in fact offer a superior grade of service. Sometimes the client obtains only an exclusive and discriminatory character in the service provided, without greater quality. On occasion, the service may be inferior to that given in more open institutions.

This study contains no data for assessing the overall quality of medical and hospital care at each hospital. All three hospitals have well-trained staffs and a good community reputation. There is no reason to suppose that obstetrical care at St. Joseph and Good Samaritan is inferior to that at Central Baptist. Therefore, whatever the community impact and financial implications of racial patterns in admissions, the black mothers probably received care of good quality.

Table 4–14
Hospital Utilization in Matched Black-White Comparison Group

| | Hospital | | | | | | | | | | | |
| | *St. Joseph* | | *Good Samaritan* | | *Central Baptist* | | *Woodford Memorial* | | *Home Delivery* | | *Total* | |
Race	N	%	N	%	N	%	N	%	N	%	N	%
Black	14	70.0	14	60.8	0	0.0	1	100.0	1	100.0	30	50.0
White	6	30.0	9	39.2	15	100.0	0	0.0	0	0.0	30	50.0
Total	20	100.0	23	100.0	15	100.0	1	100.0	1	100.0	60	100.0

Chi^2 excluding Woodford Memorial and Home Delivery = 19.24
D.F. = 2
$p < .001$

Length of Hospitalization

The long-term trend in our society toward the use of a hospital for delivery and associated care of mother and infant has placed a major new claim upon hospital facilities. The National Center for Health Statistics collects data on the extent to which patients are hospitalized for 33 different medical conditions. Data from this source showed that delivery was by far the most common single reason for hospitalization, comprising 15 percent of all the hospital admissions. In another respect, however, there has been a gradual lessening of the claim that deliveries make upon hospitals. We refer to the decline in the length of hospital stay for delivery.

Studies conducted by the Health Information Foundation of family health care in 1953, 1958, and 1963 found that median length of stays for delivery were 4.5 days, 4.4 days, and 3.7 days, respectively. These figures are based on live births occurring to families included in national samples (Andersen and Anderson, 1967: 45). The National Center for Health Statistics (1966: 20) in its household Health Interview Survey found a mean length of stay of 4.2 days. The 274 hospital deliveries in our study have a mean stay of 4.7 days, with a standard deviation of 2.31 days and a median of 4.1 days. We will now analyze some of the factors in our study that caused variations in the length of the mother's hospital stay.

Some portion of the shortening of hospital stay can be attributed to a more systematic approach to labor and delivery, regarded as medical processes. Some hospitals and obstetricians have a laissez-faire philosophy, whereby the woman labors at her own pace under surveillance, with occasional professional assistance and encouragement. More typical, however, is a hurry-up approach. The woman is placed into leg stirrups to facilitate inspection by personnel as to how far labor has progressed (other bodily positions are possible but they lack this advantage). The placenta may be ruptured if natural labor is too slow. If she is conscious, the woman may be strongly encouraged to "bear down hard." Forceps may be used. Surgical episiotomy is routinely performed in many hospitals; in addition to forestalling irregular tearing of the perineal tissues, an episiotomy facilitates presentation of the fetus. Manual manipulation of the pelvis and use of medication to stimulate contractions are common. The umbilical cord is severed immediately upon delivery and the expulsion of the placenta is hastened by manual technique.

As noted above, the basic rationale for the use of hospitals in delivery is to provide medical supervision. The delivery occurs not just anywhere in the hospital but in the operating-room-like delivery room; the atmosphere and equipment are aseptic (Zimmerman, 1975). The tempo of the labor-delivery process is surgical, with the net effect of expediting this very critical phase of the total period of hospitalization. In speaking of expediting features, we do not mean to imply that these are employed solely for the convenience of the staff. A shorter labor, if not too forced, is easier for the mother also. Likewise, it is better for the infant not to hover too lengthily at the critical point between dependent and independent life.

Recent concern among women's groups has drawn attention to the fact that the techniques used by modern obstetrics are just a fraction of the total repertoire of cultural practices associated with childbirth. Many such practices are magical, reflecting prescientific attempts to influence the mysterious generative force of life. James Frazer's classic, *The Golden Bough* (1920) cites many such practices. For example, it was the custom among some peoples to avoid the use of string or tying of knots during pregnancy and delivery, on the theory that these would impede the passage of the baby. Mead and Newton (1967) surveyed techniques and rituals currently used in nonliterate societies and found that many use the birth stool, whereby the mother squats and the expulsion of the infant is assisted by gravity. This has attracted favorable notice and may hold some potential for contemporary practice.

No feature of women's health care has received more scrutiny than the medical conduct of delivery. Many of the childbirth practices that obstetricians routinely accept are coming under increasing question. For example, should the lithotomy position, used in virtually all American hospitals, be the standard position for delivery? Is it best for mother and infant, or is it simply a matter of convenience for staff, whereby they can quickly observe the mother's progress? The Boston Women's Health Book Collective challenges the routine performance of episiotomies upon women before delivery (Boston Women's Health Book Collective, 1973: 187). There is also a serious questioning of newer, technologically sophisticated devices such as the fetal heartbeat monitor, on the grounds that they interfere with labor and delivery as a beneficial process for both mother and infant (Arms, 1975).

In relation to the focus in our study upon the length of hospitalization, it should be clear that there is no scientific rule for determining the optimum length of hospitalization. *Prenatal Care* (1967: 36) says that the average length of stay for maternity care is about five days. It observes that complications of delivery, such as Caesarean section, can increase the duration. Since that publication appeared, many hospitals have moved toward four- and three-day stays.

In practice, most hospitals have a standard length of stay for routine maternity cases. The standard varies from hospital to hospital and also between regions and cultures, though everywhere economic pressures for the containment of health-care costs are tending to reduce the length of stay. A matron in charge of maternity services at St. Thomas's, a large London teaching hospital, informed the author in 1968 that her hospital's standard was 14 days. By current American standards, 14 days is a very prolonged confinement. She acknowledged that this was longer than necessary for the safe clearance of mother and infant; the standard was set primarily in recognition of the nursing department's need to provide its student nurses with a sufficient period to observe the newborn and the mother-infant relationship.

It would be incorrect, though easy, to attribute prolongation at the London hospital entirely to the educational needs of the nursing program. English hospitals in general have tended toward long maternity stays; a 1964 survey by the Royal College of Obstetricians indicated a national average of 9.6 days (Cohen, 1964: 109). Thus, there are lengthy hospital confinements and at the same time, as noted above, many deliveries at home. Cultural values permeate health care in persistent and subtle ways. It is perhaps not too farfetched to see in the long hospital stays a lingering attachment to Victorian sentiments, whereby middle-class expectant women were treated as if ill.

In its effort to universalize good health care, the English National Health Service has attempted to extend traditional middle-class standards to all hospital maternity cases. This tends to saturate facilities to the breaking point, especially since many English hospitals are cramped and antiquated. In response to this pressure, English authorities have proposed and to some extent implemented a system of planned early discharge. Under this system, the mother is discharged within 48 hours of a normal delivery, to be supervised at home by a trained midwife in the service of the local health department. The dispatch with which a mother and infant can be discharged thus depends to some extent upon the adequacy of follow-up health supervision.

Within a single hospital, there are variations in the length of maternity stay. When beds are short in relation to the number of expected deliveries, this pressure may generate discharges that occur somewhat earlier than policy prescribes.

Though not usually given explicit medical recognition, the mother's desires and life situation form another set of forces which may influence length of stay. For example, the parity of the mother might be important. The first-time mother probably needs more time to adjust to motherhood than the veteran. While instruction in infant feeding and handling does not strictly require that the mother be in the hospital, such instruction can be carried out more easily while mother and infant are inpatients that it can subsequently. The prospect of leaving and then being on her own, with complete responsibility for the helpless infant, creates anxiety in many new mothers, while the mother with young children at home may be eager to return to them, especially if household arrangements during her absence are makeshift. On the other hand, the mother with many children and heavy responsibilities at home may welcome a few extra days' hospitalization purely as a respite before return to the household, now expanded by the addition of the infant.

The distribution of stays in Lexington hospitals of the 274 mothers in our sample is as follows:

Length of Stay (in days)	Number
1	3
2	21
3	56
4	49
5	86
6	23
7	23
8-10	5
11-19	8
	274

In this group of hospital deliveries, the clustering around three, four, and five days is so noticeable that it invites attention to the deviant cases—the brief stays as well as the protracted. An examination of the long stays reveals that medical problems are largely responsible. Here are four examples, with the mother's description of the circumstances:

(19-day stay) "When she was born, nerve tissue on the lower part of her back was exposed, spinal fluid collected on her brain, and she needed an operation." (The mother in this case was discharged without the infant, the latter remaining for the operation.)

(14-day stay) "It was a Caesarean delivery. She had convulsions about two hours after birth. Doctors examined her and couldn't find anything wrong. She was irritable and cried a lot. The doctors prescribed Dilantin and some other anti-convulsants, which had *no* effect. Also, the phenobarb didn't seem to help her any. It didn't sedate her or relieve her irritation." (The extended stay in this case was for the purpose of evaluation. The mother added that when the infant was seven months old, the family went on a trip to California, where at Stanford University Hospital physicians discovered that the infant had three kidneys and a partially obstructed urinary tract.)

(14-day stay) "The baby was fine, but I had phlebitis. It was upsetting, having to stay so long when I wanted to get home with him." (The mother in this case was hospitalized for the longer period, along with the infant, to enable the phlebitis to subside.)

(14-day stay) "She was a preemie and weighed 4 pounds and 15 ounces. She had fluid in her lungs for two weeks. They had to give her special milk. When she got home, there was so much to do with her, and the other children, it was impossible." (A readmission was arranged for the premature baby, lasting until it was of sufficient size, and mother sufficiently trained in its management, for discharge.)

The distinctive feature of the one- and two-day stays is the low social status of the families involved. Of the 24 brief stays, 17 (71 percent) are in Class V families, 6 (25 percent) are in Class IV, 1 (4 percent) is in Class III; no brief stays occurred in Classes I and II. By hospital, 5 brief stays occurred in St. Joseph, accounting for 8 percent of its admissions; 10 occurred in Good Samaritan, for 16 percent of its admissions; 3 occurred in Central Baptist, for only 2 percent of its admissions (recall, however, its low percent of Class V patients); and 6 occurred in Woodford Memorial, for 30 percent of its admissions.

The role of social class in brief stays suggests a systematic examination of length of stay in relation to class. This is presented in Table 4–15. A strong and consistent trend appears. The higher-class mothers stay longer than lower-class mothers by approximately two days. Although there is appreciable variation within each class, it appears roughly that the Class I and II mother remains in the hospital for 5½ to 6 days, the Class III and IV mother for 4½ to 5 days, and the Class V mother for slightly less than 4 days. The variation among classes is statistically significant; the significance stems not entirely from the concentration of short stays at the lower end of the class ladder, but rather from differences throughout the status ladder. While the study did not produce data on hospital expenses and insurance coverage, we believe that the economic side of class status may account for class differences in length of stay. Certainly it would be difficult to develop a case for lesser medical need by lower-class mother or infant as the basis for a shorter stay. Analysis of the 13 cases where the stay is very long—eight or more days—reveals that two are in Class I, two in Class II, one in Class III, four in Class IV, and four in Class V. These numbers, though small, suggest that long stays are found throughout the class continuum. As we noted earlier, the long stays were frequently connected with a medical exigency. Brief stays, in contrast, are concentrated in Class V; but even above Class V, there is a tendency for lower status to be accompanied by shorter stays.

Table 4–15
Length of Hospital Stay by Social Class

Social Class	Length of Stay	Standard Deviation	N
I	5.86 days	1.92 days	28
II	5.50	2.05	32
III	4.78	1.42	64
IV	4.76	2.23	74
V	3.95	2.91	76
Total	4.74	2.31	274

Analysis of variance:
F-Ratio = 5.03
D.F. = 4,269
$p < .001$

The connection established between the mother's social class and the length of her hospital confinement raises a further question: Does this trend prevail generally in the four hospitals under study, or is it more accentuated in some than in others? To investigate this question, we examine length of stay in the four hospitals; Table 4-16 presents the mean length of stay and standard deviation of length in each. It shows an appreciable variation among the hospitals. Central Baptist has the longest mean stay, 5.08 days, while Woodford Memorial has the shortest, 3.54 days. St. Joseph has a mean of 5.03 days, close to that of Central Baptist. Good Samaritan's mean of 4.18 days is the lowest of the three Lexington hospitals. The differences are statistically significant. Eliminating Woodford Memorial and confining our attention to the Lexington hospitals, we find that the analysis of variance is still significant at the .05 level.

Now we may take up the question as to whether, in a given hospital, the lower-class patients have the shortest stays. The findings bearing upon this question are presented in Table 4-17. We omit Woodford Memorial from this table, since as Table 4-11 shows, almost all its patients are from Classes IV and V. Of the three Lexington hospitals, only in Good Samaritan is there a significant class tendency. The Good Samaritan Class I patients have longer stays than their counterparts elsewhere, and its Class V patients have much shorter stays than the Class V patients elsewhere. Also noteworthy is the relatively small amount of variation in the stays of the Good Samaritan Class V patients; the 32 patients in this group comprise half the caseload, but the standard deviation is only 1.36 days. It is perhaps notable that Good Samaritan, as the hospital with the heaviest load of poor patients, is also the only hospital where class affects length of stay. We stated above that it comes the closest of the three hospitals to serving as the metropolitan hospital for indigent patients of Greater Lexington. We suggest that in conjunction with its openness and its civic responsibility toward admission of poor patients, Good Samaritan moves them through the maternity experience quickly.

Table 4-16
Length of Hospital Stay by Hospital

Hospital	N	Mean Length of Stay	Standard Deviation
St. Joseph	63	5.03 days	2.74 days
Good Samaritan	64	4.18	1.72
Central Baptist	125	5.08	2.32
Woodford Memorial	22	3.54	1.71
Total	274	4.74	2.31

Analysis of variance:	Analysis of variance excluding Woodford Memorial:
F-ratio = 4.59	F-ratio = 3.45
D.F. = 3,270	D.F. = 2,249
$p < .01$	$p < .05$

Table 4-17
Length of Stay in Lexington Hospitals, by Social Class

Social Class	St. Joseph			Good Samaritan			Central Baptist		
	N	Mean Stay (in days)	Standard Deviation (in days)	N	Mean Stay (in days)	Standard Deviation (in days)	N	Mean Stay (in days)	Standard Deviation (in days)
I-II	16	5.62	2.57	13	6.07	1.70	30	5.46	1.77
III	18	5.55	1.82	5	4.20	1.30	39	4.46	1.04
IV	13	4.38	1.80	14	4.00	1.41	37	5.48	2.54
V	16	4.37	4.06	32	3.50	1.36	19	4.94	3.92
Total	63	5.03	2.74	64	4.18	1.72	125	5.08	2.32

Analysis of variance:
F-Ratio: 1.01   9.86   1.62
D.F.: 3,59   3,60   3,121
p: $\not< .05$ $< .001$ $\not< .05$

5 Early Infant Care

The preceding chapters lead to the emergence of the infant into the foreground of the study. The focus in Chapter 4 upon pregnancy and delivery will be followed here by a sociological examination of several important features of the care of young infants. The scope of our inquiry is set by the simple and objective biosocial needs of infants. They need to be fed and to sleep. They need to be kept clean and comfortable. They need caretakers. These common needs can be satisfied in various ways. For example, young infants can be fed at the breast, whether their mother's breast or that of another lactating female. They can be given stored breast milk, not at the breast. They can be fed with non-human milk, whether by their mother or another agent of care. We shall consider varying ways of meeting this particular need and explore the effects of such social influences as social class, family size, and the birth order of the infant upon the modes of feeding employed in our sample.

In Chapter 4 we noted that pregnancy and delivery have in recent times come into medical culture, owing to the application of biomedical science. It can scarcely be claimed that there is an analogous science of infant care, whereby scientific knowledge provides unequivocal answers to the many questions that arise in the care of an infant; however, many contemporary parents and other caretakers are eager for the information and advice provided by experts who write on the subject. Such experts are usually scientifically trained as pediatricians, child psychiatrists, or child psychologists. Their authoritativeness arises not only from their own professional experience in dealing with infants but also from their ability to interpret and purvey relevant scientific information. As we consider the study findings dealing with selected features of infant care, we shall also present a picture of contemporary expert advice on the features under consideration, and we will develop a sociohistorical perspective by looking at past practice and the expert advice presented in earlier times.

The biomedical sciences cannot always give direct answers to practical problems of infant care. Other resources come into play. If the biomedical sciences do not present a decisive answer to the concerned and puzzled mother who wants to know how long she may safely let the baby cry, or whether she should bottle-feed or breast-feed, the behavioral sciences can at least tell her, through questionnaire and interview studies, what *other* mothers are doing. The results of such research filter into popular culture and become part of the informational context in which parents care for their own babies.

In order to provide research comparison, we will introduce the results of several other studies of infant care. It is of particular interest to compare our total Kentucky sample with other samples in regard to such questions as breast- or bottle-feeding. In some instances, it will be possible to make a more critical comparison, for example to determine whether an independent, or causal, variable such as social class influences infant-care behavior similarly in different, independently conducted studies.

Breast-Feeding and Bottle-Feeding: Pediatric Advice, Historical Background, and Comparative Studies

Every new mother faces immediately the question of how to feed her infant. This question does not present itself out of the blue at the time of delivery, but is anticipated beforehand. It is woven deep into the texture of prenatal fantasy. The choice between breast- and bottle-feeding looms as a large, emotionally toned issue in the minds of many mothers.

From a sheerly instrumental standpoint, feeding the infant is a means to the end of his survival and growth. From this standpoint the mode of feeding may be regarded as a neutral avenue toward that end. Almost every mother will be able to nurse her baby adequately, and almost every baby will thrive on breast milk (Berg, 1973: 99). Equally, almost every baby will thrive on a properly composed and prepared formula.

Each method has its advantages. Breast-feeding has the incomparable advantage of being natural. Benjamin Spock (1976: 93), the pediatrician whose advice has been spread to a whole generation of American parents, emphasizes this feature of breast-feeding. The chemical composition of the human mother's milk is specifically adapted to the nutritional requirements of the human infant. Breast-feeding provides milk that is fresh, sterile, and always served at the correct (i.e., body) temperature. Breast milk is more digestible than formulas and causes fewer feeding problems. It requires no extra effort in its preparation, although a mother with an adequately nourishing diet is advised to consume several supplements daily: 1,000 extra calories, extra protein, and additional minerals and vitamins that can be obtained from milk and green leafy vegetables. No special equipment is necessary for nursing. Milk for the infant need not be purchased; the relative economy of breast-feeding is attested to by many authorities (Slobody, 1968: 30; Newson and Newson, 1963: 165).

From a biological standpoint, the galactopoiesis, or milk-secreting function, of the female is extraordinarily well-protected, even in the absence of adequate diet (as during war or other extreme situations). Just as before birth the fetus enjoys a high degree of protection from stresses and deprivations that may occur in the maternal environment, following birth the mother's capacity for providing sustenance to the infant is relatively invulnerable. It has further been noted that breast-feeding, in contrast to bottle-feeding, provides greater satisfaction to the infant's sucking drive—a need over and above his direct requirements for nourishment. Breast-feeding also provides physical gratification to the mother, through the buildup of tension associated with the nipple erection reflex and its release through letdown and the baby's sucking. It also hastens the return of the uterus to its pre-pregnancy size and position.

Although breast-feeding has many advantages, bottle-feeding (also called dry, manual, or artificial feeding) has advantages too. The mother is freer to separate herself from the baby for the demands of work or other interests. Bottle-feeding can be delegated to another caretaker. Weaning from bottle to cup may be easier than weaning from breast to cup. If the mother is unable to nurse, bottle-feeding may become a matter not merely of advantage, but of necessity. Illness of the mother may render breast-feeding inadvisable, or her breasts may become sore from being sucked. From the standpoint of the infant, there are occasional contraindications: a markedly premature infant may be able to suck a bottle nipple better than the breast; rarely, an infant may be allergic to breast milk. Another advantage of bottle-feeding is that it affords an objective measure of the amount of milk consumed by the infant at each feeding. This serves to allay maternal anxiety about inadequate food intake. Dr. Spock advises that adequate nourishment is being provided if the infant seems contented at most, though not necessarily all, breast-feedings, and if over a period of days, but not necessarily every day, there is weight gain. This advice, however, has little impact upon mothers who seek tangible evidence of a certain intake at every feeding.

Bottle-feeding is a prime example of the application of an artificial technology to a natural biological function. It is not a recent invention; feeding vessels have been found among the artifacts of ancient Greece and Egypt, and artificial feeding is discussed in the writings of these cultures (Davidson, 1953). Ancient physicians and moral philosophers, however, took a dim view of bottle-feeding, recommending it only in cases of necessity. Cow's milk in earlier times was often unhygienic because of bovine infection and unsterile storage.

Before the advent of bottle-feeding on a mass scale, the wet-nurse was employed more widely than crude bottle devices when the mother herself was unable or unwilling to provide her own milk. Now a defunct role, the wet-nurse once flourished in infant care. In a review of early American infant-care practices, Caulfield writes that during the eighteenth century breast milk was the most frequently advertised commodity in American newspapers (Caulfield, 1952). Just as moral and medical authorities cautioned against the too-easy resort to bottle-feeding, so they cautioned against the use of wet-nurses. Women of style and aristocracy commonly employed wet-nurses to tend and feed their infants, fearing that breast-feeding would spoil their fashionable contours. Such behavior became the object of moral censure; reinforcing the censure was the fact that many wet-nurses were lower-class girls who had borne children out of wedlock. A belief prevailed during the eighteenth and nineteenth centuries that breast milk transmitted not only nourishment but also the moral qualities, for better or for worse, of the provider. Under this moral ideology arose the concept that every infant had the inherent right to suckle at his mother's breast.

A strong devotion to breast milk rather than dry feeding was seen during the late nineteenth and early twentieth centuries in the creation of philanthropic breast-milk banks in the larger cities. In those earlier times, the predominant reason for using artificial feeding, breast-milk banks, or wet-nurses lay not in the considerations of fashion mentioned above, but rather in the large number of infants with ill, absent, or deceased mothers. An additional reason lay in the belief, common among middle-class families in the rapidly growing and congested metropolitan areas, that the city was less healthful than the country for the rearing of young children. Many infants were sent to the countryside and wet-nursed for the first six to twelve months. Given the deplorable sanitary conditions and the high infant-mortality rates in the cities at that time, the practice probably had much to recommend it.

Although many contemporary pediatric authorities recommend breast-feeding over bottle-feeding, their recommendation does not extend to the providing of breast milk from other than the infant's own mother. The breast-milk bank and the wet-nurse are extinct social institutions. No one pleads for their restoration. This suggests that the advantage attributed to breast-feeding is regarded as a relative advantage, not an absolute to be achieved at all cost. Contemporary authorities, as seen above, agree substantially that prepared formulas can meet infant nutritional requirements almost as well as breast milk. There is the further implication that the advantage of breast over bottle lies not primarily in the substance of the milk, but in the feeding process; that is, through physical contact with the mother, the infant obtains pyschological and emotional benefits that are more difficult to achieve via bottle-feeding. The moral fervor of a century ago that insisted upon breast milk, even if provided by a wet-nurse or through a breast-milk bank, has been gradually replaced by a more modulated, pyschological view that stresses the infant's connection with its mother, preferably via breast-feeding, but failing that through bottle-feeding rather than resources outside the family.

Despite the general preference of pediatric authorities for breast-feeding, an increasing proportion of infants are bottle-fed. Davidson (1953: 86) offers the following explanation of this trend: "With the introduction in the latter nineteenth century of the pasteurization of milk, and the understanding of the sanitary handling and preservation of it, cow's milk became increasingly popular for artificial feeding. Along with this, the scientific study of infantile nutritional requirements hastened to increase the popularity of artificial feeding. Thus assured of a scientifically adequate formula, combined with hygienically pure milk, the vogue of artificial feeding became and is more widespread now than ever before in history." Another major impetus to bottle-feeding is that the baby-food industry has a commercial interest in furthering bottle-feeding:

cow's-milk preparations are vended, along with bottles and bottle-sterilizing equipment. Advertising, based upon commercial interest, has portrayed breast-feeding as unstylish and culturally backward in the United States, and currently in many developing societies (Wade, 1974).

Neonatal intensive care as practiced in contemporary centers of technologically advanced medical care constitutes a new source of demand for breast milk. Infants born at great risk of life, who would have perished ten or fifteen years ago, are maintained until they can function independently. Such infants frequently do better on breast milk than bottle milk, even if the milk comes from another mother (Pediatrics Department, 1977). But such infants comprise only a small fraction of the current total of births.

How widespread is bottle-feeding? For background and comparison with our own sample, let us view its extent in several other studies over recent decades. Bain conducted a national study in 1945 of feeding practices for all infants born during a one-week period in 2,513 American hospitals (of a maximum possible number of 3,600) with 25 or more beds (Bain, 1948). The Bain study determined the feeding mode at the time of the infant's hospital discharge. This study found that 38 percent of infants were exclusively breast-fed, 27 percent were fed by breast and bottle, and 35 percent were exclusively bottle-fed. In particular relation to our study, it was found that in Kentucky hospitals 38 percent of the infants were exclusively breast-fed, 46 percent were breast- and bottle-fed, and only 16 percent were exclusively bottle-fed. A lower percentage of breast-feeding occurred in metropolitan hospitals, as contrasted with rural or small-town hospitals.

In an interview study conducted in 1955–1956 of 1,433 mothers in upstate New York, Boek and his associates found that 24 percent of the infants were breast-fed (Boek et al., 1958). The proportion of babies who had been breast-fed was 31 percent in Class I-II, 25 percent in Class III, 21 percent in Class IV, and 21 percent in Class V (the class-ranking scheme employed is similar to that in our own study).

In a mail questionnaire study conducted in 1958, Robertson found that 30 percent of infants were either wholly or partly breast-fed at one week of age. Robertson's findings are based on questionnaires sent to a probability sample of mothers from a list that included 85 percent of the nation's births (Robertson, 1961). The Robertson and Boek studies were both conducted within a span of three years and their figures on overall extent of breast-feeding are similar. The comparable figure in the Bain study, conducted 13 years previously, was 65 percent wholly or partly breast-fed. While some allowance must be made for differing methodologies of the earlier and later studies, we believe that the later, and lower, figures reflect a true decline in the extent of breast-feeding during the interim period 1945–1958.

A study reported in 1968 by Meyer, based on a continuing survey of 2.5 million American infants, found that in 1946, 38 percent of mothers were breast-feeding (wholly or partially) upon leaving the hospital, 21 percent in

1956, and 18 percent in 1966 (Meyer, 1968). The decline over two decades was greatest in the states with lowest per-capita income; in Arkansas, for example, the decline was from 84 percent in 1946 to 22 percent in 1966.

In 1971, the New York City Department of Health conducted a survey of feeding practices for 451 infants of low socioeconomic level (Maslansky et al., 1974). Black and Puerto Rican infants accounted for 90 percent of the sample. Only 17 percent of the infants were ever breast-fed.

The decline over time in the total extent of breast-feeding is also indicated by several studies in England. John and Elizabeth Newson (1963) studied the infant-care practices of 709 mothers of year-old infants in Nottingham in 1959. The sample was a random sample stratified according to social class. They found that 50 percent of infants were breast-fed at one month, 26 percent at three months, and 12 percent at six months. The Newsons present figures from earlier English studies, going back to 1945, which show higher percentages for breast-feeding. Their figures permit the strong inference that breast-feeding declined substantially in England between 1945 and 1959.

Mode of Feeding

In our study, 208 infants (74.6 percent) are bottle-fed and 71 (25.4 percent) are breast-fed. The breast-fed group includes several infants who had been at the breast for only the first week and then shifted to the bottle. It excludes, however, a small group for whom the mothers made a brief, unsuccessful attempt at breast-feeding. The extent of breast-feeding in our study is considerably lower than in the Bain study, comparable with the Robertson study, and lower than the English study in Nottingham.

We asked the mothers why they chose their feeding mode. A variety of reasons were presented on behalf of both breast and bottle. These are classified into a set of categories presented below.

These reasons were offered by the mothers for bottle-feeding:

1. Mother is influenced by relatives or friends not to breast-feed.
2. The idea of breast-feeding is emotionally distasteful.
3. Perceived inadequacy of milk supply. ("I tried to feed the first baby by breast but my milk was no account, so I just didn't try with this one.")
4. Breast-feeding is inconvenient or impossible. It requires privacy, wets the mother's clothing, interferes with work commitments or care of other children. ("I thought maybe I would have to go back to work, and that way it would be more convenient to start with the bottle"; "I didn't have enough time to breast-feed because of the three other children"; "I was going back to work and so I just bottle-fed him. If I have another child, I'm going to breast-feed him, I think"; "People told me I'd need to eat special foods to be able to breast-feed successfully.")

5. Mother's medical problems interfered. ("I was forced to bottle-feed because of difficulties and operations I had"; "The doctor said it'd be better for the baby to be put on a bottle, because I was in bad shape for about six days after delivery"; "I had psoriasis.")
6. Medical problem of infant, such as low birth weight or infant's remaining in hospital for observation after mother's discharge.
7. Breast-feeding makes the breast sore.

These reasons were offered by the mothers for breast-feeding:

1. Recommendation of doctor, husband, mother, or other influential person.
2. Breast-feeding is better, nutritionally or emotionally, for the baby, ("I have always heard that mother's milk is better, and it brings you closer to the baby"; "Sucking the breast is good for the baby.")
3. Breast-feeding benefits the mother, physically or emotionally.
4. Breast-feeding is more convenient — no apparatus to store, saves time spent in sterilizing bottles, can be done away from home.
5. Fundamental preference for breast-feeding, no other reason offered. ("I breast-fed all the others. I just believe in it.")

In reviewing this classification of reasons offered, it should be borne in mind that these are the considerations from the mothers' own account that prompted them to act as they did. Some of the bottle-feeding mothers said they would have preferred to breast-feed but their daily schedules prevented it. Others doubted their ability to breast-feed and cited previous difficult or abortive attempts. Pediatric opinion holds that most mothers can successfully nurse, but many mothers feel otherwise. There is a considerable gap between biological potential and actual performance. The obstacles stem primarily from the mother's family situation, work responsibilities, and general life-style.

Is feeding mode related to social class? Table 5-1 answers this question. The proportion of breast-fed infants ranges from 53.1 percent in Class II to 16 percent in Class IV. In Class I, 32.1 percent of infants are breast-fed, a figure not much higher than that in Class III. While the general association of feeding mode with social class is statistically significant, there is no stepwise progression.

In our assessment of reasons for choice of feeding mode, this theme came up many times: "I want to breast-feed but can't because I have to take care of the other children." It is entirely possible, of course, that in offering this reason many mothers are resorting to a pretext; even without older children in the family, and for other reasons, they would have used bottle-feeding. This possibility prompted us to examine the mode of feeding in relation to the birth order of the infant.

Most studies of breast-feeding focus narrowly upon feeding mode for the mother's first baby, because this is a convenient category for gathering uniform data (Hirschman and Sweet, 1974: 40); families with one child can be merged

Table 5-1
Infant Feeding Mode and Social Class

	Mode of Feeding				
	Bottle		Breast		
Social Class	N in Class Who Bottle-Fed	% of Class Who Bottle-Fed	N in Class Who Breast-Fed	% in Class Who Breast-Fed	Total Number in Class
I	19	67.9	9	32.1	28
II	15	46.9	17	53.1	32
III	45	70.3	19	29.7	64
IV	63	84.0	12	16.0	75
V	66	82.5	14	17.5	80
Total	208	74.6	71	25.4	279

$Chi^2 = 20.41$
$D.F. = 4$
$p < .001$

into the same data pool with families containing more than one child. But this single category does not permit analysis that reveals changes in feeding mode through a succession of infants in the same family. Our study compares two distinct family categories: the infant-only family and the other-child-present family. Table 5-2 compares these categories. It shows that infants in an infant-only family are almost twice as likely to be breast-fed as they are in a family containing other children—39.4 percent of the former are breast-fed, compared with only 20.7 percent of the latter, a difference significant at the .01 level. This indicates that a genuine process, not a pretext, is at work behind the report of many mothers that the presence of other children in the family deters breast-feeding. On this basis, we suggest the following proposition: In a line of siblings, if any at all is breast-fed it will be the first, while a later arrival is more likely to be bottle-fed.

The study inquired also into the feeding mode for the older children, when they were infants. By cross-tabulating the feeding mode for the study-infant with the mode used previously for older children, it was possible to determine the extent to which breast-feeding declines as more children enter the family. Table 5-3 presents this cross-tabulation. Since it deals only with infants who have older siblings, the total N is 208 (cf. Table 5-2). These 208 are divided into three categories according to the mother's mode of feeding previous infants: all previous infants (one or more) bottle-fed; some previous infants bottle-fed and others breast-fed (this requires at least two older siblings); and all previous infants (one ore more) breast-fed.

According to Table 5-3, an infant with siblings all of whom have been bottle-fed has a 96.2 percent chance of being bottle-fed. Only 4 of the 105 infants whose siblings had been bottle-fed were themselves breast-fed. In the 49 cases where some siblings had had the breast and others the bottle, the results are similar. In the total group of study infants, 25.4 percent are breast-fed. But among those 54 infants whose mothers had earlier breast-fed exclusively, 34, or 63 percent, were breast-fed and the remaining 20 were bottle-fed. The drift from breast to bottle among a line of siblings is sizable, but the drift in the opposite direction, as shown in the first row of the table, is negligible.

Table 5-3 may be seen as the resultant of three kinds of influence. The first line of influence expresses how many mothers in a given social group or geographical region are basically inclined toward breast-feeding or bottle-feeding. As we saw earlier, there is a secular trend away from breast-feeding. The second influence expresses a mother's tendency to repeat for later children in the family the feeding mode she used with the first child. Third, there is a trend to shift from breast to bottle (if breast-feeding was originally used) with successive infants.

Additional comments may be made in regard to the second and third influences. It is scarcely surprising that a mother repeats the feeding mode used with her first infant. It becomes part of her repertoire: she knows it works

Table 5–2
Mode of Feeding in Relation to Number of Children in Family

Children in Family	Mode of Feeding				Total Number in Family Category
	Bottle		Breast		
	N	Percent of Family Category Who Were Bottle-Fed	N	Percent of Family Category Who Were Breast-Fed	
Infant is Only Child	43	60.6	28	39.4	71
Other Children Present	165	79.3	43	20.7	208
Total	208	74.6	71	25.4	279

Chi^2 = 9.82
D.F. = 1
$p < .01$

Table 5–3
Mode of Feeding This Infant in Relation to Mode of Feeding Previous Infants

| | | *Mode of Feeding the Study Infant* | | | |
| | | *Bottle-Fed* | | *Breast-Fed* | |
Mode of Feeding Previous Infants	*N*	*Percent of Row*	*N*	*Percent of Row*	*Total Number*
All were Bottle-Fed	101	96.2	4	3.8	105
Some were Bottle-Fed, Some were Breast-Fed	44	89.8	5	10.2	49
All were Breast-Fed	20	37.0	34	63.0	54
Total	165	79.3	43	20.7	208

$Chi^2 = 80.40$
$D.F. = 2$
$p < .001$

(or that *she* "works"), and, other things being equal, she is ready to use it again. But with a second infant, other things are not equal, because the first infant is now an older child upon the scene. This factor gives rise to the third influence. A mother of two or more children may feel that she cannot continue to breast-feed because of the demands presented by the older child or children. Even if she breast-fed previously, liked it, and felt it was good for the infant, she may now regard it as fundamentally less convenient than bottle-feeding. Beleaguered, she resorts to bottle-feeding.

Aside from its relative convenience or inconvenience, breast-feeding may heighten normal sibling rivalry. Whatever resentment the older child feels toward the infant "intruder" becomes intensified at the latter's feeding time. The obstacles that older children pose to breast-feeding are not just ordinary bids for attention, but may have behind them the force of intense jealousy. Breast-feeding entails a higher degree of physical intimacy than bottle-feeding, and the young child correctly senses the exclusiveness and sensuousness of contact between mother and infant. There are reports that fathers too "experience sexual jealousy when the baby is breast-fed" (Boston Women's Health Book Collective, 1973: 214). The mother who persists in breast-feeding can do so only by determination, ingenuity, and patience in coping with the other family members. Much also depends, of course, upon the layout of the household and the extent to which the mother feeds the infant in privacy. Neither Dr. Spock, nor *Infant Care*, the U.S. government publication, offers specific advice on how to cope with this problem, although both offer general discussions of jealousy in older children.

The feeding mode for the study-infant shows interesting correlations with variables previously considered. For the purpose of quantiative analysis, bottle-feeding is scored as 1 and breast-feeding as 2. Feeding mode, regarded here as a dependent variable, can then be correlated with other quantitative variables. The correlation with birth weight (scored in ounces) is .18. Lighter babies are more likely to be bottle-fed; the level of correlation is significant well beyond a probability of .05. Many small infants are kept in the hospital premature nursery for a week or two after birth; bottle-feeding by nurses, and temporary separation from the mother when the mother is discharged, virtually preclude establishment of a breast regime. Even in the case of tiny or small babies who are discharged with their mothers, the mother may well feel that breast-feeding is too uncertain a means of strengthening a baby who had a shaky start.

It is of interest also to look at mode of feeding in relation to the mother's state of health during pregnancy, considered in Chapter 4. Table 5-4 shows that of the 81 mothers who reported poor health during pregnancy, 14 (17.3 percent) engaged in breast-feeding subsequently. Of the 198 mothers who reported good health, 57 (29.8 percent) engaged in breast-feeding. This difference is significant at the .05 level. This finding fits in with other findings and interpretations concerning mode of feeding. We have seen that a vulnerability on the infant's part, such as low birth weight, decreases the chance of breast-feeding. It appears also that a vulnerability on the mother's part—poor health during pregnancy—has a similar effect.

Cup-Weaning and Emotional Aspects of Feeding

We have devoted considerable attention to the early mode of feeding because of the inherent significance of the topic and because data are available for every

Table 5–4

Relation Between Mother's Prenatal Health and Subsequent Mode of Infant Feeding

| | | Mode of Feeding | | |
		Breast	Bottle	Total
Prenatal	Good	57	141	198
Health	Poor	14	67	81
	Total	71	208	279

Chi^2 = 4.01
D.F. = 1
$p < .05$

infant in the study, whatever his or her age at the time of the interview. We also collected data on subsequent feeding experience. Because of the variation in age of the sample at the time of the interview, many of the infants had not yet been weaned. Nevertheless, many others had been weaned, and the relevant findings on them can be placed in sequence with the findings on the initial feeding mode.

The shift from bottle or breast to the cup as the method of ingesting liquid usually occurs during the latter half of the first year. The newborn infant cannot manipulate a cup. The gains in muscular strength and coordination which come rapidly in the first months are a necessary preparation for independent cup use. Also, many infants over time lose interest in sucking and nipple contact; they spontaneously develop interest in the more complex task of managing a cup. Further, as the transition to cup occurs, the importance of liquid intake diminishes. The eruption of teeth and changes in the digestive system enable the infant to utilize a more varied range of solid and semisolid foods. No doubt the infant also finds new food textures and flavors satisfying to his curiosity and exploratory urges.

Weaning is widely regarded as having important emotional implications (Brenner, 1973: 28; Ginsburg, 1971: 234). The Newsons (1963: 62) write that the emphasis upon the emotional import of weaning "is most obviously attributable to the influence of Freud and his followers. In psychoanalytic theory it is held that breast-feeding provides the infant with intense sensual pleasure, and it is suggested that he becomes extremely reluctant to relinquish these first pleasures of the oral body-zone. Consequently, weaning is considered to be a potentially traumatic experience, which may have unfortunate after-effects in the child's later character development. Whatever the historical reason, the subject of weaning receives a good deal of attention in manuals of infant care, and the reader is given the impression that weaning is a difficult and delicate operation which the mother must approach with circumspection."

The timing of the introduction to the cup depends on the infant's readiness as perceived by the mother (and other caring people), and on her own concept of the appropriate age, as formed from her own experience, advice from relatives and neighbors, and other social influences. In practice, these two factors—the mother's perception of the infant and her idea of timing— are intertwined. If an infant is put on the cup at an early age, such as three months, the mother will find herself constantly holding and guiding the cup because the infant is not able to negotiate it himself. Many mothers find this inconvenient, and delay until the infant is better able to manage. In some cultures, the infant remains at the breast or on the bottle for a year or longer. Many mothers and pediatricians in our society feel that too prolonged a dependence on a nipple source makes weaning more difficult and traumatic for the infant when it does occur. Hence the common emphasis on the infant's readiness: "too late" is as undesirable as "too early."

One aspect of bottle use is that there is a certain convenience for the mother in retaining the bottle. Once the infant can manipulate a bottle (much easier than manipulating a cup), it is a simple matter to give him or her the bottle and let him curl up with it in the crib. Feeding becomes less demanding upon the mother, and some mothers may tend to prolong bottle use for months. A further example of the same tendency is found in the very common pattern whereby the infant drinks from a cup during the day but receives a night bottle. This practice thus figures in sleeping as well as feeding routines. The night bottle may play the part of a reliable soporific, highly valued by harassed parents. It may be retained long after the infant has been weaned to the cup. With a keen sensitivity to possible maternal inadequacy, some mothers who prolong the use of a bottle feel embarrassed about it.

Weaning to the cup, like that other great developmental step, toilet training, is very much a matter of mother-infant cooperation and the mother's sensitivity to her baby. In both cases, premature timing means more work and strain for the mother. Other major steps, such as crawling, standing and walking, uttering words, and sleeping the night through depend more exclusively upon the infant's maturation, without need for maternal initiative or cooperation.

We found that 179 infants in our study had been weaned to the cup by the time when the interview occurred. The mean age at weaning was 6.6 months, with a standard deviation of 2.0 months. The mean age of these infants at the time of the interview was 9.7 months; thus they had been on the cup for an average of three months. The remaining 100 infants, still on breast or bottle, were, of course, a younger group at the time of the interview, with a mean age of 6.9 months.

Is there a social-class influence upon weaning to the cup? This question is answered in Table 5-5. The class I infants started latest, at 7.4 months, and the Class II infants earliest, at 5.9 months. Classes III, IV, and V fall in between these figures, with the Class V infants starting the cup at 6.9 months. The variation

Table 5-5
Age When Infant Started Cup-Drinking, by Social Class

Social Class	Mean Age (Months)	Standard Deviation	N
I	7.4	2.1	19
II	5.9	1.9	18
III	6.1	1.8	43
IV	6.6	1.8	45
V	6.9	2.2	54
Total	6.6	2.0	179

Analysis of variance:
F-Ratio = 2.30
D.F. = 4,174
$p \not< .05$

in each class is appreciable. Thus there is considerable overlapping among the social classes, and no clear trend is evident.

If an infant is bottle-fed from the start, then his subsequent move to cup-feeding is the only significant change in mode of liquid intake. If he is breast-fed, he may be weaned directly from breast to cup, or he may be moved from breast to bottle, and later on to the cup. Some mothers who emphasize the value of breast-feeding may have a particular aversion to the seeming artificiality of bottle-feeding, and attempt to maintain the breast regime until the infant can be given a cup. In this way, the mother's achievement in nourishing by breast is directly succeeded by the infant's achievement in managing the cup, and the bottle—a symbol of possible concession and defeat—is altogether avoided. The achievement motif is perhaps enhanced in such a sequence by the likelihood that an infant weaned from breast to cup is younger than one weaned from bottle to cup. Bottle-feeding, once commenced, can be prolonged indefinitely. While many mothers can breast-feed, even those with a copious milk supply find it difficult to keep pace as the exclusive source of supply with a thriving infant's need for milk after a year or so. Many, regarding breast access and mother's milk as important to give the infant a good start, intend to continue only two or three months regardless of their milk-producing capacity. Infants at this age are too young to be weaned to the cup, so a bottle regime is necessary.

The study data do not permit us to explore all the questions raised by these considerations. It is possible, however, to look at the duration of breast-feeding for the 71 infants fed in this way. Of these, eleven were still receiving breast milk at the time of the interview. These eleven have an average age of 7.6 months; they are "old" babies still to be at the breast, in comparison with the other breast-fed infants. The sixty others, whose period of breast-feeding is over, terminated at 2.6 months. Expressed in weeks, the duration of breast-feeding is 11.2 weeks with a standard deviation of 9.3 weeks. By social class, the nine infants in Class I who completed breast-feeding stopped at 7.4 weeks; the 14 in Class I at 12.1 weeks; the 17 in Class III at 11.7 weeks; the 10 in Class IV at 14.2 weeks; and the 10 in Class V at 9.7 weeks. Analysis of variance shows these differences not to be statistically significant.

Another feature of potential emotional significance in the feeding situation is the extent of physical contact between mother and infant. Breast-feeding inherently involves physical contact: there is the union of breast and mouth, with temporal fluctuations. The infant sucks hard, relaxes, and again intensifies his or her effort; the mother reacts and responds, and a preverbal communication is established. She also supports the child in her lap (although some mothers nurse with the infant beside them on a bed or couch), and there is eye contact. Many of these same points of contact are possible in a bottle regime. The mother may, however, not hold the infant, and prop the bottle with pillows or a manu-factured device that holds the bottle in position in the crib. This frees her for other activities, yet assures that the infant can proceed with his feeding. She may need to check the bottle position (and content) occasionally, especially if the infant is young, but she is not constrained to constant attendance.

It is difficult on the basis of an interview to determine the extent of bottle-propping practices. A mother might prop the bottle frequently and yet be unaware of the extent because she also frequently holds the infant for feeding; or, with a sense of maternal negligence, she might be reluctant to acknowledge her pattern. Accepting these possibilities, we simply put to the mother the direct question as to whether she usually held or propped the bottle.

Of the 218 mothers who bottle-fed their infants (this includes ten who shifted from breast- to bottle-feeding during the first two weeks), 164, or 75.2 percent, said they held the bottle during feedings and did not prop it. As Table 5-6 shows, there is a pronounced social-class effect. Although few mothers at any class level acknowledge bottle-propping, the proportion is largest among Class V mothers. Whether the higher-class mothers in Classes I, II, and III actually do less bottle-propping, or whether, affected by social-desirability considerations, they simply acknowledge it less remains an open question. Arguing for a real and not merely an apparent difference is the fact that the lower-class mothers have larger families (see Table 3-5) and are less able to devote themselves exclusively to the baby at feeding time. On the other hand, the tendency to present an image of ideal motherhood may be stronger at middle-class and upper-class levels. If we accept the social-class gradient as a real phenomenon, then it may be taken as indicative of closer feeding contact at higher class levels. More mothers in Classes I, II, and III hold baby and bottle for feeding than in

Table 5-6
Mother-Infant Contact During Feeding, by Social Class

Social Class	Percent of Bottle-Fed Infants Held with Bottle (Bottle Not Propped)	Percent Fed by Breast or Held with Bottle (Bottle Not Propped)
I	90.5 (21)[a]	92.9 (28)[b]
II	82.4 (17)	90.6 (32)
III	87.2 (47)	90.6 (64)
IV	68.8 (64)	73.3 (75)
V	66.7 (69)	71.2 (80)
Total	75.2 (218)	80.6 (279)
Chi^2:	10.82	15.87
D.F.:	4	4
p:	< .05	< .01

[a]Numbers in parentheses are the totals on which the percents are based. Thus, 90.5 percent of Class I mothers (19 of 21) did not prop the infant's bottle. The base number is the number, in each class, who bottle-fed the infant.

[b]Numbers in parentheses are the total number of infants in each class.

Classes IV and V, and their babies experience the very direct visual and physical contact attendant upon this manner of feeding.

Table 5-6 extends the analysis of feeding contact by including in the second column all those infants who are breast-fed. This part of Table 5-6 combines the first column with earlier figures on breast-feeding by social class (in Table 5-1). While the differences among Classes I, II, and III are slight, there is a considerable gap between them and Classes IV and V. Whatever the emotional benefits of close feeding contact may be, it appears that they are more widely available to the higher-class infants.

Sleeping Patterns

Sleep is a fundamental physiological need. Like needs for nourishment, attention, and body contact, it is a channel whereby the individual, starting in infancy, is socialized into his culture. Many aspects of sleep are culturally patterned.

Young children spend much time asleep. Adults may get less sleep than they need, but this rarely happens with infants. They are expected to sleep a good deal and are as a rule given ample opportunity. Internal barriers to sleep—the night fears of the older child or the insomnia of the adult—are unknown to them. External noise and commotion—loud television, the rumpus of older siblings—may at times intrude upon sleep, but the infant's capacity for sleep is so large that these are not usually serious hindrances.

When a mother describes her infant as being a "good baby," a closer inspection of her meaning frequently reveals that the infant sleeps easily and long. Discussion of the sleeping proclivities of their babies and tricks for inducing sleep are staples, along with eating patterns, and later on toilet training, of new mothers' conversation.

We have presented findings on the feeding of the infant and contact patterns during feeding. These topics are closely linked with sleeping; for the infant of two or three months, feeding is typically succeeded by sleep. Falling asleep on a full stomach in parental arms is regarded by many child psychologists as a prototypical bliss which subsequent life satisfactions can never fully duplicate.

The exploration of sleeping patterns in our study dealt with two topics: the age when the infant commenced to sleep the night through, and the physical site of sleep in the household.

It is a milestone in development when an infant begins to sleep through the night. Hunger is the drive or deficit state that arouses the neonate from sleep; the newborn typically has six distinct daily feeding periods. Rapid growth during the first weeks of life creates a larger capacity to store food and to digest it over a longer period. Feedings gradually become larger and less frequent. If on a six-times-daily basis feedings occur at 6 A.M., 10 A.M., 2 P.M., 6 P.M.,

10 P.M., and 2 A.M., the transition to five feedings will typically produce a sequence something like 5 A.M., 10 A.M., 2 P.M., 6 P.M., and 11 P.M. Fortunately for parents, it is usually the middle-of-the-night feeding that the infant drops first. (We are not here raising the question as to whether feeding times are definitely scheduled or whether it simply works out this way.)

Probably the changing pattern of the need for feeding is the product of cultural influences and organic factors such as the circadian rhythm. In the very beginning, infants function on a simple hunger-satiation-sleep-hunger cycle, and their mother adjusts her routines to accommodate their needs, feeding being the principal requirement. Within a few weeks, however, much sensory development occurs. Infants come to view their world as a source of interest and stimulation as well as food. They give evidence of enjoyment in watching moving objects. Form, color, sound, and touch preferences develop. Soon another cycle overlays the earlier hunger-based cycle, namely, stimulation-attention-exhaustion-stimulation. This new cycle is more closely attuned and responsive to the environment and its human diurnal culture. Though infants continue to sleep a good deal in the day, they sleep more at night—the time of silence and sensory deadness.

Most parents look forward to the time when their infant can reliably manage to sleep through the night. Until this occurs, it is a nightly matter of feeding, changing a diaper, returning the baby to bed, and the parent returning to bed in the hope (at times a false one) that the baby will easily fall asleep. Although the father may be involved in the process, the burden as a rule falls upon the mother. Parents may count themselves lucky if an infant starts to sleep through the night at the relatively early age of five or six weeks.

In our study, 257 of the 279 infants had reached the point of sleeping through the night. Since this point is not achieved by the infant all at once with no relapses, we counted infants among the 257 if they were, at the time of the interview, sleeping through at least half of the time. The average age at which these infants commenced sleeping through the night was 9.8 weeks—a little over two months. However, there was a great deal of variation; the standard deviation is 8.2 weeks. Four mothers reported that their babies slept the night through virtually from birth. Thirty-eight, or 14.8 percent of the 257 infants, reached this point by age two weeks. At the other extreme, 14, or 5.4 percent, took 25 weeks, and one infant took 40 weeks. Table 5-7 shows the distribution of ages.

Another important feature of infant sleep behavior is sleeping location in the household. The house or domicile is a physical space, but as a household it is also a social space used by a family in culturally prescribed ways. As part of a larger study of cultural differences between Japan and the United States, the anthropologists William Caudill and David Plath investigated the sleeping location of family members over the life cycle in the two cultures (Caudill and Plath, 1966). One important aspect of sleep behavior is, in the language of the Japanese–American study, "Who sleeps by whom?" Sleeping location in this

Table 5-7
Age When Infant Began to Sleep Through the Night

Age (Weeks)	N	Percent of Total
0–2	38	14.8
3–4	37	14.4
5–6	43	16.7
7–8	42	16.3
9–12	32	12.5
13–16	27	10.5
17–24	24	9.3
25–40	14	5.4
Total	257	99.9

social sense has two aspects: Does the infant (or other family member) sleep in a room alone or with another family member? And, if not alone, with whom?

We will present findings on these questions from our study and then we will compare them with the Caudill-Plath study and other, similar studies. In our study, to standardize for infant's age we inquired where he slept at age one to two months. We found that 217 (77.8 percent) infants shared a room with their parents, 18 (6.5 percent) shared a room with other children, and 44 (15.8 percent) were the only occupant in the room where they slept. As Table 5-8 shows, there is a close connection between sleeping location and social class. Over half the Class I infants slept alone. In every other class, only a small minority did so; only four of the 28 Class V infants slept alone.

A still closer degree of sleeping propinquity is achieved when the infant sleeps beside the mother in her bed (which, we presume, was in many cases a double bed shared with the father). The interviewer inquired, "Did you ever let him (her) sleep beside you at night when he was a month or two old?" For those mothers who responded affirmatively, there was a follow-up question: "Did he do that as a regular thing—or just now and then?" This mode of questioning, while admittedly too rough for a refined analysis of infant sleeping behavior, can nevertheless serve to establish basic parameters.

Table 5-9 presents the findings on these questions, arranged by social class. Seventy-four of the 279 infants, or 26.5 percent, are reported to have slept beside their mothers. Of these, 27 (36.5 percent) did this regularly, while the remaining 47 (63.5 percent) did so "now and then." There are differences by social class, though not a consistent pattern. In Classes I, II, and IV, approximately one quarter of the infants slept beside their mothers; in Class III, only 15 percent; but in Class V, almost 39 percent. In terms of the frequency or regularity of this contact, Class II stands highest, with five of the eight mothers reporting that their infants slept beside them regularly at the stated age.

Table 5-8
Infant's Sleeping Location, by Social Class

Social Class	Slept in Room Alone		Slept in Room With Parents		Slept in Room With Children		Total		Crowding Index[a]
	N	Percent of Class	N	Percent of Class	N	Percent of Class	N	Percent of Class	
I	16	57.1	11	39.3	1	3.6	28	100.0	.59
II	5	15.6	26	81.3	1	3.1	32	100.0	.69
III	12	18.8	47	73.4	5	7.9	64	100.1	.73
IV	7	9.3	61	81.3	7	9.3	75	99.9	.90
V	4	5.0	72	90.0	4	5.0	80	100.0	1.29
Total	44	15.8	217	77.8	18	6.5	279	100.0	.92

Chi^2 = 45.78   Chi^2 compares infants who slept alone—first heading—with those who slept either with parents or other children—second and third
D.F. = 4   headings combined.
$p < .001$

[a]Same as in Table 3–7.

Table 5-9
Infant's Sleeping Beside Mother, by Social Class

Social Class	Number in Class	Number and Percent of Class Who Slept Beside Mother		Slept Regularly Beside Mother		Slept Beside Mother "Now and Then"	
		N	*Percent*	*N^a*	*Percent*	*N^a*	*Percent*
I	28	7	25.0	1	14.3	6	85.7
II	32	8	25.0	5	62.5	3	37.5
III	64	10	15.4	1	10.0	9	90.0
IV	75	18	23.4	6	33.3	12	66.7
V	80	31	38.7	14	45.2	17	54.8
Total	279	74	26.5	27	36.5	47	63.5

Chi^2 (Sleeping Beside Mother, by Social Class) = 10.40
D.F. = 4
$p < .05$

[a]The *N*'s in these two colums sum to the *N* of infants who slept beside mother (previous column).

Having presented our findings on sleeping location, we wish to place them in an interpretive framework in relation to other studies. Four other studies will be used for comparison: a. the Newson and Newson study (1963) in Nottingham, England, of families containing one-year olds; b. a study of Caudill and Plath (1966) of middle-class Japanese families containing a three to four month-old; c. a study by Caudill and Weinstein (1969) of thirty urban middle-class American families, selected and intensively studied for comparison with a subsample of thirty Japanese families from the Caudill-Plath study; and d. an unpublished study by Martha Oleinick (1968) of an urban sample of Baltimore, Maryland, families containing young children. These studies, along with the Kentucky study, are compared in Table 5-10.

The questions asked in the several studies are somewhat disparate. For instance, the Oleinick study inquired, "Did your child ever sleep in the same room with you and his father?" The wording of the question perhaps implies that it is an unusual practice. A second point of nonstandardization is that the several studies made inquiries concerning sleep location at different ages. A gross but reasonable correction for this is to assume that in a given population and culture, the proportion of children sleeping in a room with their parents remains stationary or declines as the children age. That is, it does not increase. A third point of nonstandardization concerns the matter of whom the child slept with, if he was not alone. The most probable categories are parents, siblings, or both. Only the Caudill-Plath study offers a detailed analysis of this question.

Despite these limitations, the marked differences apparent in Table 5-10 strongly suggest that the Japanese, English, and American cultures have different answers to the question, Where does the baby sleep? Only 7 percent of the Japanese infants slept alone at age three to four months. Twenty-six percent of the English infants at one year slept alone; at age three to four months, we might hypothesize a figure of 10 to 12 percent—not far from the Japanese figure of 7 percent. The Japanese and English patterns favor the infant's sharing a bedroom; usually they slept in the parents' bedroom. The English study shows a substantial use of sibling bedrooms as well.

The three American studies do not speak with one voice, though they collectively imply a considerably higher occurrence of infants sleeping alone than holds true in England or Japan. In the Caudill-Weinstein study, 57 percent (17 of 30) of the infants at age three to four months slept alone; all were first children, lacking older siblings. The authors report that every one of the other 13 families planned to move to larger quarters, specifically to provide separate sleeping space for the infant. In the Oleinick study, 39 percent of the children had never slept in a room with their parents. Of those who had, many stopped during the first year. The percentage sleeping alone at age three to four months might be estimated at 45 to 55 percent. This study provides no information on the number who may have shared a bedroom with siblings. The present study, in Kentucky, finds 16 percent sleeping alone at age one to two months. Again,

Table 5-10
Infant's Sleeping Location: Five Studies Compared

Study	Place	Sample	Applicable Age of Child	Findings
(1) Newson & Newson	Nottingham, England	*N*=709; general urban (all social classes)	12 months	60% slept in room with parents; 14% slept with siblings; 26% slept alone.
(2) Caudill-Plath	Matsumoto, Kyoto, & Tokyo, Japan	N=297; urban & mainly middle-class	3-4 months	91% slept in room with parents or parents and siblings; 2% slept with siblings; 7% slept alone.
(3) Caudill & Weinstein	Washington, D.C.	N=30; urban, middle-class, one-child families	3-4 months	43% slept in room with parents; 57% slept alone.
(4) Oleinick	Baltimore, Maryland	N=370; general urban	birth to four years	39% never slept in room with parents; 61% had. The 61% are distributed as follows: 22% stopped during first year; 21% by end of fourth year; 17% beyond fourth year.
(5) Gallagher	Central Kentucky	N=279; general urban & rural	1-2 months	78% slept in room with parents; 6% slept with siblings; 16% slept alone.

using the three- to four-month period as a hypothetical age for standardization, we estimate that 30 percent of the Kentucky infants sleep alone by then.

Whether an infant sleeps alone or in a shared bedroom is in part a function of situational factors. It is also an expression of less tangible yet insistent cultural values concerning privacy, family structure, and the patterning of relationships between the sexes and the generations.

Among the situational factors is the total amount of space in a household and the way in which it is partitioned into rooms. Young married couples in the United States commonly live in small, one-bedroom apartments. However, when a child arrives on the scene, the parents and infant do not necessarily share the one bedroom; infant bassinets and small cribs can be placed in kitchens and living rooms, or convertible sofabeds or folding cots can be used by parents in the living room, with the infant using the bedroom. In other words, given the physical space of a household, one cannot directly infer its use by the family. Strong cultural values for privacy, for example, as expressed through the tastes and desires of the family, effectively counter the seeming dictates of architecture.

Another important pragmatic factor bearing upon the sleeping location of the infant is that it is convenient for the parents to have the infant near their sleeping site. Especially during the first months, there are likely to be many trips to cribside. Babies are wakeful and need to be cuddled or fed. Placing them closer to the parent usually means that they will be farther from older siblings and their crying will be less disrupting to the rest of the family.

The very high rate of "co-sleeping" that Caudill and Plath found in the Japanese study is interpreted by them as an expression of core cultural values, rather than sheerly expedient or necessary behavior. In Japan, it is not simply a matter of the children's co-sleeping with parents when they are infants. Of the older children in their study, 79 percent aged 6 to 10 years, slept with their parents, and 50 percent of the children aged 11 to 15 did so. In the later adolescent period, 16 to 20, the figure declined to 17 percent. Caudill and Plath point out that the Japanese can expect to spend the greater part of their life co-sleeping with other family members (in addition to spouse): first, as an infant, child, and young adolescent, with parents; then, as an older adolescent, with siblings; then, together with a spouse, with their preadolescent children; and finally, when the children have established other households, with a spouse only, or if widowed, alone. At no stage of life prior to widowhood is the individual more likely than not to sleep alone; through most of life prior to this phase, he is more likely than not to sleep in a two-generational sleeping group. Thus the Japanese infant, in being situated with parents for sleeping, is starting on a life's career of co-sleeping.

Caudill and Plath emphasize the communal, group-oriented nature of Japanese culture. They see co-sleeping as an arrangement that places the individual in biosocial intimacy and interdependency with a group. Though for the infant and child to co-sleep with parents might carry the implication of domination of the younger generation by the older, Caudill and Plath feel that Japanese co-sleeping promotes the generalized bonding of the individual to a group, without promoting any particular hierarchical structure. As a general interpretation, they write: ". . . .sleeping arrangements tend to blur the distinctions between generations and between the sexes, to emphasize the interdependence more than the separateness of individuals, and to underplay (or largely ignore) the potentiality for the growth of conjugal intimacy between husband and wife in sexual and other matters in favor of a more general familial cohesion" (Caudill and Plath, 1966: 363).

The contrast with American sleeping arrangements and character is explicitly drawn. Caudill and Plath hold that American character is more independent and self-assertive. Such a character is developed by giving the infant sleeping arrangements that are separate from the parents'—one phase of the independence-training of the American child. Many other influences are of course at work.

It is instructive to examine American infant-care texts for their advice. *Infant Care* (U.S. Children's Bureau, 1972: 16) counsels: "Everybody will get more rest if the baby does not sleep in the parents' room. . . . Even in the smallest apartment, a crib or makeshift crib can be moved to the living room, kitchen or bathroom when the parents retire for the night." Dr. Spock (1976: 200-201) offers similar advice.

If people went to bed simply to sleep, the most expedient approach for many would be to sleep in a separate bed in a separate room (assuming enough rooms). However, where one sleeps has many connotations and consequences that go beyond expediency. It is linked with other behaviors and feelings in addition to sleep, and it symbolizes interpersonal relationships. For couples, sleeping in proximity is associated with privacy and sexual activity. Anyone close to a sleeper can hear his respiratory rhythms and bodily movements; body heat and odors may also be sensed. Many individuals find the presence of another a psychological protection against bad dreams and sleep disruption. Pre-sleep maneuvers involve undressing and a change of attire; co-sleepers may be exposed to the full or partial nakedness of one another. Further, co-sleeping is usually associated with co-waking, which is a disorderly process. A waker is in a temporary state of dishabille, socially disrobed.

These aspects of the total sleep situation imply a deep biosocial interdependence between habitual co-sleepers. It thus seems plausible that cultures such as Japan, which carry co-sleeping from infancy onward into later stages of the life cycle, tend to produce an adult character that has a strong dependence upon others and a strong orientation to group values.

Having looked at co-sleeping as a cultural value and potential influence upon character development, we may again consider the still closer degree of contact between mother and infant that occurs when the infant sleeps in the mother's (or parental) bed. This behavior may, in very crowded households, be due to lack of space. It may also reflect a preference by the mother (or parents together) for physical closeness and cuddling. It may also have practical aspects; taking the baby into the bed to give it attention saves frequent trips to the crib. We saw in Table 5-9 that in 26 percent (74) of the Kentucky families the baby slept beside the mother.

We also investigated mode of feeding for its bearing upon sleeping arrangements. It seems reasonable to expect that mothers who breast-fed, with the close body contact implied, would be more likely to take the infant to sleep beside them. Table 5-11 shows that this is indeed the case. It shows that 41 percent (29 of 71) of the breast-fed infants sleep beside their mother, compared to 22 percent (45 of 208) of the bottle-fed infants. Moreover, breast-fed infants who sleep beside their mother are likely to be taken beside her regularly, as Table 5-12 shows: fifty-nine percent (17 of 29) of the breast-fed infants sleep regularly beside their mother, while only 22 percent (10 of 45) of the bottle-fed infants do; that is, most of the bottle-fed infants who sleep beside their mother do so only occasionally.

Although the Caudill-Plath study recognizes this phenomenon and categorizes it qualitatively as the closest possible sleeping access of infant to parents, figures on its extent are not provided for their entire sample. In a subsample of 73 families containing an infant and an older child, 10 percent of the infants are reported as sleeping regularly in the parents' bed (whether a traditional cot or a Western-style bed).

The Newsons (1963: 79) in their Nottingham study also investigated sleeping, and reported: "A negligible number of children officially slept in the same bed as parents or siblings; almost all babies seem to have their own sleeping place, at least until they grow too big for their cot. A fair number of the wakeful babies . . . often or occasionally spend part of the night in the bed of the parents, or sometimes an older sister, having been taken in as a quick and certain means

Table 5-11
Sleeping Beside Mother, in Relation to Feeding Mode

| | | Did Infant Sleep Beside Mother? | | |
		Yes	No	Total
	Breast	29	42	71
Mode of Feeding	Bottle	45	163	208
	Total	74	205	279

$Chi^2 = 10.02$
D.F. = 1
$p < .01$

Table 5-12
Regularity of Sleeping Beside Mother, in Relation to Feeding Mode[a]

		Degree of Regularity in Sleeping Beside Mother		
		Now and Then	Regularly	Total
	Breast	12	17	29
Mode of Feeding	Bottle	35	10	45
	Total	47	27	74

Chi^2 = 10.08
D.F. = 1
$p < .01$

[a]This table deals only with the 74 infants who slept beside the mother (Table 5-11).

of comfort. Many more come into their parents' bed in the early morning for a cuddle, a romp, a bit of love and perhaps another hour's sleep."

What do American experts advise on this practice? They are firmly against it. The possibility of taking the infant into the parents' bed as a regular practice is not contemplated at all; even as an emergency or occasional procedure, it is discouraged. Spock (1976: 201) writes: "Sometimes a small child is going through a period of waking up frightened at night . . . and is taken into the parents' bed so they can get some sleep. This seems like the most practical thing to do at the time, but it usually turns out to be a mistake. Even if the child's anxiety improves during the following weeks, he is apt to cling to the security of his parents' bed, and there is the devil to pay getting him out again. So *always* bring him promptly and firmly back into his bed. I think it's a sensible rule not to take a child in the parents' bed for any reason . . ." *Infant Care* (U.S. Children's Bureau, 1972: 16) offers similar advice.

We have seen from Table 5-10 that a substantial minority of the Kentucky families do not follow this advice. Nevertheless, if we accept Dr. Spock and *Infant Care* as representative of American culture, it may be said that there is a strong emphasis upon training for independence, starting in infancy. Of the various considerations advanced against bringing the infant into the parental bed, the most forcefully stated is the argument that the practice leads to a hard-to-break dependency.

Bathing

Another basic routine in infant care is bathing. Bathing lacks the biological significance of eating and sleeping, in that it satisfies no obvious instinctual or physiological need. Yet once the biological imperatives are listed, bathing must come soon after. In his metapsychological *Civilization and its Discontents,* Freud cites personal cleanliness as a basic feature of civilization, evident in all societies and everywhere impressed upon the young (Freud, 1962: 40-45). The bathing of infants is an early component in the varied, lifelong processes of bodily care. As in feeding, toilet training, and other aspects of personal development, the activity is at first done to them or for them, the infants themselves constituting completely passive objects of care. In the normal course, they gradually become independent and self-caring. One index of the personality depth at which habits of cleanliness lie is the fact that dirtiness and unkempt appearance are common features of severe mental illness; psychiatrists regard a mother's failure to keep her baby reasonably clean as indicative of severe depression.

Once infants attain crawling capability and especially when they are liberated from the crib, their capacity for dirtying themselves and their immediate environment is enormous. They roll on the floor and grab at sticky, messy substances—food, cigarette ashes, discarded cans and bottles. If a diaper is loosely pinned, they play with their feces as readily as with a toy. Their noses run, even in good health. Keeping the baby clean is a continuing task, periodically climaxed by a total effort: sponging and wiping him or her off intermittently throughout the day, and, with greater or lesser regularity, a bath.

Cleanliness is not the sole benefit of bathing. The bath is also an occasion for water play, temporary freedom from the bind of diapers and clothing, and for delightful sensory experiences. The infant of one or two months probably derives considerable passive gratification from the experience; by age ten to twelve months, the infant has gained muscular agility sufficient to turn the bath into a wet frolic.

Our inquiry into bathing practice focused on two specific questions. First, how frequently is the baby bathed? To obtain an age standardization for bathing frequency, we asked how often the infant was bathed at age two months. Second, what kind of equipment is used for this task? We will also subsequently look at the question of whether mother or father administered the bath, as part of an investigation into the division of infant-care tasks in the family.

Of the mothers in our study, 232 report that they bathe the infant once a day. Some mothers bathe their infants less frequently, and a substantial minority more frequently. The mean number of baths per day is 1.11, with a standard deviation of 0.44. The distribution is as follows:

Frequency	*Number*
Less than once daily	20
Once daily	212
More than once daily but less than twice daily	13
Twice or more daily	34
	279

The great volume of mass-media advertising focused upon personal hygiene implies that a faultlessly laundered, thoroughly deodorized, and carefully groomed body is a sine qua non to social acceptance and success. Nevertheless, devotion to cleanliness and cleansing routines is not evenly distributed in our society. Whatever the actual values and behavior, some social groups have a reputation for great fastidiousness, while dirtiness figures prominently in the negative stereotypes that dominant groups hold of out-groups and minority groups. Social classes above the lower class tend to stereotype lower-class families as indifferent to personal and domestic cleanliness and lax on the associated virtues of tidiness and orderliness.

The question of the bearing of social status upon bathing is obviously suggested. Table 5-13 presents the mean number of infant baths per week and the associated standard deviation within each social class. A clear stepwise progression is revealed, ranging from 6.00 baths—not quite one per day—in Class I to 9.27 in Class V. There is a substantial variation within each class; Class V, for example, with its mean of 9.27 and standard deviation of 4.12, includes a few infants who do not receive a daily bath. But the differences between classes are on the whole strong; the analysis of variance shows a highly significant degree of interclass difference.

As we have seen on several previous occasions of significant variations among the social classes, Class V lies at an extreme position in regard to the dependent variable. In this instance, Class V differs significantly from Class IV (critical ratio of difference between means equals 2.13, $p < .05$). Thus, contrary to many prevailing conceptions of lower-class life, Class V is the "cleanest" class in terms of bathing frequency.

This unanticipated finding can be accounted for in several ways. Perhaps Class V mothers simply like to scrub more. Our hunch, however, lies in factors associated with the physical environment. Middle-class and working-class homes, more spacious and less crowded with human bodies and material objects, are

Table 5-13
Frequency of Bathing the Infant, by Social Class

Social Class	Mean Number of Baths per Week	Standard Deviation	N
I	6.00	2.18	28
II	6.31	1.77	32
III	7.28	1.90	64
IV	7.92	2.52	75
V	9.27	4.12	80
Total	7.78	3.07	279

Analysis of Variance:
F-Radio = 10.73
D.F. = 4,274
$p < .001$

perhaps more conducive to the continuous cleanness of the infant than is the Class V home. Once an infant starts crawling, smooth linoleum-tile floors and clean carpeting make a difference. Tending to lack these amenities, the Class V household exposes the infant to greater dirt and mess; frequent bathing is necessary to achieve cleanliness.

Inquiry in our study dealt with the location of the bath. Infant bathing can be carried out with no equipment beyond what adults and children in the household use for themselves. Even a little infant can be bathed in an adult-size tub, though the task is arduous and awkward for the bath-giver, who must kneel on the floor. The average kitchen sink is a feasible site for infant bathing. Other ingredients in the process, such as soap and towels, can be drawn from the usual household stores without special provision.

At the other extreme, infant bathing can be made easier, safer, more effective, and more pleasurable by the use of specialized equipment. Combination bath–dressing tables, called Bathinettes, are an especially useful type of equipment. The baby is bathed in a table-height tub lined with soft, waterproof fabric. He is lifted out, a hinged, padded lid is lowered over the tub, and he is then dried, powdered, and dressed on this surface. A safety-oriented refinement in some Bathinettes is the bath seat; it attaches with suction cups to the tub floor, and the infant strapped in it is more secure against unpleasant splashes and against slipping under the water. Special mild soaps, shampoos, lotions, and powders can be employed. Bath toys, noticed and appreciated by infants at an early age, add to the occasion. Some parents check water temperature with a thermometer—another piece of equipment which can be drawn into the process.

We found that 13 percent (35) of the infants in our study are bathed in Bathinettes. Thirty-three percent (92) are bathed in special small tubs or pans; the remaining 54 percent (152) are bathed without special equipment, that is, in a kitchen or bathroom sink or bathtub. A number of infants in this latter category do not receive an immersion bath; instead, they are sponged off while being held or laid on a surface.

Table 5–14 examines bathing equipment in relation to social class. A statistically significant relationship exists. Class variation in use of a Bathinette is especially noticeable. One quarter of the Class I and II infants are bathed in Bathinettes; only one of the 80 Class V infants is. About one third of the infants in every class are bathed in plastic tubs or other apparatus which, though less convenient and complete than a Bathinette, are used for that purpose only. Every class also has a substantial number of infants who are bathed in existing facilities; this figure approaches two-thirds in Class V.

Father's Role in Infant Care

From the standpoint of biological constraints and imperatives, the father's role in infant care is an open script. Fathers are not uniquely equipped for any

Table 5-14
Type of Infant Bath Equipment Used, by Social Class

Social Class	Bathinette	Percent of Class Using Type of Equipment[a]		N
		Other Special Equipment[b]	No Special Equipment[c]	
I	25	32	43	28
II	25	31	44	32
III	19	34	47	64
IV	9	31	60	75
V	1	35	64	80
Total	13	33	54	279

Chi^2 = 22.19
D.F. = 8
$p < .01$

[a]The percentages sum to 100 horizontally.

[b]Baby bathtubs or large dishpans devoted to infant use.

[c]Adult bathtub, kitchen sink, washbowl, or sponge bath in adult's lap.

particular function. By the same token, they can provide total care, except for feeding by breast. Even at that, technology can circumvent biology: artificial feeding is inherently no more woman's work than man's work. Given this biological interdetermination, human cultures reveal a wide variety of arrangements for the participation of fathers in the daily care and rearing of infants (Gough, 1975; Minturn and Lambert, 1964).

What do American child-rearing authorities say about the father's role? The most recent edition of *Infant Care* (1972) says little explicitly, though two pictures show fathers with infants and by implication suggest that fathers should be involved. One picture (p. 8) shows the father watching as the mother bathes the infant; the other (p. 57) shows the father carrying the infant in a baby backpack (with mother not shown). The previous edition of *Infant Care* (eleventh edition, U.S. Children's Bureau, 1963) contains no direct prescriptions for the father's role either, though it also hints strongly that fathers should be interested in their infants. The cover of the booklet bears a blue-toned photograph of a mother, father, and infant. In this trinity, the mother feeds the baby by spoon from a jar; baby's eyes are fastened upon mother and his lips are pursed to receive the next bite. Father is there, not as an active participant but an an involved spectator. In a discussion of how mothers may avert postnatal feelings of depression, this booklet says (p. 11): "Many a new father is inexperienced when it comes to the actual handling of a new baby. . . . A wise mother will let her husband share in the routines of his care, from the beginning. Some fathers take over certain aspects of care regularly, giving the evening bottle, for instance. Others are more comfortable in helping with household chores, thereby freeing the mothers from these. Whichever suits, the father is part of the picture." Subsequent illustrations show father with baby, though the emphasis is on pleasurable involvement rather than routine responsibility.

The tenth edition (U.S. Children's Bureau, 1955: 6) was more pointed on this topic:

"A father wants to have some part in the care of his baby, but he doesn't want it to be only the middle-of-the-night floor walking that is such a favorite of cartoonists. He's good at more than bottle-warming and diaper-changing, though at times inexperienced mothers seem to cold-shoulder the idea that he can have any worthwhile suggestions about a baby's care. A father feels just as necessary to his son or daughter as a mother does. And a new father may be no clumsier at giving a baby a bath than his wife is. . . . Of course, he *can* feel necessary to the baby while he's doing the laundry. But he doesn't get the kick out of it that he does when he gives the baby orange juice or holds him and talks to him when he cries. . . . A baby wants to know his father as a warm, loving person. He can't learn this from having his father do laundry; he has to have direct contact with him."

An illustration accompanying the text shows a baby in the father's arms.

This comparison of successive recent editions should not lead us to infer that the emphasis upon father's role in infant care was consistently stronger further back. In the second edition, published in 1921 (Department of Labor), one looks in vain for a single reference to father as caretaker, though nurse-maids, wet-nurses, older sisters and brothers are mentioned. This lack permits the inference of a traditional middle-class segregation of sex roles. Father mediates between the family and the external world, providing the family with status and material support, while mother devotes herself to interior affairs of the family.

Dr. Spock's advice on the father's role in infant care evidences a dramatic shift within the past decade. The 1968 edition of his *Baby and Child Care* strongly recommended a major, early role for the father in infant care—for the sound development of the infant, and as a practical help to the mother. Its presumption was that the mother has the primary responsibility for the infant care, and moreover that she has unique emotional qualities to contribute to the infant's need for security and love. The most recent edition (1976) is radically cleansed of all conceptions of essential difference between the proper responsibilities and special talents of male and female parents. Its message is the following: Children need much love and attention, especially for the first three years of their life. Caring for them is a demanding job, to be undertaken only by parents who are committed to it and who will find satisfaction in it. But it makes no difference what and how much mother does, and, similarly, what and how much father does, so long as the infant's needs are met. In his espousal of the equal responsibility of mothers and fathers, Dr. Spock states: "Men, especially the husbands of women with outside jobs, have been participating increasingly in all aspects of home and child care. There is no reason why fathers shouldn't be able to do these jobs as well as mothers. . . . But the benefit is lost if this work is done as a favor to their wives, since that implies that it's really not their work but just an unusual degree of generosity on their part. The work should be done in the spirit of an equal partnership" (Spock, 1976: 46).

To obtain information on father's participation, our study focused upon three daily activities: diapering, feeding, and bathing the baby. We determined both the total amount of father participation and also the relative level of participation in each activity, then related this data to social class and other family characteristics. The questions concerned participation when the infant was one to two months old, so that the mothers would respond in terms of a standard early age of infant.

Table 5-15 shows the extent to which the fathers participate in these activities. Five mothers reported that during this period their husbands were not present in the household; these fathers are thus subtracted from the overall total, to give a base of 274 for diapering and bathing participation. A further correction was made for feeding, since 43 mothers reported that breast milk was the sole intake at this stage of the infant's life. Thus, these fathers are also excluded, giving a reduced total of 231. These several adjustments are made to obtain a standard basis for a comparison that assesses the father's actual participation in relation to the maximum possibility of such participation.

It appears that the fathers are considerably more likely to change diapers or feed their infants than to bathe them. Approximately one quarter of the fathers had never diapered or fed their infants, but 80 percent had never bathed them.

Table 5-15
Father's Participation in Infant Care: Diapering, Feeding, Bathing

Degree of Participation[a]	Percent of Fathers Who Participated in Each Activity		
	Diapering	Feeding	Bathing
Never	28	23	80
Rarely	13	12	8
Occasionally	20	29	10
Frequently	39	36	3
Total	100 (274)[b]	100 (231)[c]	101 (274)[b]

[a]To provide standardization of meaning on degree of participation, these definitions were used. For diapering, "frequently" means at least once a day; "occasionally" means less than once a day; "rarely," of course, signifies greater participation than "never." For feeding, "frequently" means once or more during the day or regularly at night; "occasionally" includes as little as once per week; "rarely" means that the father had fed the infant at least once. For bathing, "frequently" means half or more of the infant's baths; "occasionally" includes as little as once per week; "rarely" means that the father had bathed the infant at least once.

[b]Excludes five absent fathers.

[c]Excludes five absent fathers plus 43 fathers whose infants were breast-fed at age 1-2 months.

Only 3 percent of the fathers bathed their infants frequently, while more than one third frequently diapered and fed them.

These findings doubtless are related to the circumstance that bathing occurs, on the average, only once daily (see Table 5-13). In contrast, feeding occurs four or five times daily when the infant is very young, and fresh diapers are needed 10 to 15 times. Moreover, the daily bath is likely to occur when the father is away at work. Of the three activities studied here, bathing is perhaps the most complex in terms of the equipment involved, the requisite manual dexterity, and the integration in time and space of the components of the total production. This is not to say it is beyond paternal capability, but bathing the baby is not a well-stereotyped fatherly activity in our culture and in some instances maternal anxiety may discourage this employment of the father.

Another infant-care routine we investigated is the washing of diapers. Fathers' participation in this ongoing task can be a major contribution to the domestic economy. In many families with infants the daily volume of soiled infant clothing, particularly diapers, is quite large. Infant laundry forms a separate category from other family laundry because milder soaps and hotter water are usually used. It thus stands out as a distinct task in the total household work load. Though physically remote from the infant, it is a form of infant care.

We found that the burden of this task falls primarily upon the mother. In 219 families (78 percent of the total 279), the mother is principal diaper-washer. Thirty-three families (12 percent) use commercial laundering services. In 19 families (7 percent), the diapers are washed by someone other than mother or father; and in only eight families (3 percent) is the father the principal diaper-washer. In another 12 families (4 percent) the father, though not the principal diaper-washer, helps frequently.

These several categories of help in infant care were assembled into a composite Father Participation Index (FPI). The FPI takes into account the extent of participation in feeding, diapering, washing diapers, and bathing. To equalize scoring, the FPI weighs paternal participation more heavily in those activities other than feeding for the babies who were breast-fed. As constructed, the scale has a theoretical range of one (no participation) to eight (maximum participation). Because of the five fathers not present in the household when the baby was one to two months old, scores were available on only 274 fathers. (Chapter 3 reported ten absent fathers at the time of the interview. An additional five fathers were not part of the household during the months before the interview.)

The distribution of FPI scores is presented in Table 5-16. The concentration of scores is at the lower end of the scale, with a minority trailing off in the higher range of scores. There are more fathers who play no part at all in the specified infant-care activities (38 fathers with a score of one) than there are who play a slight part (18 fathers with a score of two). At the other end there are 39 fathers with scores of six or above. The mean FPI score is 3.88, with a standard deviation of 1.65. The median score is 3.46.

Table 5-16
Distribution of Scores, Father Participation Index (FPI)[a]

Score	Frequency
1 (no participation)	38
2	18
3	43
4	64
5	72
6	30
7	7
8 (maximum participation)	2
Total	274

Median = 3.46
Mean = 3.88
Standard Deviation = 1.65

[a]The FPI is a composite score based upon the father's degree of participation in diapering, feeding, and bathing the infant, and also, assisting in the washing of diapers.

Having established a considerable range of variation in the father's participation in infant care, let us look again at the broader family context and then determine how the father's participation is related to other features of the family. We have earlier indicated that the role of father-husband is in a state of transition, as are other family roles. Traditions of the past were strongly prescriptive of the roles and work of father and mother. The content of each role was sharply delineated; mother's place was in the home, while father was away breadwinning. Role tasks were segregated, and child care, especially infant care, was predominantly mother's work. This segregation was maintained by social pressures that made it seem right and natural for mothers and fathers so to define their roles. Situational exigencies further made these definitions seem practical and convenient. For example, preparing baby food was a more time-consuming task in earlier times, and the mother was the only person who knew how to go about it.

Nowadays, father as well as mother can feed the infant with commercially prepared food. Bottle sterilization is more of a chore, but nonetheless manageable by either parent. The contemporary trend is toward an overlapping and blurring of responsibility for various tasks; the greater involvement of fathers in infant care is one aspect of the broad trend. The evidence from our study is that many fathers are involved in routine care. Their participation exceeds a quick cuddle on returning from work in the evening or a ritual kiss before bedtime. Yet, as in all major social changes, the impact of the change is felt unevenly throughout society, and the earlier ways persist and coexist alongside the newer modes. In our study, for example, the 38 no-participation fathers with FPI scores of one may include many whose orientation toward the father role is highly traditional.

If the broad social trend toward greater father participation in infant care has an unequal impact through society, are there characteristic social-class differences? Prescriptions that recommend father's involvement in infant and child care emanate primarily from middle-class, professional experts, and they are directed primarily toward middle-class mothers and fathers. However, questions about child-rearing and family roles are important to working-class families and lower-class families as well, and the pronouncements of middle-class authorities may find a wide and receptive audience in the world of the common man. Despite the orientation toward middle-class parents by the experts, many middle-class fathers, bound to demanding professional or administrative responsibilities, may find themselves less able to tend and spend time with the children and the baby than are working-class fathers. Some social analysts feel that the social role of the father, particularly in the middle-class family, is dwindling to a marked degree (Beels, 1974).

These considerations, pointing in different directions, decided us not to advance a hypothesis about social class and father's participation in infant care. Table 5-17 examines the variation of FPI scores with social class; it presents mean FPI scores and uses analysis of variance as the analytical statistic. The variation is not statistically significant.

For comparison, we turn again to the Nottingham study by the Newsons. Like our own study, it provides information on the father's part in specific care tasks. The Newsons note that a great change in the father-husband role is occurring in all sectors of English society—a trend toward greater involvement of the male in domestic decisions and responsibilities (Newson and Newson, 1963: 139). Nevertheless, class differences appear, as indicated in Table 5-18 (taken

Table 5-17
Father Participation Index by Social Class

Social Class	Mean	Standard Deviation	N
I	4.18	1.12	28
II	3.72	1.61	32
III	4.05	1.53	64
IV	4.15	1.73	72
V	3.46	1.77	78
Total	3.88	1.65	274

Analysis of Variance: F-ratio = 2.27
D.F. = 4,269
$p < .05$

Table 5-18

Father's Participation in Child Care by Occupational Class, Nottingham, England

Occupational Class	Percent High Participation	Percent Moderate Participation	Percent Little or No Participation	Total N in Class (=100%)
I-II	57	24	19	37
III	59	33	8	106
IV	55	27	18	33
V	36	28	36	25
Total	55	30	15	201

$Chi^2 = 14.84$
$D.F. = 6$
$p < .05$

Source: Adapted from Newson and Newson, Table XXX, p. 213. The occupational class scheme employed by the Newsons is a slight modification of the registrar general's classification of occupations (Registrar General – General Register Office, 1960). Although the Hollingshead Two-Factor scheme used in our study bases itself on education as well as occupation, the class rankings obtained in both systems are approximately equivalent.

from their study). More than half the fathers in Classes I, II, III, and IV were highly participant; Class III had the largest proportion of highly participant fathers and the smallest proportion of fathers with little or no participation. Class V stood lowest in degree of father participation, and considerably below any of the other classes.

An interesting convergence between the English and Kentucky studies is the finding that the lower-class father participates less in infant care than do the fathers in classes above the lowest. Infant care is one of a large number of family activities and responsibilities that are divided between the marital pair in accordance with prevailing norms concerning what is the male sphere, the female sphere, and the sphere of joint activity. This finding, common to both studies, suggests that the division of tasks between mother and father remains more stereotyped along traditional sex lines at the lower-class level than at higher levels in the stratification system. Lower-class male work and recreation tend to glorify toughness, independence, and aggressiveness; further, the rigors and instabilities of lower-class family life tend to strengthen the mother-child tie, strong in any event, to the possible exclusion of father's involvement. On a practical level, the lower-class father may work a shift schedule which drastically limits time at home during baby's waking hours.

Within the context of our study, it is possible to identify several other conditions that are associated with a high level of father involvement. The number of children present in the family is a critical determinant. This fact became apparent through an inspection of correlations among the several categories of data. We noted that FPI scores correlate significantly and negatively,

— .17 ($p<$.02), with the mother's current age. That is, the husbands of younger mothers help more with the baby (i.e., had higher FPI scores) and the husbands of older mothers help less.

This suggests two possible interpretations. First, since the husbands of younger mothers tend to be younger themselves and such marriages tend to be more recent, both spouses would be more influenced than would older couples by newer, more egalitarian views of husband-wife roles. Second, and not to the detriment of the first interpretation, younger mothers tend to be infant-only mothers, while older mothers tend to have other children in addition to the infant. If participation in child care were within the father's repertoire to any extent, then we might expect the father of several children to help in care for the older children, and to relinquish most infant care to the mother. This hypothesis derives from the cultural idealization of a close mother-infant tie. Apart from this cultural factor, there is no inherent reason why the mother of a second baby could not delegate a great deal of infant care to her husband, so that he has relatively little to do with the older child and the care he gives to the second baby is as extensive as that which he gave to the first.

This suggests a contrary hypothesis, namely, that the husbands of the multipara mothers are as involved in infant care as the husbands of the primapara mothers. This hypothesis was tested by comparing the FPI scores of the two groups of fathers, as shown in Table 5-19. It appears that the primapara fathers do help more in infant care than the multipara fathers. Our conjecture about the force of the cultural stereotype finds substantial confirmation. We suggest a further hypothesis which builds upon this: namely, among a line of siblings, it is the firstborn who enjoys the greatest total amount and continuity of father care. That is, when the first baby arrives, the father pitches in—not as heavily as the mother does, but to an appreciable extent. The father continues to give care to the firstborn upon the advent of the second, and neither the second nor any subsequent sibling receives the same degree of early care from the father. A proper test of this hypothesis is not possible within the framework of our data; it would require data on father's participation in the care of successive infants in the family.

Table 5-19
Father Participation Index (FPI) in Relation to Mother's Parity

| | *Maternal Status* | | |
	Primapara	*Multipara*	*Total*
Number	71	203	274
FPI Mean Score	4.24	3.75	3.88
Standard Deviation	1.55	1.66	1.64

Critical Ratio of Difference between Means: 2.25
$p < .05$

Another factor of potential influence upon the degree of father care is race, that is, black-white differences in the cultural, nonbiological sense discussed in the previous chapter. In the light of contemporary concern with racial inequality and its remedy, it is useful to place our findings in the context of current social-science conceptualization and investigation of the problem. Many analyses of the problems of American blacks identify family structure as both cause and effect of the disadvantaged position that blacks have in income, occupational status and security, educational attainment, and other parameters of well-being (Hannerz, Ulf, 1969; U.S. Department of Labor, 1965, also known as the Moynihan Report; Banton, Michael, 1967: 334-67). Family structure is adversely affected because many blacks suffer job discrimination, being last hired and first fired, and receive lower wages for the same work done by whites. Also of critical importance is the fact that black females are on the average better-educated than black males; to a greater extent than in white families, the black wife can hold steadier employment, at a higher income, than the black husband. The Moynihan Report (U.S. Department of Labor, 1965: 34) notes, "It is clear that Negro females have established a strong position for themselves in white collar and professional employment, precisely the areas of the economy which are growing most rapidly, and to which highest prestige is accorded." These circumstances have impaired the ability of the black male to play the role of steady bread-winner and have given rise to the "matrifocal" family—mother-dominated, economically supported by the mother, and characterized by frequent illegitimacy, divorce, and domestic instability. This, in turn, may lead to inadequate socialization of the children, to low educational attainment, and to low occupational aspiration, which, reinforced by discriminatory patterns of the external society, serve to carry forward the matrifocal family into succeeding generations.

These characterizations of the black family lead to the general expectation that black fathers participate less in infant care than do white fathers. But whether this general expectation applies in our study is questionable. The black families in our study are to a high degree intact and stable; ninety-six percent of the fathers are present and employed. Thus, although the black families have much lower social status than the whites (see Table 4-13), they lack the features of gross disorganization that are frequently noted in analyses of racial problems. In an intact family structure, the black father may participate in infant care as much as his white counterpart. On the other hand, perhaps the important factor is not the physical presence of the father in the household. Even with the father present in an intact family structure, cultural factors such as discrimination and the vestigial effects of the slavery tradition may sustain the matrifocal family. Even when the father is on the scene, his role may be shadowy and ineffectual.

The black father's role can best be examined in our study through the black-white comparison group. It will be recalled that this consists of 30 black families matched with 30 white families on social class, mother's age, and number of children. In two cases, the paired black and white families both lacked the father, which reduced the comparison group to 28 pairs. The FPI mean for the

28 black fathers is 4.07; the mean for the white fathers is 3.37. The mean difference for the 28 pairs is 0.70, with the black fathers showing higher participation, though this trend is not statistically significant.

This comparison concludes our consideration of the father's direct role in early infant care. There is a general lack of studies dealing with the father's part in child care and child-rearing, and yet there is also a rising degree of public interest in the role, influence, and image of the father within the family. Many studies of social and personal ills such as crime, alcoholism, and mental illness implicate the broken home and father's absence or inadequacy as a cause, though the mechanisms whereby normal development is skewed or arrested remain obscure (Goode, 1971). The general topic is difficult to investigate; we alluded to this above in indicating that the black father's effectiveness in the family structure may be undercut by social and cultural factors external to the family. Another possibility is that the interpretation of the father's role which the mother imparts to the children is as important as the father's actual behavior and participation with them. In aristocratic and wealthy families of past and present, neither parent has carried much direct responsibility for child care (Aries, 1962: 396); servants have sustained intensive involvements with the children. The image of the parents conveyed by the servants may be more important than actual parental contact for adequate socialization of the children in their particular milieu. Definitive research on child-rearing must study the interpersonal and cultural environment of the child, as well as the main effects of direct parental contact.

Mother's Employment After Delivery

In the preceding chapter we discussed general trends in female employment and presented findings on the mothers in our sample who worked during pregnancy. Approximately 30 percent of the mothers were employed during pregnancy. The level of employment was much higher for the primaparas than the multiparas; 49 percent of the former worked, and only 23 percent of the latter. The social class of the mother also had an influence upon her employment status: higher-class women were more likely than lower-class women to work. This trend was more pronounced among the primapara mothers.

We turn now to the question of employment following the birth of the infant. Like employment during pregnancy, employment following the infant's birth is a component of female employment, but its meaning and consequence are different. Employment during pregnancy places some physical strain upon the woman, particularly as pregnancy progresses. Following the delivery, the mother regains her energy and stamina, so that she can again meet work responsibilities comfortably. But she bears a new responsibility at home—the care of her baby. If she is a first-time mother, she may be especially prone to feelings of conflict between job demands and the needs of the infant. If she already has children at home and has perhaps worked during previous pregnancies, she now has one more child to care for. Whatever the economic or psychological advantages of work following the birth, the mother who engages in it may find herself hard-pressed to resume employment and to care for the baby.

The social norm in our society assigns to the mother primary responsibility for the care of the young child. This norm is less stringently held than it once was and is being lessened somewhat by the growth (albeit slow) of day-care centers, and by increasing paternal responsibility. There has been an increase in the proportion of mothers of infants and preschool children who work. Nevertheless, the notion that the infant needs a primary attachment to its mother remains strong. There is perhaps less sentimental idealization of the mother-infant tie than there was fifty or a hundred years ago; however, a newer, more psychological conception of the infant's need for mothering has gained a strong foothold, especially through women's magazines and authorities such as Dr. Spock. Although breast-feeding may be declining as a practice, a concept of psychosocial supplies, or psychological nourishment, from the mother is replacing the older emphasis on the sheer nutritional benefit of breast milk.

The employment of women, especially mothers, in the United States has an increasingly elective character (Blake, 1974). This is directly related to basic social forces affecting female employment. The increase in male life expectancy in the decades since 1900 means that far fewer mothers are left as widows with young children to support. The general increase in living standards and the job security of male breadwinners means that fewer mothers, and fewer married women as a whole, work from economic pressure. Those who work are more free to move in and out of the labor force depending upon the availability of attractive work, changing personal motivations related to the cycle of family development, and other factors. The decision to work is frequently a woman's personal decision. There is little social pressure either for or against it.

There is also little social facilitation in the form of extensive, well-organized, child-care facilities at the community level. The most serious problem faced by many working mothers of infants is the difficulty in finding an adequate mother substitute during the hours of their work. Grandmothers or other female relatives living nearby are a major resource, but one available to relatively few mothers in today's world. Many working mothers employ infant caretakers who come to the mother's home or care for the baby in their own home. Another possibility is the use of a day nursery, but many communities have a dearth of good nurseries for infants and preschool children. Societies that rely heavily upon the employment of women have made much greater provision for community nurseries than has the United States. Some societies also positively encourage early placement of the infant in a group-care setting for the inculcation of societal values, thus avoiding the vicissitudes of value transmission in the nuclear family. It is perhaps not surprising that work in child care forms a substantial fraction of total female employment in societies with a well-developed system of nurseries and kindergartens; many women are engaged in the care of young children, but not necessarily their own.

The lack of communal infant-care facilities has been identified and deplored by leaders of the contemporary women's movement in the United States (Baxandall, 1975). The establishment of day-care facilities for children of working mothers is an important objective. This movement holds that if women can be relieved of the total (or near-total) burden of child care, they will be free to pursue other tasks that contribute to social welfare. They will also have greater scope to develop personal interests and talents. There is also recognition of the plight of poor and divorced women who work from economic necessity and whose babies might receive better food, health care, and social stimulation than they would at home. This strand of thinking emphasizes the distinction between the mother who wants to work for the sake of career, self-expression, or social contact, and the mother who works involuntarily to support herself and her family. Another argument in favor of day-care centers is strictly economic: as the social economist John Galbraith writes, "In a child care center one person cares professionally for numerous children; in the family one person cares unprofessionally for one or a very few. Thus, there can be few institutions so directly designed to increase the productivity of labor" (Galbraith, 1973: 82).

Many child-care authorities tend to discourage mothers from working unless there is overriding economic necessity. *Infant Care* states: "Every mother should carefully consider whether the money and satisfaction she gets for returning to work is worth the cost to her and her family. Good child care is always expensive, and poor child care causes a great deal of trouble and worry and can be dangerous for the baby" (U.S. Children's Bureau, 1972: 54). This source does not recognize the need of some mothers to obtain relief from the stress of infant care through the medium of employment. Neither does it recognize the interest of married career women in combining professional growth with motherhood, nor the broader concept that the national economy could not function without widespread female employment.

Given the open, partly elective nature of much female employment in our society, it is of particular interest to understand the kinds of work motivation and attitude associated with employment. By examining the relationship of postdelivery employment to previous employment, social class, and other characteristics of the mothers, we will assess the work orientation that comes into play among working mothers.

Turning from these general considerations, we will explore postdelivery employment of mothers in our study. We find that 55 mothers, or 19.7 percent of the sample, were employed within the first ten months following delivery. For most of the mothers who had postnatal employment, this was a resumption of the previous work role. However, many mothers who had been earlier employed did not return to work. Presumably, they elected to devote themselves to family and maternal roles coupled perhaps with volunteer and neighborhood activities. Moreover, some mothers who had not been employed during the pregnancy did then enter the work force.

Table 5-20 examines the relationship between employment before and after delivery. Eighty-three, or 30 percent, of the 279 mothers were employed during pregnancy. Of these 83 mothers, 36 (43 percent) subsequently returned to work. Of the 196 mothers who were not employed during pregnancy, 177 remained out of the work force and 19 entered it following the delivery. Thus, although there is movement into and away from the work force, the net effect of child-bearing and its associated roles is strongly in the direction of removing mothers from employment. This primary tendency reflects the general social norms regarding infant care. It further appears that many of those women who deviated from the general norm, that is, who worked following the birth, were influenced by another important factor, previous employment during pregnancy. Among the 55 mothers employed after delivery, 36 had worked during pregnancy; many of these mothers presumably returned to a job that was waiting for them.

Let us now dissect the components of these trends more precisely, by looking at other variables affecting employment. Table 5-21 divides the mothers into two categories according to primapara or multipara status. Looking first at the primaparas, we see that approximately half (35 of 71, or 49 percent) were employed during pregnancy, and that of this half, half again (17 of 35, or 49 percent) returned to work after delivery. Among the multiparas, 23 percent (48 of 208) were employed during pregnancy; of those so employed, 40 percent (19 of 48) returned after delivery. In both categories of parity, the advent of the infant exerts a strong effect toward removing mothers from the work force, although this effect is stronger among the multiparas than among the primaparas.

In both categories, working before the delivery is linked with working afterward, among those mothers who did work afterward. However, one point of noticeable contrast between the two categories lies in the mothers who

Table 5-20
Employment Status of Mothers Before and After Delivery

		Did Mother Work After Delivery?		
		No	Yes	Total
	No	177	19	196
Did Mother Work Before Delivery?	Yes	47	36	83
	Total	224	55	279

Chi^2 : Employment Status Before Delivery and After Delivery Compared = 41.77
D.F. = 1
$p < .001$

Table 5-21

Employment Status of Mothers Before and After Delivery, by Parity

Part A: *Primaparas*

		Did Mother Work After Delivery?		
		No	Yes	Total
Did Mother Work Before Delivery?	No	33	3	36
	Yes	18	17	35
	Total	51	20	71

Chi² = 14.20
D.F. = 1
p < .001

Part B: *Multiparas*

		Did Mother Work After Delivery?		
		No	Yes	Total
Did Mother Work Before Delivery?	No	144	16	160
	Yes	29	19	48
	Total	173	35	208

Chi² = 23.09
D.F. = 1
p < .001

worked after delivery but not before. Sixteen of the 35 multiparas, or 46 percent, with postdelivery employment had not worked before, compared with only 3 of 20 primaparas, or 15 percent. The mothers with this employment pattern, while not a numerically large group, are of particular interest because the sequence of moving from nonwork during pregnancy to work following it runs counter to the general cultural norm regarding maternal responsibility for infant care. One explanation for this countertrend is that these mothers work from economic necessity. The data support this conjecture: there were no mothers in Classes I and II who worked after the delivery but not before; of the 19 mothers who did work after the delivery but not before, 2 were in Class III, 4 were in Class IV, and 13 were in Class V.

An overview of postdelivery employment in relationship to the social class and parity of the mother can be obtained from Table 5-22. This table can be readily compared with Table 4-5, which shows parallel findings for the mothers during pregnancy. A comparisom reveals several interesting points. Among the

Table 5-22
Employment Status of Mothers After Delivery, by Social Class and Parity

Social Class	All Women		Parity			
			Primapara		Multipara	
	Total N	Percent of N Who Worked	Total N	Percent of N Who Worked	Total N	Percent of N Who Worked
I-II	60	18.3(11)[a]	17	29.4(5)	43	11.6(6)
III	64	18.7(12)	24	29.1(7)	40	12.5(5)
IV	75	18.6(14)	14	21.4(3)	61	18.0(11)
V	80	22.5(18)	16	31.3(5)	64	20.3(13)
Total	279	19.7(55)	71	28.2(20)	208	16.3(35)
	$Chi^2 = .55$		$Chi^2 = .11$		$Chi^2 = 1.39$	
	D.F. = 3		D.F. = 3		D.F. = 3	
	$p \nless .05$		$p \nless .05$		$p \nless .05$	

[a]The numbers in parentheses are the actual number in each category who worked. Thus, of the 43 multiparas in Classes I-II, 6 (11.6%) worked.

primaparas during pregnancy, the higher-class women show a greater level of employment than do the lower-class women. Among the multiparas, there is no consistent variation by social class in employment during pregnancy. Following delivery, a substantial proportion of the primaparas who had worked earlier did not return to work, except in Class V, where the proportion working is the same (31 percent) in both time periods. Among the multiparas after delivery, there is no strong overall variation in employment by social class.

It is relevant to point out that the multipara mothers have, following delivery, two or more children (including the infant) at home; that is, multiparas of Table 4-5 have one or more children at home during the pregnancy, so following the new birth their family includes two or more. The overall level of multipara employment drops from 23.1 percent during the pregnancy to 16.3 percent following delivery. The proportion declines in every class except Class V, where it increases, from 15.6 percent to 20.3 percent. This increase is related to the trend noted above, namely, that some Class V multipara mothers enter the work force following delivery without having been employed during pregnancy. We may surmise that these Class V mothers are largely lacking in special occupational skills and previous work experience. They enter employment under the domestic condition of having primary responsibility for several small children. They probably work not from an interest in job or career and not as an escape from the stress of child care, but simply because they need income.

Whatever the problems of alienation from work which afflict male workers, such problems are probably greater for the lower-class mother who works under economic duress at a stultifying job. Her situation also contrasts with the higher-class working mother, who faces some of the same work-family conflicts but who, with less economic pressure, can move in and out of the work force more freely in relation to family needs and whose work is more apt to hold intrinsic interest.

We have thus far examined employment after delivery in the light of the mother's parity, her social class, and her work experience during pregnancy. These are antecedent variables; they identify conditions that may incline mothers to undertake postdelivery employment. We interpreted the data by characterizing mothers of a given social class or parity and trying to understand what leads them to work or not to work. We will now examine a fourth variable, namely, father's participation in infant care, in relation to the mother's employment.

This variable occupies a different causal position in relation to maternal employment from the other three. The father's role in infant care proceeds concurrently with the mother's employment for those mothers who work. In this light, his contribution could be regarded as an element that makes it easier for the working mother to bear the dual burden of an outside job and domestic responsibility. Expectation of such support from the father might lead some mothers into employment; that is, in weighing the advantages and disadvantages of work, anticipation of the father's help might be a decisive, positive element.

Dr. Spock, in his most recent advice, states that mothers and fathers "have an equal right to a career if they want one . . . and an equal obligation to share in the care of their child, with or without the help of others" (Spock, 1976: 37). He notes approvingly that many husbands of women with outside jobs have been participating increasingly in all aspects of home and child care. *Infant Care,* the U.S. government publication, makes no mention of modifications of the father's role in relation to the mother's employment; the implication is that the mother's employment is her own doing and that she need expect no extra help at home if she works.

In order to examine the father's role when the wife is employed, we use the Father Participation Index. (It will be recalled that this index generates a composite score ranging from one—no participation—to eight—high participation—which reflects the father's level of participation in the selected standard infant-care tasks.) The FPI mean for the entire sample is 3.88, as shown in Table 5-23. For the husbands of the 53 mothers who worked following the advent of the baby, the mean is 4.23; for the husbands of nonworking mothers, the mean is 3.79. Thus, the husbands of working mothers were more involved in infant care than the husbands of mothers who did not work, although as the table shows the difference is not statistically significant.

The question may be pursued further by inquiring how infant care by the father is related jointly to the mother's employment and number of children. Earlier, in Table 5-19, we examined the question of father's infant care in relation to number of children (husbands of primapara mothers compared with husbands of multipara mothers). Now a fuller view is taken by looking at father care in relation to both independent variables, which may be expected to modify the father role.

By dichotomizing mothers according to work-nonwork status and primapara-multipara status, we constitute four distinct groups: the working primapara, the working multipara, the nonworking primapara, and the nonworking multipara. According to the logic of our analysis, of these four groups the working multipara mother should receive the most help from the father. Because of her job, she has less time and energy to devote to her family. Moreover, with two or more children to care for, she needs more help than the mother with one child. At the other extreme, the primapara mother who does not work has, presumably, few claims upon her other than the responsibility for her baby. She would have less need for help from her husband. Of course, husbands may participate not only in relation to the wife's need, but also out of interest and satisfaction in being with the baby.

Table 5-23 shows that the fathers in our study did not distribute their infant-care assistance in accordance with the foregoing expectations. The husbands of the multipara working mothers have a mean score of 4.18, as compared with a mean of 4.30 for the husbands of the primapara working mothers. The group of husbands with the lowest FPI mean, 3.67, are those with wives in the

Table 5-23
Father Participation Index (FPI) in Relation to Mother's Employment Status and Parity

	Working Mothers			Nonworking Mothers			All Mothers		
	Primapara	Multipara	Total	Primapara	Multipara	Total	Primapara	Multipara	Total
Number	20	33	53	51	170	221	71	203	274
FPI Mean Score	4.30	4.18	4.23	4.21	3.67	3.79	4.24	3.75	3.88
FPI Standard Deviation	1.88	2.00	1.85	1.42	1.56	1.54	1.55	1.66	1.64

Comparison Groups

	Critical Ratio of Difference Between Means
1. Working Primapara and Working Multipara	0.22
2. Nonworking Primapara and Nonworking Multipara	2.33 ($p < .05$)
3. Working Primapara and Nonworking Primapara	0.19
4. Working Multipara and Nonworking Multipara	1.39
5. Working and Nonworking	1.59
6. Primapara and Multipara	2.25 ($p < .05$)

nonworking multipara group. In essence, the other three groups have statistically similar means, while the nonworking multipara group is distinctly different. (As noted previously, the FPI fixes specifically upon infant care and ignores other dimensions of father's participation in domestic affairs. It may be that many fathers with two or more children in the family devote considerable effort to the older children so that the mother can devote herself to the infant.)

By examining the pattern of critical ratios, we see that both status and parity status affect the father's participation in infant care, though neither factor exerts a consistently significant effect. The husbands of working mothers, in general, help more in infant care than the husbands of nonworking mothers (4.23 compared with 3.79). But the difference is very slight in the primapara category (4.30 compared with 4.21). The husbands of the multipara mothers in general help *less* with the infant than the husbands of the primapara mothers. However, the husbands of the working multipara mothers help with the infant a good deal more than the husbands of the nonworking multipara mothers.

It appears from Table 5-23 that maternal parity has a stronger influence upon the husband's infant-care performance than the mother's work status. This suggests that the traditional rootedness of the mother's role in reproductive and child-care functions commands high recognition and support within the family. Her occupational performance, on the other hand, whatever its contribution to family standard of living, is more in the nature of a personal activity, which she does on her own with less support from her husband.

The evidence from this study indicates that the husband's role in infant care is to some extent aligned with the wife's degree of need, as this is construed in terms of her responsibility for work and other children. It appears that husbands participate in the care of a first baby to virtually the same extent whether the wife works or not. If she is not working, she can presumably devote herself more fully to care of the baby, and according to the traditional rationale of male-female roles the husband would have little part in infant care. The relatively high participation of many husbands in care of the first baby suggests that the husband wants a share in an activity that defines the family unit in a fundamentally new way. The traditional division of labor then asserts itself more strongly with children after the first. The mother is less likely to work. If she does work, the husband helps more with the infant than if she does not. The husband's help in this case may reflect the mother's need for help rather than the father's independent, personal disposition to help, that disposition being stronger with the novelty of the first infant. On the other hand, if the multipara mother does not work, then the husband's participation drops off to a great extent.

6

The Health Care of the Infant

A church in Kent, England, contains a monumental brass bearing the inscription, "Anne the daughter and onely child of Thom Consant person of Deale & of Lydeth his wife (after 13 years maried) was borne ye 18th of lune & died sodenly at nurse ye 20th of luly 1606." Anne Consant's early death in the seventeenth century typifies the melancholy lot of many infants in times and places that lack the material and scientific advantages of industrial society.

The health care of the infant is an important component within the total scope of modern medicine. Just as medical supervision during pregnancy is of significant benefit to fetus and to mother, so is medical supervision of the infant a vital and widely accepted part of health care. As with a host of diseases and disabling conditions which affect adults, scientific methods of early disease detection, prevention, and treatment have made infancy a more biologically secure phase of life. Vital statistics from the nineteenth century are not accurate, but estimates place infant mortality in the United States at 150 to 200 deaths per thousand live births at midcentury, declining to 100 to 120 per thousand by 1900. Further decline is evident in the rate of 56 in 1932 as compared with 25 in 1962 (National Center for Health Statistics, 1965: 61). Kentucky figures parallel the national figures, dropping from 75 in 1915 to 29 in 1961 (Ford, 1964: 111). Information on morbidity is less available than on mortality, but it appears that along with mortality reduction has come lessened morbidity and disability from infectious diseases such as influenza, cholera, smallpox, syphilis, and polio.

Much of the progress in infant health is a part of the improvement in the health status of the general population, without specific medical intervention (Fuchs, 1974). A series of notable public health advances were made, starting around 1875, in water supply, food and milk handling, and in waste disposal. Infants benefited as much from these as older age groups—perhaps they benefited more, for infants are especially vulnerable to gastrointestinal and respiratory infections which adults withstand more easily. The nineteenth century saw a general improvement in quantity and quality of the food supply available to the general population; better nutrition is thought to have been even more important in the decline of deaths from tuberculosis than were sanitary improvements (Powles, 1972). Infants have also benefited from preventive inoculations against a number of diseases that formerly took a heavy toll—diphtheria, whooping cough, tetanus, smallpox, polio, and most recently measles. A further line of advance in infant health care has come in the antibiotic treatment of infections.

Along with these general advances in health care, there has developed a more specific conception of the diseases and health needs of infants. It has been previously noted that middle-class, urban families of the mid-nineteenth century sent their infants to live in the country, where the air, water, food, and general environment were presumed to be more wholesome. We have also referred to the strong interest among contemporary parents and professional caretakers of the young in acquiring a scientifically based understanding of infant and child development. Dr. Benjamin Spock has been identified as an important authority for a whole generation of parents.

The base of knowledge, concepts, and data which underlies the contemporary understanding of infancy and childhood has been built by many scientists (such as Piaget, Binet, Freud, Gesell, and Bowlby) in studies of intellectual, emotional, behavioral, and physiological development. This knowledge base covers normal development as well as developmental deviations and pathology. The newer concepts in child development give greater recognition than was earlier the case to the individuality of the child, to the broad range of variation that is encompassed in normal development, and to the importance of parent-child relationships.

The foregoing, brief review of progress in infant health care forms one context for the investigation of infant health status in our study. A second context lies in the organization of medical services that deal with infant health problems. In the current period, the delivery of health services poses issues that have aroused much controversy and provoked extensive social analysis (Saward, 1973). Any resolution of problems in provision of health services must obviously reckon with broad population needs for infant and child health care and with the existing apparatus for delivering such care.

A major historical development in the organization of medical care for children has been the emergence of pediatrics as a medical specialty. Pediatrics was the fifth such specialty to gain recognition in the United States; the American Board of Pediatrics was recognized by the American Medical Association in 1934 (Stevens, 1971: 542). Pediatric specialization is one branch of the significant trend toward specialization and away from general practice, having its basis in the recognition that children are not simply little adults or homunculi. Certain diseases are limited to childhood or have a more severe course than in adulthood, and dosage levels for many medications cannot simply be proportioned to the body weight of the child as compared with that of the adult, but must be determined in relation to the age-specific biological organization of the child.

While pediatrics is by now a large and firmly established branch of medicine, questions persist as to the proper and distinctive province of the pediatrician. In her comprehensive analysis of the structure of American medicine, Stevens (1971: 219) views the emergence of pediatrics as "an expression of a relatively narrow professionalism, whose roots lay rather in the evolution of specialist interest in the past, than in any new approach to functional delineations in the profession which would be appropriate to the demands of modern medicine." She notes further that most other specialties are defined by their focus on a body system or a specific technology (such as the obstetrician's forceps, the anesthesiologist's gases, and the pathologist's stains). In contrast, the pediatrician's specialty is determined only by age of the patient; otherwise, he functions as a general practitioner.

Beyond the issue of general practice versus specialization in medicine, other current issues in health-care delivery are the role of paramedical personnel; inadequate medical care for the poor, the black, and rural dwellers; and the widespread difficulty of obtaining care at times and places convenient to patients (Bowers, 1977). All these topics have particular relevance to infant and child health services.

Our study will focus upon these four specific questions:

1. What health problems are found in the sample of infants?
2. How is the social class of the infant related to the health care he receives?
3. How is the race of the infant related to the health care he receives?
4. What social patterns are associated with professional house-calls to the infant's home?

Health care may be examined from the perspective of the recipient of health services, who is variously designated as the patient, patron, client, or consumer. It may also be examined from the perspective of the provider, variously designated as a professional worker, a purveyor of services, or a servant of the client.

As a trained expert, the health-care provider views his or her work as an orderly set of tasks that implement scientific principles. He or she is concerned about providing a valid, effective service and about the material rewards and the dignity of the work. On the other hand, the health-care provider tends to view as unquestionable the physical and organizational context in which he or she renders services and the social mechanisms whereby he or she receives patients. The patient, in contrast, is more aware of contextual and social factors as they impinge upon the individual, while he or she may have little comprehension of the professional content of the services received. The perspectives of both provider and patient are important for a rounded view. By focusing upon concrete data, we hope to avoid the polemical biases of much current discussion, and to contribute to a growing body of knowledge and concepts about health care.

Infant Health Problems

By now the reader is aware that the sample of infants selected for this study is essentially a normal group. A survey of health status in a representative group of 279 infants is unlikely to report a case of cystic fibrosis or leukemia. Thus our intent here is to assess the occurrence of common infant health problems. To this end, we devised a list of complaints and symptoms which infants frequently present. As a set of general categories under which specific items could be arrayed, we used the following: accidents, harmful behavioral patterns, and somatic symptoms and complaints. To obtain a comprehensive set of items familiar to (within the experience of) mothers and usable in an interview situation, we consulted pediatric sources, child-care manuals, and parent education materials. The list employed is shown in Table 6-1

In eliciting responses from the mothers, the interviewers said, "Here is a list of different things that can happen with babies. Most babies have had some of these things. Has your baby ever had (name of health problem)?" Discussion of infant problems is a sensitive matter to mothers, whose role imposes primary responsibility for the feeding, daily care, health, and total welfare of the baby.

Table 6-1
Infant Health Problems

Type of Health Problem	Frequency Reported	Percentage of Sample
Accidents		
Fall	30	11
Burn or scald	11	4
Accidents not listed elsewhere	9	3
Poison	0	0
Behavioral Patterns		
Excessive thumb-sucking	70	25
Head-banging	59	21
Dirt-eating	28	10
Breath-holding	8	3
Harmful behavioral patterns not listed elsewhere	4	1
Somatic Symptoms		
Bad cough or cold	182	65
Diaper rash	150	54
Diarrhea	139	50
Constipation	119	43
Vomiting	103	37
Labored breathing	102	37
Skin problems not listed elsewhere	89	32
Lack of weight gain	55	20
Ear trouble	55	20
Serious illness not listed elsewhere	35	12
Anemia	14	5
Parasites	3	1

Mean number of problems reported per infant: 4.5
Range in number of problems reported per infant: 0 to 13

The interviewers were instructed to put the mothers at ease in identifying health problems.

Our findings on infant health problems register the mother's response to the interview questions, rather than objective, clinically validated assessments. Accepting the findings in these terms, let us turn again to Table 6-1 to examine the results in terms of frequency. The health problems most frequently reported are bad cough or cold (65 percent), diaper rash (54 percent), diarrhea (50 percent), and constipation (43 percent). At the other extreme, no infant is reported to have swallowed a poisonous substance (though 10 percent were said to have engaged in dirt-eating). One percent had had parasites, 3 percent had had breath-holding spells to the point of passing out, and 5 percent are cited as having been anemic.

Several questions were asked to elicit residual health problems not explicitly designated by the interviewer. The kinds of responses given include the following. Four infants engaged in harmful behavioral patterns other than excessive thumb-sucking, head-banging, breath-holding, and dirt-eating. Of these, one engaged in hair-pulling, two scratched their skin heavily, and one, according to the mother's response, "turns her head from side to side constantly" (but no reference was made by the mother to actual harm). Skin problems in addition to diaper rash are common, reported by 32 percent. Many allergic rashes were reported, sometimes to specific foods such as orange juice and wheat cereal. Heat rash, dust allergies, and scalp infections were also reported.

Twelve percent of the mothers reported serious illnesses not otherwise enumerated. Pneumonia is the most common entity reported. Infectious diseases typical of later childhood were also reported: measles, mumps, chicken-pox, and whooping cough. Infancy is not the best time for contracting infectious diseases, because the infant tends to be afflicted more severely than the older child. No complications or aftereffects were reported in this group. And the residual accident question drew nine positive responses. Of these, most involved the infant pulling a heavy or sharp object onto itself. The episode was thus a type of fall but not the infant's own falling.

According to developmental data acquired on the sample, only one third of the infants could stand alone at the time of the interview, and only one fifth could walk. Many accidents cannot occur until the infant becomes a mobile, active toddler. Only a toddler can reach into the medicine cabinet and get hold of pills. A crawler can fall down steps, but a toddler is more likely to have such a mishap. Burns are more likely to occur to mobile infants who can pull hot liquids off the stove or a hot iron off the ironing board. Burns can also be passively received, as when the mother, holding the baby, burns it with a cigarette or spills hot water from a bottle sterilizer.

Many of the falls sustained by infants in this study seem, from spontaneous comments offered by the mothers, to be related to developmental thresholds achieved by the infant without the mother's recognition. For example, the mother changes the diapers uneventfully for several months, with the infant lying on a changing-table or a bed. Then the infant acquires the capacity to roll from front to back, or, a little later, from back to front. Instead of lying passively while the mother steps away to fetch pins or talcum powder, the infant rolls over and falls to the floor. Once this happens, the mother readies her materials in advance so as not to step away. None of the "bad falls" reported had caused fractures or dislocations; many were "bad" only in the sense that an adult could have prevented them. Inasmuch as the infant is completely dependent upon adults for its care and safety, virtually all accidents come down to adult responsibility.

Table 6-1 shows that the mean of problems per infant was 4.5, with a range of zero to thirteen problems. The rank order of health problems by frequency corresponds with information provided by the American Academy of Pediatrics (Schade, 1962: 14) to physicians potentially interested in a pediatric career: "The most common diseases that affect children are those of the respiratory tract. Other common entities include feeding problems, allergic conditions, acute diarrhea, enteric conditions of other types, acute viral illnesses, common contagious diseases, various forms of anemia and heart disease, and infections of the urinary tract, often associated with obstructive malformations."

The Health Difficulty Index: Construction and Analysis

To gain a more systematic view of the health status of the infant, and to study health status in relation to quantitative parameters of the study, we constructed a composite statistical index called the Health Difficulty (HD) Index. It is based upon the health information described above, plus four developmental categories. The HD index embraces the following categories:

1. All the health-problem categories shown in Table 6-1, except poison (because it had a zero frequency in the sample). This group thus has 20 categories of data.
2. Four categories related to difficulties in behavioral development:
   a. Failure to sleep through the night, for infants over four months old.
   b. Failure to attain sit-up position, for infants over eight months old.
   c. Difficulty in teething, for infants over eight months old.
   d. Difficulty in accepting or adjusting to the most "advanced" food the infant currently eats—whether prepared baby vegetables, meats, or family table food.

It will be noted that there are 24 categories of information, and that three of these (2a, 2b, and 2c) apply only to those infants who had reached specified ages. The age norms were set conservatively, to allow for a wide range of developmental variation. For example, with regard to sleeping, an infant was counted as having a developmental difficulty only if by five months he or she still was not sleeping through the night. Similar considerations apply to not sitting up by nine months. The category of teething trouble is different, in that the question is not whether the infant had erupted teeth but instead whether in the process of teething the infant had evidenced considerable fussiness or sensitivity. It was assumed that by age nine months an infant would have begun teething, or would be in an immediate preeruptive phase.

From the index construction, a hypothetical infant who was nine months or older and who had a negative or unfavorable score in every category (that is, had had a bad fall, been burned, had other accidents, been an excessive thumb-sucker, and so on) would have an HD score of 24. Another infant of the same age might, at the other extreme, have a score of zero—no difficulties at all. The raw scores of younger infants are arithmetically weighted upward by the appropriate multiplier to give them a theoretical range of zero to 24. All items are equally weighted.

The HD index provides a convenient summary measure of health and development problems encountered by the infant. By means of HD scores, two infants or two groups of infants could be compared, and various social background factors could be assessed for their significance in relation to the infant health status. It must be acknowledged that the index is an imperfect device for conveying quantitative information about a complex phenomenon. The HD index rests upon the accuracy of the mother's recall of her infant's health and developmental history. Presumably errors of recall, so far as they are random and not systematic, have small impact in an extensive composite index.

Let us turn now to the use of the HD index in the study. Table 6-2 shows that the average infant in the survey has slightly more than five health problems. The median index score is 4.4. The highest score is 15, and seven other scores exceeded 10. At the other extreme, that is low scores indicative of good health, there are seven scores of zero, and 47 scores of one or two.

We shall examine the connection of health status as represented by the Health Difficulty index with social class, maternal attitude toward pregnancy, pregnancy history, and other factors which may affect the infant's status. First, let us look at Table 6-3, which presents HD score means within social classes. We see that infants in Class II have the lowest frequency of health problems reported, 4.2, and those in Class V have the highest frequency, 5.8, for a mean difference of 1.6 problems between the two classes. Each class has an appreciable amount of internal variation. There is nonetheless a trend, statistically significant at the 5 percent level by analysis of variance, for the infants of lower social status to have a greater number of health problems. This overall trend suggested the value of turning back to the separate constituents of the HD index in order to determine which were most strongly associated with social status. While many of the specific health

Table 6-2
Health Difficulty Index (HD)

Score Interval	Frequency
0	7
1–2	47
3–4	68
5–6	65
7–8	54
9–10	30
11–15	8
16–24	0
Total	279

Mean Score: 5.2
Standard Deviation: 2.7
Range: 0 to 15 (Theoretical Range: 0 to 24)
Median Score: 4.4

Table 6-3
Health Difficulty Index by Social Class

Social Class	Mean HD Score	Standard Deviation	N
I	4.7	1.9	28
II	4.2	2.0	32
III	4.8	2.5	64
IV	5.4	2.7	75
V	5.8	3.1	80
Total	5.2	2.7	279

Analysis of Variance: F-Ratio = 2.87
D.F. = 4,274
$p < .05$

problems are somewhat overrepresented at lower-class levels, only four have a connection with social class that is significant at the 5 percent level. These are lack of weight gain, bad cough or cold, labored breathing, and diaper rash.

Empirical relationships between health status and social status are never easy to interpret unless the health entity under study has a specific cause which is firmly linked with the occupation, diet, life-style, or physical habitat of particular status groups. When established, class-disease correlations usually take the form seen here: lower-status persons are more likely to be affected than higher-status persons (Coe, 1970: 58). Our study does not deal with diagnosed disease entities but rather with adverse health conditions in the infants which are, for the most part, self-limited incidents and episodes, unconnected with significant morbidity. It is nevertheless of interest that infants in lower-status families have a greater burden of reported health problems than those of higher status. Studies of infant mortality and morbidity have found that greater risk accompanies lower social status (National Center for Health Statistics, 1967: 67-8; Lerner and Anderson, 1963: 23-8). The findings here, at a milder level of health impairment, are consistent with these studies.

We can examine the effect upon the infant's health status of other factors, in addition to social status. Other possibilities to be explored are that those infants with more health problems were the outcome of difficult pregnancies, were less likely to have been intentionally conceived, and were subject to adverse attitudinal and emotional pressures. We may designate these latter as "psychosomatic" effects. The question at issue is not that of the direct effect of the infant's emotions and stress reactions upon his or her bodily function. Rather, we may in a broader sense view the mother's attitudinal-emotional state, her sense of competence, and her own health as constituting a field within which the infant flourishes or languishes. Talbot and Howell (1971: 1) write, "To thrive, human beings must draw upon certain 'psychosocial supplies,' such as attention, affection, approval and control. Without an appropriate balance of these supplies, the individual may suffer from forms of 'psychosocial malnutrition' which can produce results as disastrous to his health as is physical malnutrition induced by dietary imbalances." If the mother experiences emotional conflicts or negative attitudes toward the infant, the latter's psychosocial supplies may be diminished, rendering him or her more vulnerable to illness episodes and poor health.

To investigate this possibility, we examined the relationship between the infant's HD score and several parameters descriptive of the mother's attitudes and health. These are presented in Table 6-4. This table bears upon a general hypothesis that the infant's health status is affected by maternal influences and precursor features of the pregnancy. Those mothers whose attitude toward the pregnancy was negative and who experienced physical and emotional difficulties tended to report more health problems in the infant than mothers whose attitudes were more favorable. The correlation of .24 between the PD index and the HD index indicates a moderately strong relationship between pregnancy and subsequent infant health. The general hypothesis finds considerable confirmation.

Table 6-4 also looks at current contextual influences on infant health. It shows that mothers who experience poor health currently also report more infant health problems, the correlation being −.28. Table 6-4 also explores the relationship between HD score and three characteristics of the infant that are not health or developmental features: birth weight, early feeding mode, and disposition as to quiet or "cry-ey." No significant relationship emerges between birth weight of infant and HD score. Also, no relationship appears between feeding mode and HD score. There is a significant tendency, however, for the infants regarded by their mothers as cry-ey to have higher HD scores.

Table 6–4

Relation of HD Index to Maternal and Infant Characteristics

Maternal-Infant Characteristic	Correlation with HD Score[a]	Meaning
Mother's attitude toward pregnancy	−.18	Infants whose mothers held a negative attitude toward the pregnancy had higher HD scores.
Mother's health during pregnancy	−.34	Infants whose mothers reported poor health during the pregnancy had higher HD scores.
Mother's emotional state during pregnancy	−.17	Infants whose mothers often felt low or blue during the pregnancy had higher HD scores.
Pregnancy Difficulty (PD) Index Score	+.24	Infants coming from a difficult pregnancy had higher HD scores.
Current health of mother	−.28	Infants whose mothers reported poor current health had higher HD scores.
Infant's birth weight	−.04	No relation between infant's birth weight and HD score.
Mode of infant feeding	−.10	No relation between mode of feeding (bottle or breast) and HD score.
Infant characterized by mother as "cry-ey" or "quiet"	−.14	Infants characterized as "cry-ey" had higher HD scores.

Maternal-infant characteristics are quantified as follows in calculating correlations with HD:

(1) Mother's attitude toward pregnancy: "hoping to be pregnant" − 3; "manage all right" − 2; "pregnancy interferes with plans" − 1.

(2) Mother's health during pregnancy: good − 2; not so good − 1.

(3) Mother's emotional state during pregnancy: not often low or blue − 2; often low or blue − 1.

(4) Pregnancy Difficulty Index: score indicates number of problems encountered, ranging from zero to six. See Chapter 4.

(5) Current health of mother: no health problem, good health − 1; health problem present − 0.

(6) Infant's birth weight: actual weight in ounces.

(7) Mode of infant feeding: breast − 2; bottle − 1.

(8) Infant characterization: "quiet baby" − 2; "cry-ey baby" − 1.

[a]Correlations greater than ± .12 are significant at the 5% level; those exceeding ±.18 are significant at the 1% level.

Health Care of the Infant

Contemporary health standards recommend the periodic examination of infants for early detection of sensory-motor impairments, metabolic disorders, growth retardation, and other deviations from normal development. In addition, it is recommended that infants receive diphtheria-pertussis-tetanus inoculations and measles, smallpox, and polio vaccines. These provide easily obtained protection against major, historical sources of high infant mortality and morbidity.

The utilization of these preventive health measures was assessed by asking the mothers whether they took their babies for health checkups and shots. Table 6-5 shows that such preventive care is widespread in the sample. Only 13 percent, or 35 infants, did not receive shots and checkups. All Class I and II infants received preventive care; almost all did in Class III; in Classes IV and V, preventive care is substantially predominant. However, the minority who did not receive such care are heavily concentrated in the lower classes. Almost one third of the Class V infants did not receive it.

Why did these mothers not obtain preventive care for their infants? An answer was sought in the interview. A few mothers expressed a fear of doctors. Many had no concept of routine health supervision for infants: they had never heard of the idea, or they did not accept it as valid. One mother who had taken her infant to the Baby Health Clinic (a free facility for indigent families) said it was a waste of health-clinic time: "He is not sick and they have other babies that is sick and needs to see the doctor." Another spoke of the trouble that her other children, whom she had taken for preventive care, had had after their shots. She referred to their discomfort following vaccination; she did not know that this was a common sequela.

Two other broad reasons were frequently cited for not obtaining preventive care: situational barriers and expense. The major situational barriers were transportation difficulties and the difficulty of obtaining baby-sitters for the other children. With regard to expense, free preventive care is available for infants in each of the three counties. However, many Class IV and V mothers preferred to go to private physicians. Choosing thus, they tended to take the infant only when necessary—that is, when he or she was obviously sick or

Table 6-5
Preventive Checkups, Sabin Vaccination, and Mother's Knowledge of Sabin Vaccine, by Social Class

Social Class	Percent of Infants Who Received Preventive Shots and Checkups	Percent of Infants Who Received Sabin Vaccine	Percent of Mothers Who Knew About Sabin Vaccine	Total
I	100	86	100	28
II	100	91	100	32
III	98	91	97	64
IV	88	79	91	75
V	69	66	88	80
Total	87	80	93	279
	$Chi^2 = 41.16$ D.F. = 4 $p < .001$	$Chi^2 = 16.82$ D.F. = 4 $p < .01$	$Chi^2 = 10.56$ D.F. = 4 $p < .05$	

hurt. Several mothers said, in effect, "It costs too much . . . and besides, it's not really necessary."

Most of the infants who lacked routine preventive care had indeed been seen by physicians (or public-health nurses) on the occasion of evident illness or symptoms. Only five of the 35 had not been seen at all by physicians since the immediate postnatal period. These mothers did not accept the idea of preventive care, and their infants had presented no symptoms that in their view warranted medical attention.

Another feature of health care investigated was Sabin oral polio vaccination of the infant. Our study was conducted two months after a series of "mass Sabin clinics" in the three-county area. These clinics were widely publicized by the newspapers and radio and television media. They were held in numerous convenient locations—schools, churches, and hospitals. Free vaccination against all three types of polio virus was offered. While Sabin vaccine had been used in earlier public-school campaigns (for school children) and by private physicians (for all ages), these mass clinics were the first time when infants included in this survey were eligible for free vaccination.

We asked mothers whether they had heard of Sabin vaccine and knew its purpose. In view of the recent publicity, it was expected that most mothers would respond with accurate information; those who did not would then constitute a group who stood outside the mass media and popular communication channels of the community. In addition, we were interested in the connection between the mother's information and whether or not her infant had been vaccinated. Presumably, many of the unvaccinated infants were those of mothers who did not know about the vaccine. Further, both these aspects of health care—infant Sabin vaccination and mother's knowledge of Sabin—were investigated in relation to social class.

Table 6-5 shows that most mothers knew about Sabin vaccine. Only 7 percent (19 mothers) failed to recognize and correctly identify it. Further questioning of this group revealed that some had heard about an oral preventive of polio but failed to recognize it by the label "Sabin vaccine." These mothers were for data analysis counted among those who possessed the knowledge; that is, recognition of the specific name was not required. Sabin vaccination reached 80 percent, or 223 infants. We counted an infant as vaccinated if he or she received one or more of the three types of vaccine, effective against the three strains of virus. Both variables showed a significant class gradient. Of the 19 mothers who did not know about Sabin vaccine, 17 are in Class IV and V. Of the 56 unvaccinated infants, 43 are in these two classes.

To what extent is lack of vaccination associated with the mother's lack of information about it? Ten of the unvaccinated infants belong to mothers who did not know about Sabin vaccine; with the other 46, the mother did know about it. Thus, the greater number of unvaccinated cases could not be attributed to sheer lack of information. As in regard to lack of prenatal care, many people whose care is substandard do not lack adequate knowledge. The principal barriers to better care lie instead in the realm of apathy and alienation, situational obstacles, and inconvenient packaging of health services.

The Inadequate Health-Care Constellation

We have examined two components of infant health care: shots and checkups, and Sabin vaccination of the infant. Now we consider these components in combination with two components of maternal care considered in Chapter 4, namely, prenatal care and hospital delivery (these are aspects of maternal health care, but we may equally regard them as aspects of infant health care). In the same network of relationships we shall consider a fifth element, whether or not the mother knew about Sabin vaccine.

Each of these variables describes a basic element in contemporary health care. It is a matter of community and professional expectation, particularly in areas with abundant health facilities such as the Lexington metropolitan area, that infants will be born in hospitals, that adults will know about polio vaccine, and so forth. Our attention here focuses upon the infants in the sample who lacked these basics of health care. Through this focus, we can tentatively answer an important health question: Is there in the sample (and, by extension, in the community) a group of infants whose health care is deficient in all respects? Alternatively, is the pattern of deficiency more dispersed? How sharp is the line between the health "haves" and the health "have-nots"?

Figure 6-1 presents the relationship between each pair of the five health-care variables. It also relates each variable to social class. Because this figure presents many findings compactly, we shall not discuss each finding separately. But let us examine one connection, that between no prenatal care and no infant checkups. As we saw in Chapter 4, nine of the 279 mothers had no prenatal care. Also, 35 of the 279 infants did not have routine health examinations and shots. The line connecting these two boxes shows that four of the nine infants whose mothers did not have prenatal care were among the 35 infants who lacked checkups. (It could be said equivalently that four of the 35 infants without checkups are found in the group of nine mothers who had no prenatal care.) The figure shows further that this is a statistically significant association between the two variables; the probability of chance occurrence is less than 5 percent.

Scanning the interrelationships among the health-care variables, we see that while there is a pattern of association, it is not a tight pattern. For example, there is a highly significant association ($p < 0.01$) between no checkups and no Sabin. Seventeen of the 279 infants had neither. But the remaining 18 without checkups did have Sabin; and the other 39 without Sabin did have checkups. Figure 6-1 leads to the general conclusion that the infants in the sample who lacked adequate prenatal and infant health care are a scattered minority, with

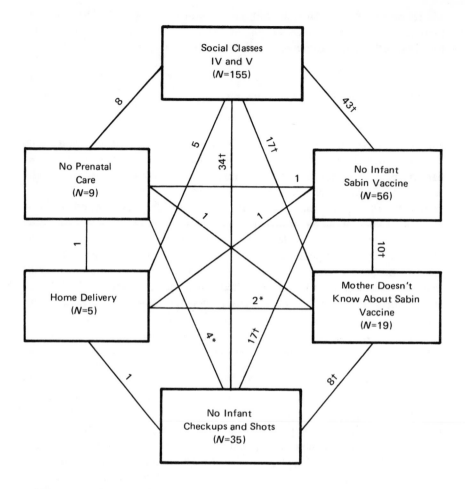

*Means that Chi-square for the two connected variables has a probability of less than 0.05.
†Means that Chi-square for the two connected variables has a probability of less than 0.01.

Figure 6-1. The Inadequate Health-Care Constellation

some members lacking this feature and other members lacking that feature. There is no hard-core group that lacked every constituent of adequate care.

What is the relationship of health care to social class? Figure 6-1 gives an overview. It shows that an overwhelming amount of inadequate health care is found in Classes IV and V. For example, 34 of the 35 infants with no checkups are found in these classes, as are 43 of the 56 infants without Sabin. Caution is necessary in interpreting these findings. While the mothers and infants with inadequate health care are preponderantly from Classes IV and V, we cannot reverse this proposition and assert that inadequate health care is characteristic in these classes. Most of Classes IV and V received adequate care.

This phenomenon of intraclass variation has particular relevance for the sociological understanding of the behavior and situation of the lower class. It provides a corrective to overgeneralized formulations which see lower-class orientations as being uniformly indifferent toward good health practice. At the same time, we conjecture that the health "have-nots" in Classes IV and V constitute a particularly deprived and isolated segment where the culture of poverty, with its apathy, lack of long-term goals, and marginal economic-educational status, exists in relatively full-blown form. Identification of barriers to health care, of the dominant health values, and of the major avenues of communication within this segment could provide clues for strategies by which the health "have-nots" can be encouraged to improve their infant and maternal health status.

Source of Infant Health Care

In the preceding section we focused upon several elements of infant health care with only incidental attention to the sources of such care. Now we shall examine this latter question.

To investigate the source of care, the interviewers asked, "If the baby is sick and needs to see someone, where do you take him?" This elicited a response from all the mothers except a few who said the infant had never been sick. From this group, we obtained information on the source of care for checkup visits. By combining these two kinds of responses, we were able to obtain for each infant the name of a specific physician or other agent who served as the child's principal source of health care. The identified physicians were then classified according to specialty status, by use of the *American Medical Association Directory,* and by race, by use of the *Kentucky Medical Directory.* Racial classification is of interest in connection with the health care of infants in the 32 black families of the sample. (In Chapter 4 we looked at hospital utilization in the community from the standpoint of black-white differences.)

The infant's source of health care was categorized first as to whether it was a private, individual source or a public source. Then, among the private, individual sources further determinations were made. Table 6-6 presents the results of this classification.

This table shows that 29 infants received free public care. All 29 reside in Fayette County and are clients of the Baby Health Clinic. The clinic is a charity organization with roots deep in the community. It was started in 1914 by women of Lexington's social elite, for the single purpose of providing pasteurized milk to infants of poor families who otherwise would be without an adequate milk supply (it was at first called the Baby Milk Supply). During the

Table 6-6
Source of Infant Health Care, by Medical Classification

Type of Practice	Number of Practitioners	Number of Infants
Pediatrics:		
Board-Certified Pediatrician	8	107
Board-Eligible Pediatrician	4	56
Total	12	163
General Practice:		
Primary Specialty GP (M.D.)	20	57
Other Primary Specialty (M.D.)	11	26
Osteopath	1	2
Chiropractor	1	1
Unidentified	1	1
Total	34	87
Total for Individual Sources (above combined)	46	250
Baby Health Clinic	–	29
Total	–	279

next five decades, its mission expanded to include a full range of well-baby health services and the name was changed to the Baby Health Clinic. Staff services are donated by part-time nurses and pediatricians; clinic policy is established by a board of female community leaders who also give service and financial support. The clinic has free housing at St. Joseph Hospital and obtains a small amount of money from city and county tax revenues. It still supplies milk, or, more accurately, pays a local dairy to deliver it to client families.

Table 6-6 also shows that 163 infants were seen by 12 pediatricians. We further distinguished between those pediatricians who are board-certified and those who are board-eligible. This distinction may be regarded as a matter of differential professional recognition. The minimum training and qualification of a pediatrician consist of four years of undergraduate medical education, one year's internship, two years of pediatric residency, and two years of practice or advanced residency. After the final two years of practice or advanced residency, the aspiring pediatrician becomes eligible to take the examinations formulated by the American Academy of Pediatrics; successful completion of the examinations gives him board-certified status. Eight board-certified pediatricians were used by 107 families in the sample, and the four board-eligibles were used by 56 families.

All other individual medical professionals were classified in this study as general practitioners. Listings in the *American Medical Association Directory* provided the basis for classification of 31 physicians in this group. Twenty listed general practice (GP) as their primary specialty, with or without a secondary listing. Eleven other physicians were listed as practicing in a primary specialty area other than general practice, such as otolaryngology, obstetrics, or internal medicine. None of these practitioners claimed any specialization in pediatrics. To this group of physicians we added an osteopath, a chiropractor, and one other practitioner who could not be further identified. The 34 practitioners in the general-practice category served 87 infants in the sample.

Fifty-eight percent of the infants have a pediatrician as the principal source of health care, 31 percent have a general practitioner, and 11 percent use the free service provided by the Baby Health Clinic. That such a large proportion of the infants—an essentially healthy population—use specialist medical services rather than general practice is a matter of current concern in relation to medical manpower.

Pediatrician or General Practitioner?

What do the popular authorities say about the choice between a pediatrician and a general practitioner as the source of professional health care for infants? We examined Dr. Spock's *Baby and Child Care* (1968 and 1976 editions) and the U.S. Children's Bureau's *Infant Care* (1963 and 1972 editions). Both impart extensive advice on the desirable components of infant health care, but say little about who should provide it.

Infant Care does not indicate that the selection of a doctor for the baby can be problematic. The 1963 edition refers to the two kinds of physicians in an incidental statement within the context of a general recommendation of the value of preventive, regular medical care rather than sick care: "Even though things are going well, it is important to take the baby regularly to the doctor. There is wisdom in seeing the doctor to keep the baby well instead of seeing him only when the baby is sick. You may see a specialist in the care of babies, a pediatrician, in his office or at a well-baby clinic conducted by the health department in your community, or you may choose a general family doctor" (*Infant Care*, 1963: 3). The 1963 and 1972 editions both refer to the source of care consistently as "the doctor" without characterization by type of practice or specialization. In view of the obvious intention to make the pamphlet practical and responsive to the questions of parents, lack of guidance on this very wide-spread concern may seem a curious omission. Yet we presume the omission is intentional, reflecting lack of consensus on the part of government and professional experts about proper advice for the large and heterogeneous public which the pamphlet reaches.

Dr. Spock addresses the question of pediatrician versus general practitioner in a section of his book entitled "Who's to Be the Doctor?" (Spock, 1968: 50; 1976: 70). He says, "A family doctor who is used to taking care of babies can do just as good a job as the specialist, unless some unusual problem comes up.

In large cities the mother may have been delivered by a specialist in obstetrics who doesn't take care of the baby afterward. Then she will want to find a children's specialist . . ." Spock also advises low-income parents to seek out the services of a well-baby clinic (such as Lexington's Baby Health Clinic). In subsequent discussion of such topics as the doctor-patient relationship and when to call the doctor, the reference is consistently to "doctor" without further elaboration.

While Spock's explicit advice is noncommittal and his tone bland on the generalist versus specialist issue, his bias is prospecialist. No positive considerations are cited in favor of generalists, such as the value of having one doctor get to know the family by treating different family members; nor is an attempt made to delineate the potential role of the general practitioner in family medicine or as guide and advocate for the patient in relation to the complex of medical, paramedical, and social support services that may be needed in the event of serious illness. On the other hand, potential difficulties in the use of a general practitioner, such as the discomfort that parents may feel in requesting an outside consultation and the possibility that some general practitioners may not like to deal with infants, are hinted at.

Contemporary concern and planning about the rational deployment of medical manpower has led to innovative programs for training of physicians' assistants and other paramedical personnel to participate significantly in the delivery of health services, including child and infant health. Since physicians' assistants and other paramedical workers frequently function as the point of first contact with mother and infant, wide public acceptance of these roles will facilitate the success of such ideas. Another new development is the renewal of interest on the part of medical educators and organized medicine in the concepts of primary care and family practice (Bornemeier, 1970). Many medical faculties now include departments of family practice, which hold the potential of training many doctors who will be able to deal with a wide range of family health problems, including the medical care of children and infants. Robert Ebert recently predicted that training programs for medical specialists will eventually be eclipsed by training for generalists, thus reversing the trend of the past five decades (Ebert, 1973: 148).

A second broad contemporary trend in health care, with many implications for infant health care, is consumerism (Reeder, 1972). In general terms, consumerism argues that the interest and welfare of the patient have been subordinated to the convenience and advantage of providers—physicians, hospitals, and professional organizations. It urges a better balance between provider and consumer of health care. Applied to infant health care, this would lead to such changes as a freer use of home visits by doctors, easier access to doctors' offices in terms of office hours and neighborhood location, and more time devoted to explanation and counseling.

Consumerism diagnoses many ills in the health-care system and makes many demands (Twaddle and Hessler, 1977). Many of the remedies it seeks impinge upon principles of professional practice and organization which, under the aegis of professional autonomy, have become firmly established and elaborately rationalized (Freidson, 1970). By contrast, consumerism, though it reflects deep public dissatisfactions, is at present a loosely framed ideology that lacks the coherent formulation, organized thrust, and broad popular appeal necessary to challenge vested professional interests. Moreover, it runs counter to the general direction of health manpower planning. For an extreme yet realistic example, if an infant develops acute respiratory or gastric distress in the middle of the night, anxious parents might prefer to have the attention of a highly trained expert, and they might prefer that he or she make a house call, to taking the patient to the doctor's office or hospital. From the standpoint of rational resource deployment, it can be argued that house calls misuse the specialized skills of the pediatrician—he cannot function at highest effectiveness outside his professional setting. According to this argument, house calls waste professional time and effort, but there would be less waste if a less-skilled professional provided the service. The consumer, on the other hand, is not so concerned about inefficiency and waste (Gallagher, 1976). For himself and his dependents, he wants readily accessible, highly skilled expertise.

Considerable impetus to this consumer philosophy already exists in the form of the extensive private market for medical services. The affluent consumer can buy his way into expensive specialist services, without preliminary screening and without regard to his clinical need. Since the services are priced and paid for the question of waste does not arise, any more than expensive housing is considered wasteful in a market economy. Yet market forces are not able to generate convenient, responsive, high-quality services even for the affluent, and market performance in regard to the poor is grossly inadequate.

Another set of considerations fits into this examination of the specialist-generalist issue in the provision of infant care. Is pediatrics a satisfying field of work and career for the pediatrician? How does this field of vocational endeavor appear to the professional who provides the services? What are the work motivations and satisfactions associated with pediatric practice? These questions take for granted that pediatricians are well rewarded materially and that their services are socially valuable. We assume that the pediatrician, as a professional person, identifies himself with his work. Accordingly, the work should ideally embrace a nexus of skill and service that provides stimulation, challenge, recognition, satisfaction, and other forms of psychic income over the several decades of practice which constitute a professional lifetime.

We have described general practice–pediatrics as a dichotomy; to do so is somewhat misleading, because pediatrics is in itself a type of general practice within a particular patient age span. No other area of medical specialization is defined by age of patient, with the exception of geriatrics (which has a very small number of practitioners). Like the general practitioner, the pediatrician must know a little bit about a lot of things—infectious diseases, allergy, immunology, orthopedics, pathology, neurology, pharmacology, cardiology, and radiology. He or she must refer difficult cases to other specialists, who may be pediatric subspecialists.

Like physicians in many other fields of medicine, most pediatricians engage in private, office-based practice. Health manpower statistics for 1972 indicate that 72 percent of the nation's pediatricians are so engaged (U.S. Department of Health, Education, and Welfare, 1974: 178). Although it ordinarily includes a component of hospital practice with seriously ill chidren, their work is primarily office-based. If the pediatrician is to find stimulation and meaning in his or her work, he or she must find it in dealing with the ordinary health problems of infancy and childhood. Single visits—not part of a series—account for 45 percent of all patient visits to a pediatrician (Wechsler, 1976: 167), a larger figure than for any other medical specialty. This suggests that many visits are for minor illnesses, examinations, or preventive measures. There is a significant difference between the pediatrician and general practitioner with a primarily adult practice. Cultural norms about health care and the preventive benefits of medical science bring many healthy children to the pediatrician; adults, on the other hand, tend to seek medical service only if they feel ill. The implication of this contrast is that the pediatrician spends much of his or her time dealing with well children. To a significant extent pediatric practice is based upon skill and knowledge concerning preventive medicine and child development.

In advice to prospective pediatricians, the American Academy of Pediatrics (Schade, 1962: 13-14) states: "It is estimated that about one-third of the private practice of pediatrics is concerned with routine health supervision and growth and development. . . . Unless one enjoys dealing with families and children, unless one appreciates the importance of supervising health properly and preventing diseases, and unless one has a warm and sympathetic interest in people, it would be better not to enter the private practice of pediatrics. . . . In fact, some who have been trained in pediatric departments stressing mainly the esoteric illnesses may be disappointed later in practice when they find so much of it devoted to the supervision of the relatively normal child and the treatment of commonly occurring diseases." The academy's advice on pediatric practice is intended as realistic counsel for physicians trained in the scientific, intellectual culture of the medical school. The purport of such advice is twofold: to attract doctors whose motivation and skills match the demands and opportunities of the field, and equally, to dissuade unsuited individuals from entry.

The considerations that from the standpoint of a professional organization bear upon recruitment into the profession are of a different order from those that concern individual consumers in seeking professional services, and are different again from those considerations important to manpower planners and authorities concerned with rational public policy.

In the preceding discussion, we have looked at the major sources of infant health care and attempted to determine circumstances under which various sources might be used. The fact that much infant health care is preventive has been noted and this element is identified as a prominent characteristic of pediatric practice. A rational perspective on medical care would hold that the sickest patients, or those with established disease, should receive the most specialized care. Against this expectation, it is anomalous that well babies should be taken to pediatricians.

A national survey conducted in 1964 showed that out of the total life span, children were the age group most likely to have a specialist as their regular source of medical care (Andersen, 1967: 14). Thirty-six percent of children one to five years old used a specialist, while no more than 32 percent of persons in any other age category did so. Infants (that is persons under one year) were not included in these tabulations, but it seems reasonable to suppose that infants would stand just as high in their use of specialist services as children who were older. In fact, if we think of the social and consumer values that regulate demand for medical services, as distinct from rationally determined need, we might expect an even heavier use of specialist services by infants than by older children. Parents probably regard their infants as being more delicate than toddlers and school children. They may well want specialized medical attention for their infants, in health as well as illness.

If pediatricians have become an important source of infant health care, further questions arise concerning which segments of the population use them. Evidence indicates that the economic status of a family is strongly related to the use of pediatric services. A national study conducted by the National Health Survey of 42,000 households demonstrated this clearly. It showed that for all economic levels, 20 percent of children under 15 years of age had been examined or treated by a pediatrician during the twelve months preceding the interview. Among families with incomes under $2,000, the figure was 10 percent; among those with incomes from $2,000 to $3,999, 13 percent; among those with incomes from $4,000 to $6,999, 22 percent; and among those with incomes over $7,000, 29 percent (National Center for Health Statistics, 1964: 29). This survey gathered data on the utilization of several other specialty services in addition to pediatrics. It found that pediatrics was the most widely used specialty and that only one other specialty, obstetrics-gynecology, had a utilization rate that was more strongly related to income level.

We suppose that these findings indicate more than the sheer effect of income, or money as purchasing power, in the medical-care market. More affluent families tend to have health values that favor preventive care and, moreover, favor the obtaining of such care from specialists. Within the framework of our own study, we earlier saw that infants in lower-class families were less likely to have routine health exams and polio vaccination than those in higher strata. Let us turn to our study and focus now upon the source of health care in relation to social class and other social determinants.

Social Class and Source of Infant Health Care

Table 6-7 shows the number and percent of infants within each social class who received health care from the three categories of providers given in Table 6-6: pediatricians, general practitioners, and the Baby Health Clinic. The figures indicate that Class I and II families mainly use pediatricians, and very few of them use general practitioners. Class III families use pediatricians predominantly,

Table 6-7
Source of Infant Health Care, by Social Class

Social Class	Baby Health Clinic	Individual Source General Practitioner	Pediatrician	Total
I	0 (0%)	2 (7%)	26 (93%)	28 (100%)
II	0 (0%)	3 (9%)	29 (91%)	32 (100%)
III	1 (2%)	14 (22%)	49 (77%)	64 (101%)
IV	7 (9%)	32 (43%)	36 (48%)	75 (100%)
V	21 (26%)	36 (45%)	23 (29%)	80 (100%)
Total	29 (10%)	87 (31%)	163 (58%)	279 (99%)
Mean Age of Source	–	48.8	43.9	47.5
Mean Income of All Families Using Source (1971 dollars)	$3,217	$5,813	$9,691	$7,799
Mean Fee per Routine Visit Actual or Estimated (1971 dollars)	FREE	$5.64	$6.55	$6.22[a]

Chi^2: Clinic, general practitioner, or pediatrician by social class = 78.85
D.F. = 8
$p < .001$

Chi^2: General practitioner or pediatrician by social class = 45.32
D.F. = 4
$p < .001$

[a]This mean was based upon an N of 235 rather than 279. The 44 cases excluded fall into three categories: first, the 29 infants who receive free care at the Baby Health Clinic; second, eight physicians' infants who receive free courtesy care (these eight families are all Class I and the infants all go to pediatricians); third, seven other cases in which the mother was unable to provide information regarding the fee for a visit. By social class and health-care source, these families are: two Class III using pediatricians; one Class III using general practitioner; one Class IV using pediatrician; one Class IV using general practitioner; one Class V using pediatrician, and one Class V using general practitioner. These seven cases are also excluded from the means for general practitioner and pediatrician. The medical courtesy cases are likewise excluded.

but a sizable minority use general practitioners. In Class IV, 48 percent of the families use pediatricians, 43 percent use general practitioners, and 9 percent use the Baby Health Clinic. In Class V, 26 percent use the Baby Health Clinic, 45 percent use general practitioners, and 29 percent use pediatricians.

Table 6-7 shows that although there is a statistically significant association between higher class and use of pediatric services, such services are used throughout the class structure. It is a striking fact that over one quarter of the Class V families took their infants to pediatricians. Doubtless many of the Class V families, like families of higher status, feel that specialized care is preferable; moreover, they are prepared to meet the fees of the private specialist. It also appears from this table that the Baby Health Clinic functions as intended in the medical ecology of the community. Almost three quarters (21 of 29) of its patients included in the sample are from Class V. It is of interest, however, that Class V families demonstrate more range of choice than any other class— almost half went to general practitioners, with the balance going nearly equally to the Baby Health Clinic and to pediatricians. (In an earlier description of the staffing of the Baby Health Clinic, we noted that pediatric service and surveillance were available as needed there; however, routine infant care was conducted by nurses.)

Table 6-7 also presents findings on family income and medical fees for families using the different categories of infant health care. The mothers were asked what basic charge was made for a routine visit, without any extra charge for immunizations, diagnostic tests, or other, concurrent services. Most of the mothers were able to produce a definite figure; the others were asked to provide an estimate. Thus the fee data should be regarded as approximate. (The method of obtaining family-income figures was discussed in Chapter 3.)

We see in Table 6-7 that the mean incomes of families using the different sources stand in the rank order that would be expected on the basis of social class. The families using the Baby Health Clinic have a mean income of $3,217, as compared to $5,813 for those using general practitioners and $9,691 for those using pediatricians. It is of interest also to relate family income to the cost of private medical services. The mean fee for a routine visit to a pediatrician is $6.55, and to a general practitioner, $5.64. The families using pediatricians have 167 percent ($9,691 divided by $5,813) of the income that families using general practitioners have, but the former group pays only 116 percent ($6.55 divided by $5.64) of the fee that the latter group pays for a routine visit. From this it might be argued that the economic burden fell more heavily upon the families that used general practitioners than upon the pediatrician users. The cost of such doctor visits, whether to pediatricians or to general practitioners, is admittedly a small fraction of family disposable income and only one component of health-care outlays. Nevertheless, in view of the steadily rising cost of health care and intense public discussion about equitable financing, such figures are revealing.

We have focused upon the social class of the family and the medical classification of the health-care provider in order to assess the extent to which family choices were guided by preferences for specialized care and for "quality" care (insofar as professional status bespeaks quality). In general, higher-class families sought specialized care. We also examined the cost of medical visits in relation to medical classification and family income. It appeared that variations in choice of practitioner could not be satisfactorily accounted for on sheer economic terms; even in Class V, where many families used the Baby Health Clinic, many other families went to general practitioners and pediatricians, paying the requisite fee.

Racial Factors and Health-Care Source

In our examination of hospital utilization for birth of the infant, we looked at racial patterns and found that the racial status of the family influenced their selection of hospital. Similar questions can be raised in regard to the health care of the infant. The community significance of racial patterns may in fact be more penetrating in regard to infant health care than in regard to maternity hospitalization. As institutions, hospitals are not susceptible to characterization in terms of race, so the only question raised earlier was whether patients, as individuals with racial characteristics, use or do not use a particular hospital. As we saw, there was no hospital that was used exclusively or predominantly by the black mothers in the sample; one hospital was, however, not used by them.

In examining health care provided by individual practitioners, it is possible to look at racial characteristics of both provider and patient as significant parameters in the distribution of care. Table 6-8 presents findings on this question. It shows that of the 46 different practitioners who provide care to the study-infants, 44 are white and two are black. Both black practitioners are classified in the general-practice category; one is an osteopathic physician and the other is a medical general practitioner.

The number of black physicians in a community is an important consideration from the standpoint of social and racial equity. The dearth of black physicians in the United States in an integral part of the black cultural heritage of deprivation. Ralph Hines states that there are four times as many physicians in relation to the general population as there are black physicians in proportion to the black population (Hines, 1972: 40-50). The situation is similar in Kentucky, where black physicians comprise 2.3 percent of the total active physician supply (including osteopathic physicians) and blacks comprise 7.2 percent of the total population. The deficiency is much greater in the three-county area of the study, where only 1.8 percent of the practicing physicians are black, as compared with 14 percent of the population.

Table 6–8
Utilization of Health-Care Source in Relation to Race of Source and of Infant

Medical Classification	Total Number of Physicians	Number of White/Black Physicians	Total Number of Infants Using Source	Number of White/Black Infants Using Source
Pediatrician	12	12/0	163	152/11
General Practitioner	34	32/2	87	76/11
Baby Health Clinic	–	–	29	19/10
Total	46	44/2	279	247/32

Does the dearth of black physicians imply that the medical needs of the black population, including black infants, are inadequately met? The provision of medical care is a professional activity drawing upon the objective skill and knowledge of the physician, yet the provision of care occurs within the context of the doctor-patient relationship, which could scarcely be called an impersonal relationship. The Spanish physician-historian Entralgo has written of medical "philia," or the friendship of the physician for the patient, which, while not fully developed in every encounter, nevertheless has a continuous latent significance (Entralgo, 1969: 17).

In our earlier discussion of the lack of support in our data for the hypothesis of a unilateral patient demand for the most highly trained type of physician (to the exclusion of other physician attributes), we advanced the notion that the patient might prefer a physician with whom he or she felt rapport or communicative ease. Where medical care focuses upon the patient's emotional distress, communication becomes of paramount importance: early studies of the distribution of psychiatric care convincingly document the cultural and communicative gap between the psychiatrist, who from his very profession is a high-status person, and the lower-class or working-class patient (Hollingshead and Redlich, 1958; Myers and Schaffer, 1954); the class position and outlook of the psychiatrist vis-à-vis such patients creates awkwardness in the relationship. Many distressed, disturbed individuals from these classes simply fail to seek psychiatric care, and thus the dissimilarity between the physician's cultural position and that of the potential beneficiary population leads ultimately to a deficiency in care. Psychiatry is a small part of medical care. It is perhaps unique in its requirement for communicative rapport and its sensitivity to status. There is evidence, however, from other branches of medicine and in relation to other patient populations, that discrepancies in doctor-patient status skew the distribution of treatment and create anomalies in treatment relationships.

National studies of health-services utilization support the generalization that blacks receive less medical care than whites, even allowing for their disadvantaged income position (Aday, 1972: 20). Hines (1972: 43) writes: "As an object of social prejudice in American society, the Negro has been discouraged from approaching agencies and facilities providing health care. The Negro has been so sensitive about his status as a second-class citizen than even in cases of serious illness, he has been hesitant to utilize agencies which have been perceived as unsympathetic or unfriendly." There is a dual point in his statement: first, black individuals limit their seeking of health care in a predominantly white health establishment; second, when they do seek health care, it is with a hesitation and sensitivity that may impair the effectiveness of care.

A clear implication of the foregoing comments is that a greater number of black physicians would be desirable from the standpoint of medical care of the black population. This presumes that whatever its scientific and objective components, medical care is facilitated by a sociocultural similarity between patient and doctor. Hines (1972: 41) states directly, "While this comparison [of the black-white differences in ratio of physicians to population] is not intended to mean nor imply that Negroes should seek or have medical care exclusively by Negro physicians, the nature of social relations in our nation has been such that the quality of health care provided the Negro population has been, and is, directly related to the number and quality of Negro physicians available to the Negro community."

The notion of physician availability to a culturally defined community suggests that culture is an important parameter of practice which cannot be taken for granted in reckoning whether or not a given community is adequately served. The concept of adequate service can be best delineated in relation to primary medical care. Adequate service can be said to be provided when medical attention is available for everyday health problems and when recognized preventive services are available. Health supervision of infants, children, and expectant women is frequently included in the framework of primary medical care.

The decisive trend toward specialization in medical practice has drastically curtailed the supply of primary-care doctors. However, the situation of population groups underrepresented in the medical profession, such as blacks, is aided somewhat by the tendency of physicians from these groups to enter primary care or general practice rather than specialized practice. Lieberson (1958), in a study of ethnic factors in medical practice in Chicago, hypothesized such a tendency; his findings confirmed it. He found that doctors of Anglo-Saxon and Jewish origin, both overrepresented in medicine, conducted specialized practice to a greater than average extent, while doctors of Irish, Italian, and Polish origin, underrepresented in medicine, conducted general practice to a greater than average extent. While his study did not include black physicians, we believe the logic of his analysis applies with equal force to them. Lieberson reasons,

Specialization has several advantages for physicians in their relations with patients who are members of ethnic groups other than their own. Specialization involves a more specific relationship between doctor and patient. Whereas the specialist is limited in his interaction with a patient to the health problems which are his specialty, the functions of the general practitioner are less clearly defined. For specialists, relatively rapid turnover means that they are less likely to know patients on an informal basis. The general practitioner, moreover, is more likely than the specialist to treat all members of a family. Specialists, when called in through the referrals of general practitioners, have had their competence validated, at least implicitly, by a qualified intermediary—the family physician. Therefore, patients do not need to use extraneous criteria.

The foregoing considerations bearing upon black physicians and the health needs of the black population are relevant to our study. We noted above that black physicians were underrepresented in relation to the population, both in Kentucky as a whole and in the three-county study area. Within the sample, 11.5 percent (32 of 279) of the families are black, but only 4.3 percent (2 of 46) of the physicians are. A more precise statement would compare only on the basis of families using individual sources for infant health care, that is, excluding families using the Baby Health Clinic. By that comparison, 8.8 percent of the families (22 of 250) are black, compared with 4.3 percent of the physicians.

A still more precise comparison will be framed shortly, but first let us ask how patients were distributed among the physicians by race. Table 6-9 shows that of the 22 black infants who were seen by private physicians, 16 went to white physicians and six went to black physicians. Three black infants went to each of the two black physicians. Every one of the 228 white infants went to a

Table 6-9
Number of Black/White Infants Under Care of Black/White Physician Source[a]

	Race of Infant's Physician		
Race of Infant	Black	White	Total
Black	6[b]	16	22
White	0	228	228
Total	6	244	250

Chi² (with correction for continuity): Race of Infant by Race of Infant's Physician = 52.60
D.F. = 1
$p < .001$

[a]The 29 infants who go to the Baby Health Clinic are not included in this table.

[b]The cell frequencies refer to infants, not physicians. Thus, six black infants went to black physicians; sixteen black infants went to white physicians.

white physician. By the standard of this table, the actual caseload of the black physician is 2.4 percent (6 of 250) of the total sample. From this it could be argued that although black physicians are in relative short supply as compared with the frequency of black families in the sample, those black physicians present in the sample are nevertheless underutilized in the ratio of 2.4 percent (the proportion of infants they saw) to 4.3 percent (the proportion of total physician supply that they constitute), or only .56 of capacity.

The comparison confined to race alone overlooks other factors requisite to a fuller understanding of the distribution of medical care. The medical classification of the physician is relevant. The two black physicians are classified as general practitioners; Table 6-10 shows that in seeing three patients each, their quota of patients is exactly the average number for all general practitioners in the sample. Pediatricians, with an age-specialized practice, see more patients, as the table indicates. Since there are no black pediatricians in the sample, any family desiring pediatric attention for their infant perforce goes to a white pediatrician. Eleven black families elect to do so; in all, 50 percent of the black families (11 of 22) using individual physicians go to pediatricians, as compared with 66 percent of the white families. Thus there is a stronger trend toward pediatrician preference among white families, but it is nonsignificant by a critical ratio test of the difference between proportions.

While six black families go to a black physician, another five go to a white general practitioner. Their preference lies across the race line even when no greater level of certified skill is at issue. None of the 76 white infants taken to general practitioners goes to a black general practitioner. The white physicians have a monopoly of service to the white families, plus many black families as well. The black physicians, all of whom are general practitioners, are far from having a monopoly of black families. If the underlying economic model for distribution of patients is not racial monopoly but something more akin to an open-market circulation of patients without regard to race of physician, that model also fails to fit the facts, for then there would be an entry of some white infants into the practice of the black physicians. It is ironic that while the sample reveals a deficit of black physicians, it also shows that the few black physicians present are underutilized by black patients. On the other hand, if the black physicians had their own monopoly closure in dealing with black

Table 6-10
Number of Patients Under Care of Physician Source, by Medical Classification

Medical Classification	Number of Physicians in Classification	Range in Number of Patients	Mean Number of Patients
Pediatrician	12	2-30	13.6
General Practitioner	34	1-8	3.0

155

patients, analogous to that of white physicians and white patients, their caseload might then become overwhelmingly large.

Our analysis of racial factors in health care extends to the Baby Health Clinic as well as to individual sources of care. Earlier description of the history and community orientation of the clinic made clear its aim to serve needy infants without reference to race. In its earlier days, it maintained separate "white clinics" and "colored clinics," although patients of both races were seen concurrently in the weekly immunization clinics. Information at our disposal permits no judgment as to whether white and black infants in fact received an equal quality of care. It can be said, however, that all care was provided with the same personnel and physical facilities. Even if in objective terms quality of care was the same, the possibility remains of a lower utilization rate by black clients, for reasons suggested earlier by Hines.

We examined comparative black-white utilization rates. The Baby Health Clinic was not available to infants outside Fayette County. Nine of the 30 Fayette County blacks, or 30 percent, use it, compared with 20 of the 208 whites, or 9.6 percent. Comparing in this fashion, however, ignores the differential in social-class distribution between blacks and whites and the fact that by policy the clinic was oriented toward poor families. Use of the black-white matched comparison group allows a more critical test. Since the black half of the comparison includes all 30 Fayette County black families, the black utilization rate in the matched comparison is 30 percent, as above. Among the 30 matching white families, 7, or 23 percent, use the clinic. This difference in utilization proportions is not statistically significant. Among Class V comparison families, the utilization rate is the same—60 percent—for both blacks and whites.

Our investigation of racial factors in the health care of the infants has revealed several basic facts. The physician-providers are almost all white. All of the pediatricians are white. Black families make substantial use of white physicians. The Baby Health Clinic is staffed by white personnel. It is used to the same extent by white and black families of comparable social-class level.

Are social equity and effective medical care two separate issues (Yerby, 1977)? One might argue that the race of the provider of care is immaterial for the quality of medical care rendered. The health problems of black infants are largely the same as those presented by white infants; even if there is some characteristic difference (such as the sickle-cell trait), the competent physician can cope with it, and if each physician is a competent practitioner the racial composition of a group of physicians has little significance for the adequacy of medical care in a community. Further, while from the standpoint of equity the racial composition of the physician group may reflect an undesirable state of affairs, it is still inadvertent and not so adverse as are the positive patterns of segregation that bear directly upon patient care, such as separate facilities.

In our opinion, the foregoing argument attempts to make the most of a weak case. Enlightened social policy requires correction of the racial imbalances revealed by the findings of the study. Since the findings do not extend to quality of care, we cannot say whether the health care of the black infants was or was not affected by these imbalances. Our impression here is similar to that regarding hospitalization: notwithstanding the evidence of racial patterns in hospital admission, the black families may well have received a level of care equivalent to that received by the white families.

House Calls

Historically, the patient's home was an important site for medical care. The doctor traveling about the countryside on house calls is part of the lore of medical care in predominantly rural society. In the last century, he traveled by horse; in the early decades of the twentieth century, he relied upon the motor car. Now he remains in his office, and the patient comes to him. With the concentration of population and medical resources in urban areas, patients are willing to transport themselves for the purpose of obtaining medical care, and they accept the shift away from the home. It is on the whole easier for the patient to get to the doctor's location now than it was at one time. By the same token, it is easier for doctors to get to patients, but they do it infrequently. However difficult the travel to patients was for doctors in the earlier era, they defined it as part of their task; it is no longer so defined (Wolfe and Badgley, 1972: 56).

House calls have not disappeared entirely. As we shall see, the doctors in our sample made a number of them. But in the broad picture of health care, the trend is strongly toward the demise of the house call. In 1928-1931, 40 percent of all outpatient contacts between doctor and patient were in the home; by 1957, only 8 percent were in the home (Somers and Somers, 1961: 48). The true decrease of house calls in the total picture of medical care is probably greater than this comparison suggests, because it is framed only in terms of outpatient visits and thus ignores the fact that patients are now hospitalized for many diseases and health problems that were formerly dealt with on an outpatient basis. The use of hospitals for infant deliveries is a leading example (discussed in Chapter 4).

Why have house calls declined in importance? A major factor is the expanded scientific base of medical practice. Increasingly the doctor's diagnostic judgment is based upon laboratory tests, X-rays, and the instrumented reading of various physiological parameters. The doctor may feel that he or she can accomplish little that will benefit the patient through a house call. Similar considerations apply to treatment. Just as a doctor cannot transport diagnostic X-ray apparatus with him, neither can he carry in his little black bag very many of the pharmaceutical products in current use.

Along with the more intensive application of science to medical care has come a more thorough rationalization of the doctor's work. Paramedical personnel, medical equipment and facilities, the architecture of hospitals and office suites, communication and paging systems, and quick reference catalogues of prescription drugs are deployed to enhance the efficiency of his or her activity. Great importance is attached to increasing the doctor's productivity, removing hindrances to rapid performance and defining carefully which activities are essential medical functions and which other activities may be delegated (LaDou and Likens, 1977). The organization of roles and activities around the figure of the doctor is similar to the judge's position in the courtroom; each party becomes significant as he presents information that becomes the focus of judicial attention and decision. With the intense emphasis upon physician productivity and upon objectively based decisionmaking, it seems inevitable that the tradition of house calls should dwindle. Yet there are certain sectors of medical care where it might be expected to maintain viability, such as the care of elderly patients, those with a physical handicap or disabling illness, and infants.

There are several reasons why house calls for infant patients are more justifiable than house calls for older children or adults. Infant care, including health care, tends to be the special responsibility of the mother; the logistics of getting the infant to the doctor's office during normal business hours can be complex and stressful for her. Discussions of the low efficiency of house calls as a physician activity do not take into account the loss of productivity sustained by the patient in terms of the time, effort, stress, and money involved in transporting herself or himself to the doctor's office. The effort and stress may be especially great when the mother takes her baby and other children must also be taken, or left behind at home.

Psychological considerations also suggest the value of house calls for infants. "Stranger anxiety" is a well-recognized phenomenon, variable yet normal, in infants 6 to 15 months old; when manifest in relation to the doctor, stranger anxiety can lead the infant into disruptive, resistant behavior that thwarts the doctor's physical examination (Spock, 1968: 234). It is relieved most by the close presence of parents, but the infant's familiarity with the physical environment can also reduce the anxiety. A doctor's office is more anxiety-provoking than home. This factor is presented by James Greene (1964), a pediatrician, in a discussion of the basis on which he makes house calls:

I always see children with possible contagion at home. I also call on those with medical emergencies, such as croup and convulsions—that may be caused by or associated with infection. That cuts down the risk of cross-infection in my office. Also, a very young child with significant abdominal pain is better seen at home, especially when he doesn't know me. I can get a toddler's cooperation better when I examine his abdomen in his own familiar surroundings. And though such a child usually doesn't have appendicitis or intussusception, it's often hard to be sure. Finally, I do make occasional calls that aren't medically necessary. They are to comfort hysterical mothers who don't know the first thing about their babies.

Dr. Greene's overall policy aims to limit the number of house calls in his urban pediatric practice. The foregoing criteria represented his professional judgment of the minimum criteria. (His statement appeared originally in *Medical Economics,* a medical trade journal, and was intended for a physician readership.)

Dr. Spock, writing for a large popular audience, takes a firm anti-house-call stance. In *Baby and Child Care* (Spock, 1976: 72), he fails to identify a single circumstance that in his opinion warrants a house call. His position is frankly stated: an office visit is more convenient for the "busy doctor," of no harm to the child ("in these days of heated cars"), and sometimes essential, as when an X-ray is to be taken. In an earlier article, he viewed the desire for a house call as "mostly an emotional problem. Perhaps we'll all stop expecting house calls for children's ordinary infections eventually but it will take some of us another ten or twenty years to outgrow the habit" (Spock, 1961).

Our study concerns itself with home visits made by nurses operating out of the Baby Health Clinic as well as house calls made by physicians. Although home visits and house calls are made by both kinds of full-time, highly trained health professionals, there are distinctive differences in the house calls. These differences are in keeping with the common conception of the roles of the nurse and doctor in our society.

The doctor's house call is a delimited mission focused upon the actual or potential illness of a designated individual. It occurs at the patient's residence in lieu of an alternative, medically controlled site, such as the doctor's office or outpatient clinic. The value of the house call tends to be assessed by the same criteria that apply to doctor-patient contact in the other sites. If the doctor has difficulty making a diagnosis for lack of equipment in the patient's home, then, according to the foregoing framework of evaluation, he or she may regard a house call as useless. If the medical purpose can be carried out equally well by the doctor's house call or by the patient's office visit, the doctor may well feel that the latter is preferable because it saves medical time and effort.

The nurse on a home visit does not conceive of the visit as one that can equally well be accomplished at his or her own health-department base. Nurses traditionally provide "care," which is more diffuse than the doctor's "diagnosis and treatment." Urban areas with adequate, tax-supported, public-health services have for several decades had a cadre of public-health nurses who make home visits to assess infant health and, in a more general sense, to help the mother care for the infant in the total family constellation and household ecology. These home visits provide first-line expertise in the care of sick infants, but are not as specifically focused as the doctor's house call; if the mother or an older child has a health problem, the nurse may attend to that also.

Another major difference is that the services of visiting public-health nurses, like many other tax-supported public-health services, have traditionally been directed toward poor families. Community medical practitioners, influential in many health-care processes beyond their immediate practice, tend to oppose the delivery of free health care (whether preventive or sick care) to families above the poverty level. Their feeling is that families who can afford private health care should not depend upon services supported by the local tax base. This sentiment is shared by the broad middle-class stratum in many communities.

A related and more pronounced feature may figure into the context of visiting-nurse services: not only are such services restricted to lower socioeconomic targets, but an aura of disrespectability may infuse the receipt of the services. Further, the very diffuseness of care rendered in the home visit provides a wedge for the nurse to engage in efforts to improve the domestic situation of needy mothers, such as better housekeeping and orderly scheduling of family meals. Some poor mothers may perceive the nurse as an obtrusive representative of middle-class society; his or her health care may be appreciated, but not any broader, "reform" activities. In contrast, the doctor's house call, as a more specific medical encounter, has an isolating and empirical quality devoid of socioeconomic nuances. The potentials of a medical call are less caring and protective, but also less meddlesome and moralizing—although probably very few nurses are indeed meddlesome and moralizing. Furthermore, the effect of a nurse's visit depends not only upon his or her own conduct but also upon the attitude of the family; the mother, for example, may welcome advice about nutrition or sterilizing bottles but be hypersensitive to any suggestion that her kitchen is unsanitary.

In our study, 50 infants received a total of 92 visits (we use "visit" here to cover both physician house calls and nurse home visits). Twenty-five infants were visited once; at the other extreme, one infant was visited eight times. The 92 visits were distributed among families as shown in Table 6-11; Table 6-12 presents findings that analyze those figures in terms of social class of family and

Table 6-11
Distribution of Home Visits of Infants

Number of Visits	Number of Families Receiving Given Number of Visits	Total Number of Visits
0	229	0
1	25	25
2	18	36
3	3	9
4	2	8
5	0	0
6	1	6
7	0	0
8	1	8
Total	279	92

Table 6-12
Number of Infants Receiving Health-Care Visits, by Social Class of Family and Professional Classification of Visitor

| Social Class | Professional Classification[a] | | | (D) Total Number of Families Receiving Visits[b] | (E) Total Number of Families in Class | (F) Percentage of All Families in Class Receiving Visits[c] | (G) Percentage of All Families in Class Receiving Pediatrician Visits[d] |
	(A) Nurse (Baby Health Clinic)	(B) General Practitioner	(C) Pediatrician				
I	0 (0)	0 (2)	4 (26)	4	28	14%	14%
II	0 (0)	0 (3)	2 (29)	2	32	6%	6%
III	1 (1)	1 (14)	7 (49)	9	64	14%	11%
IV	3 (7)	5 (32)	7 (36)	15	75	20%	9%
V	12 (21)	4 (36)	4 (23)	20	80	25%	5%
Total	16 (29)	10 (87)	24 (163)	50	279	18%	9%

Chi^2: Families Receiving Visit, by Social Class = 6.79

D.F. = 4
$p < .05$

Chi^2: Families Receiving Pediatrician Visit, by Social Class = 2.10

D.F. = 4
$p \not< .05$

[a]Numbers in parentheses are taken from Table 6–7. Each number tells how many families in the class use the type of professional listed in the column. Thus, 26 Class I families use pediatricians and four of the 26 were visited by their pediatrician. Two Class I families use general practitioners and neither was visited. No Class I families use the Baby Health Clinic.

[b]Column D equals the sum of Columns A, B, and C.

[c]Column F equals Column D divided by Column E.

[d]Column G equals Column C divided by Column E.

medical classification of visitor. It shows the number of families who were visited, regardless of number of visits, in each class.

In the bottom row of Table 6–12 it is seen that of the 50 families who have been visited, 16 were visited by nurses from the Baby Health Clinic, 10 were visited by general practitioners, and 24 were visited by pediatricians. The meaning of these figures can be appropriately gauged by comparing them with the total number of families who use each infant health-care service (this was shown in Table 6–7, and the same figures are repeated in parentheses in Table 6–12). Sixteen of the 29 families using the Baby Health Clinic, or 55 percent, received a visit—one visit or more—from clinic nurses. Ten of the 87 families using general practitioners, or 11 percent, received a visit. Twenty-four of the 163 families using pediatricians, or 15 percent, received a visit.

It thus appears that the Baby Health Clinic families are much more likely to be visited than the families using either of the two physician sources. This finding conforms with the discussion above of the visiting nurse's role. Public-health nursing developed in urban areas during the nineteenth century to meet the health, domestic, and welfare needs of the poor. Medical practice during the same period underwent changes which tended to outmode the once-familiar house call. One important change in medicine is the growth of specialized practice, which in its emphasis upon technique tends to make the doctor more remote from the patient. House calls expose the doctor to the physical and social environment of the patient; by immersing him or her in a somewhat alien culture, the house call erodes the crispness of the doctor's role definition. Presumably medical house calls have declined because the doctor increasingly feels there is little he or she can do qua doctor in the domestic setting. This would account for the lower frequency in our study of medical than nursing visits. It is, however, surprising, and in clear exception to the foregoing considerations, that a higher proportion of families using pediatricians had visits than those using general practitioners. The pediatrician's role is, of course, the more specialized.

Several class-related trends appear in Table 6–12. Class II has the lowest percent of families receiving visits, 6 percent, and Class V has the highest percent, 25 percent. The greater number of Class V visits are made by nurses. This is consistent with our early observation that not only do visiting nurses visit, but their professional traditions, coupled with community expectations and the particular background of the Baby Health Clinic, led them to target their visits particularly on Class V infants and mothers. Despite the obvious clustering of nurse visits among Class V infants, the chi-square value that compares the number of families visited with families not visited by social class, is nonsignificant (chi-square equals 6.79, degrees of freedom equals 4).

It is of interest also to note the percent of pediatrician visits by social class. The figures range from a high of 14 percent for Class I to a low of 5 percent for Class V. Stated in that form, the figures fuse two distinct elements: the extent to which families of a given class utilize pediatricians, and the extent to which pediatricians visit infants at home. Thus the low percent in Class V primarily reflects the fact that so many of the Class V families rely upon the Baby Health Clinic rather than upon pediatricians for infant health care. Of the 23 Class V families who do use pediatricians, four, or 19 percent, have been visited at home. Comparable percents for the other classes are: Class IV, 19 percent (7 of 36 families); Class III, 14 percent (7 of 49); Class II, 7 percent (2 of 29); and Class I, 15 percent (4 of 26). Thus, Class IV and V infants are more likely than infants from other classes to receive pediatrician visits. However, the chi-square value based upon the number of pediatrician-using families in a social class that have and have not received pediatrician visits is nonsignificant (chi-square equals 2.10, degrees of freedom equals 4).

Other findings shed additional light upon the phenomenon of professional health care in the home. The 163 infants whose health care is in the hands of pediatricians are served by twelve different pediatricians in the community (cf. Table 6-6). Eleven of the twelve pediatricians made house calls to infants in the study. These eleven pediatricians made a total of 32 calls among the 24 receiving infants. The average figures are thus 2.9 calls per pediatrician and 1.3 calls per infant. Two infants received three pediatrician visits, four infants received two visits each, and the remaining 18 infants each received one visit.

Comparable figures for house calls by general practitioners are as follows. Only seven of the 34 general practitioners (cf. Table 6-6) dealing with infants in the sample made house calls for the infants. These seven general practitioners made a total of 23 calls among the ten infants seen, for an average of 3.3 calls per practitioner and 2.3 calls per infant. One infant was visited at home six times by its practitioner, another received four visits, five infants received two visits each, and the remaining three infants were each visited once.

Several points of differentiation in the pattern of house calls made by the two types of physician are suggested by these findings. It appears that the trend toward obsolescence of the house call notwithstanding, most pediatricians do engage in the practice. Our data do not permit us to state the complaint or clinical occasion which led to these calls; perhaps they were in keeping with Dr. Greene's "common-sense criteria" noted earlier. Although house calls are a small, possibly vestigial, part of pediatric practice, they remain within the pediatric role. In contrast, a much smaller proportion of the general practitioners made house calls, but the number of calls made per infant was greater than with the pediatricians. This suggests that house calls were an elective part of general practice, and further, that among the general practitioners who incorporated this element into their practice its use was less controlled and selective than among the pediatricians. Three quarters of the infants visited by pediatricians received only one visit, compared with 30 percent of the infants visited by general practitioners.

The foregoing interpretation is offered tentatively, befitting the relatively small number of infants, physicians, and visits involved. More research is needed on the "natural behavior" of physicians in ongoing community practice, as distinct from the somewhat more abundant research on medical practice in academic centers and on the impact of various innovations upon practice.

In addition to the tempering of interpretation based on small numbers, two other points should be noted. First, the infants under the care of the 34 general practitioners probably constitute a much smaller part of their total patient load than those under the care of the 12 pediatricians. Therefore, the propensity of the pediatricians for making house calls is more adequately sampled in our data than that of the general practitioners. Second, we have discussed house calls as if each call were an independent behavioral event reflecting the outcome of a complex of factors, including the family's request for such a call, the illness status of the infant as reported by the parents, the physician's assessment of that report, and his general policy in regard to house calls. An alternative idea is that the physician was selected by the family partly on the basis of his willingness to make such calls. This interpretation allows that many physicians simply do not make house calls within their professional practice. Those families who value house calls would gravitate toward those physicians who do make them. If our findings can be accepted as representative on this point, we suggest another interpretation which also utilizes the selection principle: many parents select pediatricians, rather than general practitioners, for the medical care of their infants because of the more consistent disposition of pediatricians to make house calls.

7

Family Health Care

We earlier presented basic sociological characteristics of the families of this study in order to provide an analytical picture of the social context of infant care. In this chapter we return to the family to regard it not as the social context of infant care, but rather as an explicit focus of investigation. Our interest lies in the health care of the family—what health care is provided from its own resources and professional resources, and the involvement of family members in preventive care. As in the preceding chapters, the greatest amount of attention will be focused upon the mother. This emphasis on the mother role within the family started in Chapter 4 with a focus on prenatal care, and has continued with the reporting of findings about the mother's mode of infant feeding and her post-delivery employment. In this chapter, we will deal with her health and health care.

As in Chapter 6, this chapter maintains a dual interest in the recipient of health services and the service providers. The mother's choice of a physician will be examined in relation to her social class and race, in a framework parallel to that developed in Chapter 6 to analyze infant health care. We will here identify the convergent phenomenon of both mother and infant going to the same doctor. Use of the same doctor by different family members seems to be a natural outcome of the family's social solidarity, which resists the fragmentation of care posed by the growth of medical specialization. One strong counter-current in medicine is the family-practice movement, which is considered from the vantage point of the study findings on mother and infant health care.

This chapter examines how families orient to the existing health resources of the community and provide in part for their health through their own remedies. Coming from an *in vivo* community base, and without vested connections to a particular innovation or service-delivery program, the findings of this study can contribute useful information to current public discussions about health-care manpower, the regulation of drugs, preventive health care, and other concerns.

Health Aids in the Household

As the organized material environment of the infant and family, the household contains numerous health assets and liabilities. We earlier considered some of the liabilities. Our review of infant health problems looked at accidents, a

165

major health risk rising out of physical facilities and arrangements in the household. Ventilation, heating, and sanitation can play a major part in the propagation of infections. A household safe enough for adult occupants may need additional protections for the special vulnerabilities of the infant.

This section focuses upon household resources that are explicitly acquired for managing and relieving minor health problems. We will deal principally with nonprescription medications. Before presenting specific findings, let us consider the ways in which the nuclear family may be regarded as a self-sustaining collective unit in the maintenance of health and in coping with health problems.

When a physician is consulted, the family reaches outside for professional help. Obviously, many health problems arise and subside without professional attention, being managed entirely within the scope of family resources. Family norms, perhaps related to traditions from earlier generations and to mass media and cultural influences, define what symptoms and malaises shall be regarded as illnesses. Family remedies, again from the stock of tradition and also from the influence of the mass media, are applied to bring relief from these minor illnesses. The magnitude of minor-illness episodes is enormous and shallow at the same time: enormous because the average person has, in the course of a year, a number of days of "not feeling well," and yet shallow because such episodes are of transient significance.

The line between minor and major health problems is not sharp. Much depends upon the subjective evaluation of the sick person and the manner in which his or her evaluation is in turn communicated to and evaluated by family members and other significant reference persons. Further, as we have seen in this study, the threshold for resort to outside health services, whether prenatal care or vaccination, varies from one family to another. To one family, an infant fever lasting three days might be defined as a major problem and a pediatrician might be consulted. A second family might similarly view this as a major problem, and yet handle it without medical assistance. A third family might view it as a minor reverse, not requiring medical attention.

Many episodes of illness are defined as falling within an interstitial zone in which the sufferer should do something (rather than carry on as usual), and yet not consult a physician (Pratt, 1973). Into this zone fall everyday maladies such as headaches, nervous conditions, muscular soreness, and colds. In our society, a vast number of nonprescription medications are marketed by pharmaceutical manufacturers and stocked by families in household medicine cabinets for use when these maladies occur. In one sense, medications are outside resources, which like professional service have a point of origin external to the family. However, unlike physicians' services, which are provided behaviorally by a human being imbued with clinical judgment and responsibility, medications become the fully accessible and passive instruments of their user. Because of the potential for the misuse and abuse of medications, many drugs are available only on prescription by a physician; even over-the-counter medications have potential for damage through overuse, cumulative side effects, synergistic effects, and allergic reactions of the user. After presenting our findings, we shall comment on the ambiguous features of household medications. Although we refer to "health aids," this does not mean they are necessarily beneficial.

In our study we investigated the family's possession of items in the following twelve categories: analgesic, adhesive tape, antiseptic, burn remedy, cold remedy, laxative, stomach medicine, eye lotion, kidney medicine, tonic, fever thermometer, and scales. Nine of these are orally ingested medications, one (adhesive tape) is externally applied, and two (fever thermometer and scales) provide information only. For an item to be counted in the study, it was necessary that the family usually have it, whether or not it was present in the household on the day of the interview.

Table 7-1 shows the total percentage of families possessing each of the twelve items, and the percentage within each social class. The rows of the table are ordered in terms of decreasing percentage in the total sample. Thus, the most common item is an analgesic (98 percent), followed closely by adhesive tape (96 percent) and an antiseptic (92 percent). At the other end, only 8 percent of the families have tonic medicine.

There is no significant difference among the five social classes in possession of analgesics, antiseptics, laxatives, cough remedies, eye lotion, stomach medicine, kidney medicine, and tonic. Significant differences appear for adhesive tape, burn remedies, thermometers, and scales. In every instance where there is a significant difference among the social classes, a greater proportion of the higher-status families than of the lower-status families possess the particular health aid. This might be expected simply on an economic basis—the higher-status families have more money to spend. However, most of these health aids are relatively inexpensive, costing at most a dollar or two. We believe that the differences noted reflect the health values of the social classes rather than an exclusive economic factor. Such an explanation seems particularly applicable to thermometers and scales, which give only information and no relief from distress. Middle- and upper-class persons who phone the physician about a sick child may be asked for the child's temperature; such families are accustomed to using this instrument and being asked, while many lower-status families may not be so accustomed. With scales, the explanation may be different; it is the single health aid among the twelve that is an item of appreciable expense, costing seven dollars or more. Even so, spending money for an object that merely registers body weight and provides no direct benefit probably does not comport with the values of many lower-status families.

Having surveyed social-class differentials in these health aids, let us consider several aspects of nonprescription medications in the context of family use. We alluded earlier to negative features of such medications. Consider the following newspaper advertisement:

Table 7-1

Percentage of Families Reporting Specified Health Aids in the Household, by Social Class

| Health Aid | All Classes (N = 279) | Social Class | | | | | Chi square | p^a |
		I (28)	II (32)	III (64)	IV (75)	V (80)		
Analgesic ("anything to kill pain")	98	96	100	100	97	96	3.44	< .05
Adhesive tape or band-aids	96	100	97	98	100	88	18.98	> .001
Antiseptic	92	89	97	88	97	89	6.90	< .05
Burn remedy	83	86	97	86	96	62	38.01	< .001
Cough or cold remedy	79	82	88	78	81	74	3.21	< .05
Laxative	73	64	56	75	73	79	7.02	< .05
Fever thermometer	70	96	94	91	71	32	83.72	< .001
Scales	54	93	69	62	53	28	44.30	< .001
Stomach medicine	48	46	56	56	51	36	7.31	< .05
Eye lotion	42	43	44	47	49	30	7.08	< .05
Kidney medicine ("kidney pills")	14	14	12	8	20	14	4.28	< .05
Tonic ("tonic or anything to pep you up")	8	0	6	5	11	11	5.48	< .05

[a] Degrees of freedom = 4 in every row

KIDNEY DANGER SIGNALS
SUCH AS BACKACHE,
GETTING UP NIGHTS

May warn of functional disorders—"Danger Ahead." Help nature FLUSH kidneys and REGULATE passage with gentle NEPHRETS. Feel GOOD again in 12 hours or your 75¢ back. NOW at all Drug Stores.

A person with disturbed kidney function due to renal disease would be ill-advised to place much reliance upon such a medication. Even if NEPHRETS produces its claimed symptomatic relief, such a person would be better served by consulting a physician and having his symptoms diagnosed and his disease properly treated.

On the other hand, let us suppose that this person has insomnia as part of a mild emotional upset. If his medication gives him undisturbed sleep, he will regard it as beneficial. Further, because it provides him this relief, other members of his family may well encourage him to use it. In general, the family as a socioemotional group oriented to symptoms and feelings rather than to objective canons of medical practice does not bring any appreciable objectivity to the use of medications. However, health values vary. In some families, medications are critically evaluated and cautiously used.

The demarcation of prescription and nonprescription medicines limits the options of individuals and families. Of their own initiative they can only purchase nonprescription medicines, which have mild effects when used as directed. This restriction on individual and family choice is made in the interest of public health and safety. Through political authority, society decides to restrict the availability of medicines, and it charges a scientific-regulatory agency of the government (the federal Food and Drug Administration) with responsibility for drawing the prescription-nonprescription line. Any such demarcation has some arbitrariness to it. Given adequate package instructions, many individuals would be able to self-medicate themselves with codeine compounds, which are prescribed analgesics, while others abuse aspirin, a nonprescribed analgesic.

There is a rising tide of drug advertising through all the mass media, which parallels the increase in expenditure for medicines, both prescribed and nonprescribed. In terms of family roles, a disproportionately large share of expenditure is made by women and much of the advertising is directed at women: the familiar image is one of a distressed female, variously anxious, depressed, tense, sleepless, perplexed, or overwhelmed, who will be marvelously helped by a specific pharmaceutical product. If the product is an over-the-counter one, to be purchased by the woman herself, the advertising frequently flatters her by suggesting that her distress is the direct consequence of her efforts to be a good mother, wife, housekeeper, community worker, and general servant to humanity. If the product is a prescription medicine, the advertising appears in a medical journal and is directed toward an audience of predominantly male physicians who have discretionary authority to prescribe it to their patients: the image in this case is usually far less flattering, portraying the distressed woman as a habitual malcontent—and also suggesting broadly that the doctor's life could be vastly eased if he had one good drug which he could prescribe to his many, many patients exactly like her.

The upward curve of medication consumption has led some physicians and public-health authorities to regard the United States as an "overmedicated" society (Muller, 1972). This concern extends to prescription as well as non-prescription medications. The average doctor in concluding an average appointment with an average patient makes a prescription. He or she thereby intervenes in relation to the patient's problem, fulfilling the patient's expectation and his or her own concept of the doctor's role. Whether the prescribed drug is related in terms of known pharmacological action to the patient's problem is a moot question. Psychiatrist Michael Balint (1960, 1970) suggests that much prescription behavior by the doctor, especially the prescription of tranquilizers and sedatives, can be viewed as a hasty, faulty substitute for doctor–patient communication rather than as sound treatment. A medical mystique surrounds the doctor's behavior. Prescription medications originate with the physician's prescribing act, then continue on in their healing influence as a disembodied projection of his or her benign authority. The benign quality of the physician-patient encounter is repeated every time the patient takes the medicine. Under the persuasion of this mystique, the physician's own critical judgment may be overridden by the force of a desire to help, and by the patient's dependency upon him or her.

Lennard (1971) and his associates show with their concept of "mystification" how prescribing behavior can come to appear highly rational and scientific, without actually being so. For example, the process of fixing attention upon and giving a technical appellation to various patient complaints ("hyperkinesis," "agitated depression," "compulsive overeating," "minimal brain damage") can create the definite sense of a disease or pathology, which then, according to a model of rational action, invites intervention by the physician-as-expert using a medication precisely tooled for the purpose. Professional behavior patterned upon such a model may carry with it the illusory conviction of decisive action that resolves the patient's specific problem. Analogous processes of mystification occur in the mass advertising of nonprescribed medication, by the fabrication of a disease that a particular nostrum will cure, by the identification of a fictitious bodily site that will be therapeutically affected, or by the naming of a wholly imaginary chemical ingredient.

The mere generation and diffusion of advertising copy is no guarantee that individuals and families will be moved to purchase and consume the medications so touted. The din of advertising is not the only pressure that leads to the general increase in the use of medications: strong contemporary social values favor it. People medicate themselves, especially with tranquilizers and stimulants, to become more patient, cheerful, alert, and socially acceptable. Within families, they medicate their dependents for the same purposes. They also turn to the hard-pressed physician, who prescribes abundantly as an efficient means of meeting patient expectations and maintaining the brisk flow of patients through his consulting room.

With respect to nonprescription, over-the-counter medications, some physicians feel that if a person's complaint can be thus managed without recourse to other medical attention, then the complaint was indeed trivial and not worth a physician's time. In this view, nonprescribed medications form a first-line resource with which families screen out minor and self-limiting illnesses. They thus constitute a mechanism that restricts the public need for medical attention and qualitatively channels only the more serious problems to the physician. In contrast to the foregoing line of thinking, there is the cautionary consideration that medications may provide symptomatic relief that obscures or delays the recognition of serious disease. While that possibility may occur with prescribed medication, even under careful medical surveillance, the risks are perhaps greater with over-the-counter medications and a regime of self-medication.

Mother's Health

In the preceding chapter, attention focused upon the infant's state of health, the various health problems encountered, and the professional resources used for infant health. Our study also investigated similar questions about other family members. Because the mother is usually the primary caretaker of the infant, her own health and source of health care are of particular interest. As with the infants, the sample of mothers is an essentially healthy cross section of the community, yet there is a range of variation in their health status.

The mother's health was assessed by self-report: "How has your health been in the last month?" Seventy-one percent, or 198, of the 279 mothers reported themselves to be in good health. The other 29 percent, or 81, of the mothers reported having health problems. No serious illnesses were reported. A number of episodic illnesses such as flu and colds were reported, but most problems were of a chronic character—insomnia, menstrual cramps, hypertension, varicose veins, backache, and urinary infection. Lower-status mothers tended to report health problems more than higher-status mothers. By social class, the percentage with health problems was: Class I, 21 percent; Class II, 22 percent; Class III, 25 percent; Class IV, 27 percent; and Class V, 40 percent. Chi-square for this social class distribution is 7.00, nonsignificant at the 5 percent level. However, a comparison of Class V with Classes I-IV combined yields a chi-square of 6.55, significant at the 5 percent level. As we have seen in previous instances, Class V occupies a unique ledge in the social scale.

The mothers who reported good health had to a statistically significant degree more favorable pregnancy histories. They are more likely to have had a positive attitude toward the pregnancy ($r = .13$, $p<.05$) and their Pregnancy Difficulty Index is lower ($r = .31, p<.001$). (These aspects of the pregnancy were discussed in Chapter 4.) Another significant correlate of good maternal health, more contemporary with the current self-report than the pregnancy, is the infant's Health Difficulty Index (HD) score. The reader will recall from Chapter 6 that the infants were scored on a standard list according to the number of health problems they had exhibited. The infants whose mothers reported maternal health problems had a significantly higher number of health problems ($r = .43$, $p<.001$).

The mothers were also questioned about their opportunities for relaxation: "Can you get enough time to relax and take it easy?" This question was intended to touch upon the mother's mental health and sense of well-being. One premise underlying the question is that infant care is a demanding task, even for the non-working primapara mother. The demands lie partly in the physical exertions of infant care and partly in the requirement for sensitive accommodation to the infant's moods and sleep and hunger cycles. If the mother cannot find some inherent "job satisfaction" in servicing the infant and being with it, then the opportunities for relaxation that she might find or seize during its naps or periods of self-absorption may be insufficient for her own needs. Relaxation is not a simple matter of the number of clock hours or time alone, but depends upon the mother's emotional balance. We wanted to find out in a general way whether the mother felt herself to be relaxed or hard-pressed in her maternal role.

Seventy-one percent, or 198, of the mothers reported that they had enough time to relax; the remaining 29 percent, or 81, said they did not. By social class, the percentage of mothers reporting sufficient time was: Class I, 82 percent; Class II, 72 percent; Class III, 67 percent; Class IV, 73 percent; and Class V, 69 percent. The greatest class differential lies between Class I and Class III. The overall class distribution is nonsignificant (chi-square = 2.50, D.F. = 4, $p\not<.05$).

This characteristic of the mother, which may be regarded as an aspect of her mental health, reveals a pattern of significant correlations similar to those reported for her physical health. It correlates .27 ($p<.001$) with the Pregnancy Difficulty Index; .20 ($p<.001$) with a positive attitude toward the pregnancy; .24 ($p<.001$) with current health status; and .17 ($p<.01$) with the infant's Health Difficulty Index. Additionally, working mothers are considerably more likely than nonworking mothers to report insufficient time for relaxation ($r = .22$, $p<.001$). We may also ask what relationship the father's participation in infant care (Chapter 4) has to the mother's sense of having enough time to relax. The correlation is .11, in the expected direction, but it falls short of 5 percent statistical significance.

We asked the mothers what they like to do for relaxation. The most common response was, "watch television." Other frequent responses were cooking, baking, reading, and napping. One mother, either very energetic or very concerned to keep up with perceived demands, said she scrubs the floor for relaxation. Another said, "sit down and look at the wall."

A number of mothers said their favorite relaxation activity was smoking. Because cigarette smoking is increasingly a matter of health concern, we investigated this behavior systematically, determining first whether or not the mother smoked, and second the number of packs smoked daily by smokers. Of the total 279 mothers, 133, or 48 percent, smoked. By social class, the percentage of smokers was: Class I, 39 percent; Class II, 44 percent; Class III, 47 percent; Class IV, 40 percent; and Class V, 60 percent. The overall chi-square distribution of smoking by social class is nonsignificant (chi-square = 7.59, D.F. = 4, $p \not< .05$), but Class V, with its 60 percent of mothers who smoked, is significantly different from Class I-IV combined (chi-square = 6.84, D.F. = 1, $p < .01$).

Mothers who smoked were asked to estimate to the nearest half-pack how many packs of cigarettes they smoked per day. Although per-capita cigarette smoking in our society is not decreasing, smokers seem to be increasingly on the defensive about their habit. We recognize that social-desirability biases may affect the information obtained in the direction of low estimates. Accepting for analysis the figures as given, we found the frequency distribution shown in Table 7-2. There is slight variation by social class: Class I, .86 pack per day; Class II, .89; Class III, .87; Class IV, .87; and Class V, .86. In effect, this means that every class has a near-identical balance between smoking mothers who report one-half pack and those who report one pack daily. Only 13 of the 133 smokers reported a higher daily figure than one pack, and they were scattered on the social-class ladder.

The use of cigarettes correlates negatively with reported good physical health ($r = -.18$, $p < .01$). However, it correlates positively with mother's report

Table 7-2
Cigarette Smoking Among Mothers

Number of Packs Per Day	Number of Mothers	Percentage
.5	56	42
1.0	64	48
1.5	8	6
2.0	3	2
2.5	1	1
3.0	1	1
Total	133	100

Mean = .87 pack/day
Mode = 1 pack/day

of enough time for relaxation (r = .15, $p<.05$). Mothers who smoke are more likely than those who do not to have ample relaxing time. Perhaps the fact that smoking has no ulterior constructive purpose gives the smoker a definite sense of time spent in relaxation.

Mother's Source of Medical Care

Our discussion of the mother's source of medical care follows the scheme of analysis employed in Chapter 6 when we examined the source of infant health care. On a descriptive level, we are interested in the types of physicians the mothers use, and how the mothers are distributed numerically among the various types. Social-class and race differences in use of physicians will be examined. The various descriptive findings will also be considered from the standpoint of contemporary issues in health care.

Table 7-3 presents findings on the types and numbers of physicians and the number of mothers who use each. The basis for this information is a series of

Table 7-3

Source of Mother's Health Care, by Medical Classification

Type of Practice	Number of Practitioners	Number of Mothers
General Surgery		
Board-certified general surgeon	4	4
General surgeon, not board-certified	5	16
Total	9	20
Internal Medicine		
Board-certified internist	9	16
Internal medicine specialist, not board-certified	12	18
Total	21	34
Obstetrics and Gynecology		
Board-certified obstetrician	6	18
Obstetrics-gynecology specialist, not board-certified	12	44
Total	18	62
General Practice		
Medical physician	33	118
Osteopathic physician	1	6
Chiropractic physician	2	2
Total	36	126
Total for Individual Sources (above combined)	84	242
No individual source of health care given	–	37
Total	–	279

questions that established the mother's principal source of medical help. Most of the mothers had occasional illness or health problems which they took to an individual physician, whom they readily identified in the interview. Others, though never ill, had occasional medical checkups. Thirty mothers said they had had no medical contacts since delivery of the baby and that they never go to a doctor, even when sick. Another seven said they obtained health care at the health department. Through analysis of the responses, we were able in the case of 242 mothers to identify a physician who was the mother's principal source of medical care. By using physician directories we were then able to classify the physicians according to their type of practice, and for those with specialized practice, to ascertain whether or not they had achieved certification by their national specialty board.

A major difference between the mothers and infants is that the mothers go to a greater number of different physicians, and a wider variety of physicians, than do the infants. Forty-six different physicians are used by the 250 infants who have individual sources of care. In comparison, 84 different physicians are used by the 242 mothers who have individual sources. The infant's physicians can be dichotomized into pediatricians and general practitioners; the array of physicians used by the mother is more diverse and not so simply categorized.

One hundred and twenty-six of the 242 mothers, or 52 percent, used 36 different general practitioners as thier source of medical care. (It will be noted in Table 7–3 that three of these doctors were not medically trained: an osteopathic physician saw six of the 126 mothers, and two chiropractors saw one mother each.) Of the 33 medical general practitioners, nine combined general practice with a secondary focus upon a specialty area. Cardiology, neurology, psychiatry, and anesthesiology were among the specialty areas represented. The other 24 of the 33 conducted a general practice with no secondary specialization.

Sixty-two, or 26 percent, of the mothers used 18 physicians who specialize in obstetrics-gynecology. Physicians with this specialization came second to the general practitioners as the type of physician most used by the mothers. Six of the ob.-gyn. physicians had national-board certification; the other twelve limited their practice to this area but lacked board certification.

In frequency of use, the third category was internal medicine. Thirty-four mothers, or 14 percent, saw 21 internists. Nine of the 21 internists had board certification; the others also limited their practice to internal medicine but without certification. The final specialty category was general surgery. Twenty mothers, or 8 percent, saw nine general surgeons, of whom five were board-certified in their specialty.

Why did the mothers go to the specialists? What factors determine the type of specialists seen? Before we answer these questions from our study data, we wish to discuss their significance in relation to the public interest in optimum use of health manpower. Efficient allocation of professional manpower dictates that board-certified specialists should be reserved for patients whose medical problems transcend the capability of general practitioners. Under this model of allocation, the patient goes first to a general practitioner who then makes appropriately screened referrals to the specialist. While board certification is a clear index of specialized skill deserving judicious utilization, similar considerations also apply to the noncertified specialist with accumulated experience in the treatment and management of a certain type of patient.

Most nations have a system of medical care that is more highly centralized than that of the United States, and that provides greater emphasis upon primary care and orderly access to specialist services. In England's National Health Service, for example, specialists are attached to hospital staffs and can scarcely be approached by patients without referral by a general practitioner. As a general rule patients are referred by their family doctors, who make arrangements for specialist advice, and the specialist in turn arranges for hospital admission or treatment on an outpatient basis (Committee on Ways and Means, U.S. House of Representatives, 1974: 384). Unlike his or her American counterpart who engages in extensive practice with ambulatory patients, the English specialist deals primarily with patients in a hospital, though he or she may then follow them after discharge. Such centralized systems can function only with much greater control over medical training, over the distribution of health manpower, and over the expression of consumer preference than presently exists in the United States.

It is difficult to maximize efficient allocation of manpower and to achieve other goals at the same time. For example, to the seriously ill patient who requires hospital treatment, the shift from a community general practitioner to a hospital specialist may be a jarring discontinuity. While one manpower strategy emphasizes the training of primary-care physicians, another favors the production of paramedical personnel (urologic technicians, cytoscopic technicians, dialysis technicians) to assist the specialist in his routine work. The latter strategy preserves the existing specialty distribution of physicians and does nothing about primary medical care. Since physicians of all kinds in contemporary society find their services in demand, economic logic would argue that their services are already well-allocated in the existing form and quantity. Models of rational manpower allocation and orderly access do not accord well with the play of supply and demand. Changes in disease patterns or age distributions and innovations in medical technique may convert a scarcity of service into a surplus, or vice versa. A declining birthrate may mean a lessened claim upon pediatric services: according to strict economic logic, fewer doctors will go into pediatrics and the supply will diminish. But the interim period during which pediatric services are abundant could last for decades.

Another standpoint for assessing medical services is that of the consumer. It seems that the individual consumer would always prefer the greater skill of the specialist, provided that the specialist and the generalist are equal in terms of other, noncognitive qualities such as empathy, accessibility, and cost. A more informed public will be more discerning regarding the technical qualification of doctors. Also, given two doctors equal in technical qualification, the consumer would prefer the one with greater empathy or who charges less.

In our study, the 116 mothers who used specialists went to three different kinds: internists, obstetrician-gynecologists, and general surgeons. The predominance of ob.-gyn. physicians among specialists in Table 7-3 is related to the fact that the mothers were in the reproductive phase of life. All had recently borne a child. Many were preparing to do so again or were in the intermittent stage of expectation that they might be pregnant. To be under the care of the most appropriate specialist seems reasonable under the circumstances. Another factor is an inertia in the doctor-patient relationship; the expectant mother seeks an obstetrician and remains with him whether or not she still needs ob.-gyn. expertise. (Some mothers said that they were treated by their ob.-gyn. physician for colds and headaches.)

This phenomenon adds a layer of complexity to discussions of medical care. The medical-care planner may shake his head and deplore the unrestricted, disorderly access of patients to specialist services without referral by a primary-care physician. But things are not what they seem, for it may turn out that the specialist is functioning not as a true specialist but rather as a primary-care physician with a previously established patient.

The internists utilized by the mothers were for the most part general internists without a subspecialty emphasis. Since the contemporary internist frequently functions as a high-level diagnostician and broad-range therapist, his role is that of an especially well-trained generalist. From the standpoint of rational utilization of medical manpower, this seems to be an appropriate source of care for the 34 mothers who so availed themselves. The same can scarcely be said for the 20 mothers whose source of care was a general surgeon. As with the ob.-gyn. physicians, an inertia is at work. These mothers had earlier needed surgical expertise; they simply remained under the surgeon's care, sometimes for continuing observation of a potential surgical condition but more frequently for treatment of episodic minor ills.

Social Patterns in Mother's Choice of Physician

In this section, we will first examine the relation between the mother's social class and her choice of physician. In Chapter 6 (Table 6-7) we saw that there is a strong association between higher social class and the use of specialist (pediatric) medical care for the infant. Although many Class IV and V families did use pediatricians, there was nevertheless a statistically significant association—probably because very few Class I and II families did not use pediatricians. Applied to adult medical care, this pattern would lead us to expect that the higher-status mothers are more prone to go to specialists for their own medical care. A tempering consideration, however, is the previously cited fact that specialist care is sought more for children than it is for older age groups.

Table 7–4 shows that 65 percent of the Class I mothers went to specialists; in Class II, only 36 percent; in Class III, 60 percent; and in both Class IV and V, 42 percent. The overall trend is not statistically significant at the 5 percent level. Table 7-5 refines Table 7–4 by dividing the specialists into two categories, those who are board-certified and those who lack board-certification. It shows that 38, or 30 percent, of the specialists seen by the 116 mothers using specialists were board-certified. The figure varies from a high of 56 percent among the Class II mothers to a low of 14 percent in Class V (it should be noted that the Class II figure is based on a small total number, nine). There is no noticeable trend among Classes I through IV, but Class V's very low rate of use of board-certified specalists is statistically different from that of the four classes above it. Tables 7–4 and 7-5 show that there is no strong connection overall between the social class of the mother and the type of doctor she used.

These findings do not indicate a pattern of choice that reflects an articulate preference on the mother's part concerning the type of physician she goes to. It seems unlikely that many of the mothers know whether their doctor is a board-certified specialist. Probably more mothers are informed with regard to the other distinction, whether the physician has a specialized or general practice. Some of the physicians in question publicly label their practice as limited to a specialty through telephone-book listings and signs at their offices. Others do not give such public cues, though in the American Medical Association directory they indicate a specialization.

Table 7–4
Social Class and Type of Physician Used by Mother

| Social Class | Number and Percentage of Mothers Using Specialists and General Practitioners | | |
	Specialist	General Practitioner	Total
I	15 (65%)	8 (35%)	23 (100%)
II	9 (36%)	16 (64%)	25 (100%)
III	34 (60%)	23 (40%)	57 (100%)
IV	30 (42%)	41 (58%)	71 (100%)
V	28 (42%)	38 (58%)	66 (100%)
Total	116 (48%)	126 (52%)	242 (100%)[a]

$Chi^2 = 9.04$
D.F. = 4
$p \nless .05$

[a]Excludes thirty mothers who said they had no physicians and seven who received medical care from their county health department.

Table 7-5
Social Class and Type of Specialist Used by Mother

Social Class	Board-Certified Specialist	Other Specialist (Not Board-Certified)	Total[a]
	Number and Percentage of Mothers Using Board-Certified and Other Specialists		
I	6 (40%)	9 (60%)	15 (100%)
II	5 (56%)	4 (44%)	9 (100%)
III	12 (35%)	22 (65%)	34 (100%)
IV	11 (37%)	19 (63%)	30 (100%)
V	4 (14%)	24 (86%)	28 (100%)
Total	38 (30%)	78 (70%)	116 (100%)

Chi^2 : Type of specialist by mother's social class = 7.11
D.F. = 4
$p < .05$
Chi^2 : Type of specialist by mother's social class, Classes I–IV combined = 5.72
D.F. = 1
$p < .05$

[a]These total figures are the same as those that appear in the "Specialist" column of Table 7-4.

Many mothers do make a satisfactory choice, though lacking full information of this sort. This conclusion is important though not surprising; Mechanic (1968: 164), on the basis of his studies of medical care, observes that patients are concerned about the doctor's competence and qualifications but they form their impressions on many bases other than formal evidence of training and experience. Some of the behaviors considered to be evidence of competence are whether or not the doctor demonstrates personal interest in the patient, takes time to explain procedures, and listens to the patient. Such considerations have particular applicability to the next social pattern we examine—namely, the mother's choice of physician in relation to her own race and the race of the physician. Not only the physician's demeanor, but also his sociocultural similarity to the patient may be an important factor in the patient's preference.

We reviewed in Chapter 6 a number of sociological considerations and salient empirical facts pertaining to the health care of black patients. Many of the factors that influence the health care of black infants also influence the care of black adults. Table 7-6 presents findings on the racial composition of the physician population that serves the mothers of the sample, and the distribution of the mothers among the different physician categories. Table 7-7 presents a cross-tabulation showing the number of mothers of each race (white/black) who see a physician of either race (white/black). These two tables are formulated in the same manner as Tables 6-8 and 6-9, respectively. The reader is invited to make his own comparison of these tables, which will reveal the impact of

Table 7-6
Utilization of Health-Care Source in Relation to Race of Source and of Mother

Medical Classification	Total Number of Physicians	Number of White/Black Physicians	Total Number of Mothers Using Source	Number of White/Black Mothers Using Source
Board-Certified Specialist	19	19/0	38	33/5
Specialist but not Board-Certified	29	27/2	78	65/13
General Practitioner	36	33/3	126	114/12
No Individual Source Given	–	–	37	35/2
Total	84	79/5	279	247/32

Table 7-7

Number of Black/White Mothers Under Care of Black/White Physician Source

	Race of Mother's Physician[a]		
Race of Mother	*Black*	*White*	*Total*
Black	16	14	30
White	0	212	212
Total	16	226	242

Chi^2 (with correction for continuity): Race of Mother by Race of Mother's Physician =
112.59
D.F. = 1
$p < .001$

Note: The 37 mothers (35 white and 2 black) who did not have an individual source of care are not included in this table.

[a]The cell frequencies refer to mothers, not physicians. Thus, 16 black mothers went to black physicians; 14 black mothers went to white physicians.

racial factors on medical care at the two different age levels (infant and adult) of the patient.

Let us first look at the way in which the white and black mothers select physician types, shown on the right half of Table 7-6. The most notable difference between the two groups is that many more, proportionately, of the white mothers (35 of 247, or 14 percent) than of the black mothers (2 of 32, or 8 percent) used a nonindividual, institutional source or said they had no source of health care. Otherwise, the proportion using different kinds of physicians is similar; for example, 33 of the 247 white mothers (13 percent) and 5 of the 32 black mothers (16 percent) went to a board-certified specialist.

Turning to the supply and distribution of physicians by race, shown in Table 7-6, we see that 5 of the 84 physicians who provided medical care to the mothers were black. All five maintained offices in those sections of Lexington that are residentially black. None of the black physicians had board certification. Two had a practice specialty in obstetrics; the other three functioned as general practitioners. (One of these was the third oldest physician in the total group of 84. At age 70, he maintains a sizable practice and is one of the most widely known members of the Lexington black community, partly because his father was a Lexington physician also.)

Table 7-6 shows how many black and white physicians fell in each physician category, and how many black and white mothers went to each category of physician, but it does not tell how many black mothers went to a black physician and how many to white physicians. Table 7-7 provides this cross-tabulated information. It shows that 16 of the 30 black mothers went to the five black physicians. The other 14 black mothers went to a white physician. None of the 212 white mothers went to a black physician. From the standpoint of the market for professional services, this means that the black physicians were entirely dependent upon patronage from black patients. The black mother who uses a white physician cannot be duplicated by a white mother who uses a black physician.

This consideration prompts us to inquire whether the black mothers who go to white physicians seek a service that the black physicians do not provide. We can answer this question in terms of the physicians' medical classification. The five black mothers who went to a board-certified specialist perforce went to a white physician, since there were no such black physicians. However, of the 13 black mothers who went to a nonboard specialist, five went to a black physician and eight went to a white physician. These latter eight thus used a physician who in terms of professional qualification had no higher level than physicians available in the group of black physicians. A much higher degree of closure by race occurs among the black mothers who used general practitioners; of the 13 mothers in this group, 12 went to black physicians and only one to a white physician.

It is also of interest to compare Table 7-7 with Table 6-9. This comparison shows that 53 percent (16 of 30) of the black mothers and 30 percent (6 of 22) of the black infants used a black physician. The difference between these proportions is significant at the 5 percent level of probability. One may ask why this difference occurs: does it perhaps indicate a shift during the life cycle of black patients, from seeing a white doctor as a baby to seeing a black doctor as an adult? Our data do not permit a full answer, but one obvious factor in the difference is the lesser use of general practitioners for infant health care (evident among the white families as well as the black families) than for mother's health care. Only 35 percent (87 of 250, ignoring 29 infants who went to the Baby Health Clinic) of the infants, both white and black, were taken to general practitioners, while 52 percent (126 of 242, ignoring the 37 mothers who lacked an individual source of care) of all the mothers, both white and black, used a general practitioner. The difference between these proportions is significant at the 1 percent level. The difference is even more extreme when we compare utilization of the board-certified specialists: 43 percent of the infants, compared with only 16 percent of the mothers, used a board-certified physician. These findings lead us to suppose that if black pediatricians were available, many black infants would be taken to them. Consequently, the phenomenon whereby more black mothers use black physicians than do black infants would be less pronounced. (The foregoing analysis does not imply that black mothers and infants should, from the standpoint of sociomedical policy, use only black physicians. Our intention here has been simply to present the findings and to draw out some of their implications for the distribution of medical care.)

Thus far we have studied social patterns in the mother's medical care that reveal the influence of her social-class position and race. Next we deal with "mother-infant medical pairs," that is, a paired mother and infant who use the same physician as the source of health care. How common is this phenomenon in the sample, and how is it socially patterned? The question here concerns not the type of physician used, but whether the particular physician used is the same for both mother and infant; indirectly, however, the type of physician is at issue. If an infant goes to a pediatrician and the infant's mother goes to a gynecologist, then obviously they do not use the same physician. Those physicians who serve mother-infant pairs cannot be highly specialized physicians. The phenomenon under study here is thus related broadly to the generalist versus specialist question, which we have looked at earlier.

We identified 69 mother-infant pairs in which both parties used the same physician. To arrive at this figure, we first eliminated all instances where either mother or infant used a nonindividual source. This struck 37 mothers and 29 infants from the total of 279, leaving the potential maximum of mother-infant pairs at 242 (279 minus 37, which is the greater number as between 37 and 29). Next we eliminated those mothers and infants who went to specialists: 116 mothers and 163 infants. This left a maximum potential total of 79 mother-infant medical pairs (242 minus 163, which is the greater number as between 116 and 163). In 126 families, the mothers went to a general practitioner and in 87 families the infant went to a general practitioner; in only 79 families did both the mother and the infant go to a general practitioner. Only 69 of those 79 families fit the specification of a mother-infant medical pair: only in these families did the mother and infant use the *same* general practitioner. These 69 families constitute only 25 percent of the total sample, but they comprise 80 percent of those families where both mother and infant used general practitioners. In other words, where both family members go to a general practitioner, the tendency for them to use the same doctor is very strong.

As we have previously noted, there is great contemporary concern among the medical profession, legislators, the politically organized public, and individual consumers about the appropriate level of specialization in medical care. The physician who offers a broader, less specialized range of services is presumably equipped to deal with a wider spectrum of problems and patients, including the mother-infant pairs of particular interest here. The 69 mother-infant medical pairs constitute a natural, unplanned distribution of this particular medical-care phenomenon among the existing supply of general practitioners in the community.

Let us examine social factors associated with this distribution. By social class, the percentage of mothers and infants with the same physician is: Class I, 4 percent (1); Class II, 3 percent (1); Class III, 16 percent (10); Class IV, 36 percent (27); and Class V, 38 percent (30). The strong class gradient is significant at the 1 percent level (chi-square = 29.70, D.F. = 4). Over one third of the Class IV and V families use the same physician for both mother and infant; the percentage is much lower in Class III, and negligible in Classes I and II.

Looking at the same phenomenon in terms of race, we find that in six of the 32 black families (19 percent) mother and infant had the same physician, as compared with 63 of the 247 white families (26 percent). This difference in proportions is statistically non-significant.

We examined a third independent variable, the family's rural or urban status, to determine whether this has a strong influence upon the tendency of mother and infant to have the same physician. It will be recalled that in Chapter 4 we regarded rural residence as a predisposing factor in the five home deliveries. It was also considered in regard to choice of hospital for those infants with hospital deliveries. In the present instance, we use county of residence as an approximate index of rural–urban status. It will be recalled that two (Jessamine and Woodford) of the three counties in the study are predominantly rural, while the third (Fayette) is heavily urban.

There is a close connection between the family's rural–urban status and use of the same physician by mother and infant. Of the 41 families who resided in the two rural counties, 31 (76 percent) used the same physician; of the 238 families who reside in urbanized Fayette County, only 38 (16 percent) did. This difference is significant at the .01 probability level (chi-square = 66.84, D.F. = 1). Examination of the physicians' patient lists showed that one general practitioner in Jessamine County saw eight mother-infant pairs. Another eight physicians saw the remaining 23 rural mother-infant pairs. In general, the physicians in the two rural counties had a higher density of patients in the sample than did the physicians in Fayette County. The ratio of physicians to total population is lower in Jessamine and Woodford counties than in Fayette; also the supply of specialist physicians is lower. The scarcity factor in the rural counties may generate a tendency for patients in the same family to "double up" on the same doctor.

In our thinking, this tendency is somewhat independent of the previously posited, general family preference for the same source of care. We believe that yet another force is at work, namely, the bias in rural areas toward a more traditional mode of medical service. Before the advent of medical specialization and in the period when the population was predominantly rural, the modal relationship in medical care was that between one general practitioner and several members of a family. Of course, none of the rural families is truly isolated from specialist services as are families in remote parts of Appalachia, the Southwest, or Maine. Our interpretation concerning mother-infant utilization of the same physician is similar to that concerning the delivery of the infant at home: the rural status of the family is an important factor, but its importance lies more in its association with a traditional orientation toward medical care than in its association with sheer physician scarcity.

Mother-Infant Medical Care and Family Practice

In Chapter 6 we looked at the question of specialist versus generalist medical care of the infant from the standpoints of manpower policy in health care, the consumer, and the physician-provider of service. The emergence within our study of a sizable number of mother-infant medical pairs can be regarded as an empirical phenomenon that stands by itself as an important fact in medical care and also as an event linked to persisting and developing trends in health care. The family as a solitary social unit tends to seek health care from a single source insofar as the latter can provide services appropriate to the defined needs; this is a form of consumer preference. The consumer whose preference is thus enunciated is not animated by the sole desire to obtain maximum quality and quantity for a minimum price. He is, rather, a socially linked consumer whose family ties exert a force in the medical-care marketplace.

Public policy is best served when good care is available to the population at low cost (or minimum resource allocation). The proliferation of medical specialties, especially beyond that division of labor necessary to implement biomedical knowledge, is perhaps not in the public interest. A high degree of specialization creates the need for an apparatus to screen and refer patients, and to coordinate services, in a technically rational, humane, and efficient manner. The rationale for highly differentiated, specialized services can be easily and persuasively stated. However, many of the consequences, such as fragmentation of care, depersonalization of the patient, and ineffective, discontinuous professional service, are inconspicuous and difficult to assess.

A line of public interest can also be built upon the consumer and family preference for a more unitary, continuous mode of medical care than specialized service can provide. The rationale for this is based not only upon the difficulty and wastefulness of coordinating multiple, differentiated providers, but also upon the way in which a primary-care generalist can satisfy psychosocial needs of the patient, and of an interrelated group of patients. A significant recent development in this direction was the formation in 1971 of the American Academy of Family Physicians and the development of training opportunities for family practice in a number of medical schools and teaching hospitals.

While this new field of medicine has many features of a medical specialty, it is a "general specialty" and calls upon its practitioners for an integrative competence in all the specialty areas that meet the ordinary medical needs of families, specifically internal medicine, pediatrics, obstetrics, gynecology, psychiatry, and general surgery (Walsh, 1970). In dealing with an essentially healthy mother-infant pair, the family physician would give advice concerning everyday health care and feeding of the infant, and would do it with greater alertness to the mother's own needs than would a specialized pediatrician. If the infant is ill, then under this mandate the family physician can formulate his prescription and advice in the light of the total family situation more readily than can a specialist who focuses upon the sick infant or the disease process. In their training, family physicians are exposed to concepts of the family group as a psychological and emotional field for its members, family relationships as a source of both stress and support, and similar perspectives that emphasize inter-personal, behavioral, and psychosomatic aspects of illness (Worby, 1971).

It took the strenuous effort and organizational ability of a small group of physicians to found the American Board of Family Practice (in 1969) and the American Academy of Family Physicians in the face of indifference and hostility from some sectors of the medical profession, but with the growing support of influential segments of the public. Not long after the establishment of these bodies, several state legislatures took the unusual step of mandating family practice as a component in the curricula of state medical schools. The public desire for family practice is in part a reaction against the trend toward greater specialization and fragmentation in medical care. Keen public interest has buoyed the family medicine movement, but strong support from the ranks of established medicine is necessary for its long-term viability.

The findings of our study are suggestive as to the family physician's probable clientele. It will be slanted toward the working and lower classes and toward rurality in residence. Physicians as middle-class professionals tend to move into practice situations where they work with a compatible middle-class clientele unless—a very significant exception—they specialize, whereby the technical praxis of the specialty impersonalizes the doctor-patient relationship, transforming the patient into a case. Thus, a surgeon can practice his craft on a lower-class patient as well as a middle-class patient; the anatomy and pathology are the same.

While the implications of these tendencies for family medicine are not en-couraging, there are countervailing forces at work in medical education and in the movement of young physicians into fields of future practice. Pediatrics has in the decades since its establishment as a specialty field been a popular career option among physicians. We noted in a previous chapter that most pediatric practice revolves around the normal health and development problems of child-hood, rather than around serious diseases. The emergent field of family medicine will draw upon the same medical aspirations that draw physicians into pediatrics. Although the family physician is prepared to meet the medical needs of the total family at the level of primary care, the health supervision of the infant and mother constitute a substantial fraction of the total family needs.

Sabin Vaccination of Family Members

In the preceding chapter we focused upon Sabin polio vaccination of the infant as an important feature of its preventive health care. We found that most of the infants had received such vaccination, and that for the minority who had not, lack of vaccination was part of an inadequate health-care constellation. We wish to return to Sabin vaccination and to look at it here in relation to family roles and the family's social status.

Sociological investigations have sought to determine those demographic, socioeconomic, and social-psychological factors that influence this behavior. In a comprehensive review of this literature, Moody and Gray (1972) identify and categorize various factors positively associated with polio vaccination. In general, higher socioeconomic status predisposes toward vaccination. Sociopsychological influences, such as one's sense of vulnerability to the disease and the social approval one receives from others, have also been demonstrated to be important. A study by Tyroler (1965) and associates dealt explicitly with family roles in a sample of intact nuclear families with preschool children. They concluded that the mother's decision in favor of vaccination is influential in promoting the vaccination of other family members; however, in families of lower social status, low acceptance by the father leads to generally low levels of vaccination for other family members.

Table 7-8 presents findings from our study. Let us attend first to the proportion, by family-role category, of individuals who have been vaccinated. Of the 269 fathers present at the time of the interview, 195, or 72 percent, had received Sabin vaccine. Eighty percent of the mothers and infants had received vaccine. Among the 210 families where the infant had one or more siblings, 179, or 85 percent, had been vaccinated. More precisely, this figure means that in 85 percent of such families at least one of the siblings had been vaccinated (not that 85 percent of all the siblings had been vaccinated).

Let us turn to the social-class findings. Table 7-8 shows a class gradient which first becomes pronounced, moving downward, between Class III (90 percent) and Class IV (78 percent). In turn, Class V's overall vaccination level (62 percent) is substantially lower than that of Class IV. These percentages represent the extent to which the actual vaccination level in a class approaches the maximum possible level. They are based on the summed components across the four family-role categories—mother, father, infant, and siblings—in each class.

Having looked at the separate effect of social class and of family role, we now look at their interrelated effects. Table 7-9 presents a chi-square analysis of the figures in Table 7-8. It shows that the social-class variation within each family role, for percentage vaccinated, is statistically significant. The largest chi-square value occurs in the case of the fathers, whose variation is greatest, running from 96 percent vaccinated in Class I down to 41 percent in Class V. The overall variation by social class (combining all family roles) is likewise significant.

A second mode of analysis tests whether there is a significant variation according to family role within the same social class (and within all the social classes combined, that is, the entire sample). According to the concepts developed earlier, the family is a homogeneous unit in social status, residence, economic consumption, and other life chances. Under this conception, there

Table 7-8
Family Role, Social Class, and Sabin Vaccination

Social Class	Number and Percentage of Family Members Receiving Sabin Vaccination				
	Mother	Father	Siblings	Infant[d]	Total[e]
I	26/28 (93%)[a]	27/28 (96%)	22/22 (100%)	24/28 (86%)	99/106 (93%)
II	29/32 (91%)	30/32 (94%)	20/21 (95%)	29/32 (91%)	108/117 (92%)
III	57/64 (89%)	56/64 (88%)	37/40 (92%)	58/64 (91%)	208/232 (90%)
IV	61/75 (81%)	52/72 (72%)	50/63 (79%)	59/75 (79%)	222/285 (78%)
V	50/80 (62%)	30/73 (41%)	50/64 (78%)	53/80 (66%)	183/299 (62%)
Total	223/279 (80%)	195/269[b] (72%)	179/210[c] (85%)	223/279 (80%)	820/1,037 (79%)

[a]This means that there are 28 Class I mothers, of whom 26, or 93%, have been vaccinated.

[b]This total excludes ten fathers absent at time of the interview.

[c]This total includes all families where the infant at the time of its birth had an older sibling, plus two families where a new birth occurred between the birth of the study-infant and the interview.

[d]These findings on the infant also appear in Table 6-5.

[e]The numbers in this column are the sums of corresponding numbers across each row. Thus, 99 = 26 + 27 + 22 + 24, and 106 = 28 + 28 + 22 +28. The derived percentage represents the extent to which each class realized its summed potential opportunities for vaccination.

Table 7-9
Chi-Square Analysis of Table 7-8

Variables Analyzed	Chi² Value	Degrees of Freedom	Probability
Vaccination Percentage by Social Class, Combining all Family Roles	96.13	4	< .001
Percentage of Mothers Vaccinated, by Social Class	23.82	4	< .001
Percentage of Fathers Vaccinated, by Social Class	58.61	4	< .001
Percentage of Siblings Vaccinated, by Social Class	11.48	4	< .05
Percentage of Infants Vaccinated, by Social Class	16.82	4	< .01
Vaccination Percentage by Family Role, Combining All Social Classes	12.12	3	< .01
Vaccination Percentage by Family Role, Within Social Class I	4.66	3	⊀ .05
Vaccination Percentage by Family Role, Within Social Class II	.62	3	⊀ .05
Vaccination Percentage by Family Role, Within Social Class III	.76	3	⊀ .05
Vaccination Percentage by Family Role, Within Social Class IV	1.97	3	⊀ .05
Vaccination Percentage by Family Role, Within Social Class V	21.13	3	< .001

would be a strong trend also toward similar health behavior on the part of all family members. As a specific health behavior, polio vaccination affords a particularly valuable means of testing this idea because it is a uniform, convenient treatment, valuable for males and females of all age levels. These features of polio vaccination served to arouse the interest of sociological and public-health investigators, resulting in the numerous studies referred to above. With a rationale based upon a scientific conception of the disease menace and the benefit to be derived from the vaccine, the public-health authorities recommended mass immunization. If the values of a family resonated to the scientific rationale and public-health appeal, then the family as a whole would be immunized; if the family values were opposed or indifferent, then none of the members would be immunized.

This conception is tested in the second part of Table 7–9. The family-role analysis shows that there is in fact a statistically significant variation among family roles in percentage vaccinated within the total sample (chi-square = 12.12, D.F. = 3, $p<.01$). That is, the levels of vaccination, ranging from 85 percent for the siblings down to 72 percent for the fathers, vary more than random chance would allow. This defeats the hypothesis of family homogeneity. Looking within the separate social classes, however, it appears that there is no significant variation by family role within Classes I, II, III, and IV. Significant variation appears only within Class V (chi-square = 21.13, D.F. = 3, $p<.001$). The Class V variation is due to the low level for the fathers, 41 percent, and to the relatively high level for the siblings, 78 percent, both relative to the class norm of 62 percent. It is also notable that the only class with statistically significant intraclass variation (Class V) is that which has the lowest class norm. The higher levels of vaccination in Classes I, II, III, and IV impose a statistical curb upon the possibility of significant variation in these classes.

The generally low level of vaccination in Class V can be related to considerations advanced in Chapter 6 concerning the inadequate health-care constellation. The basic factor postulated there for the low level of vaccination was the social isolation of Class V in the community. What Table 7–8 reveals to supplement this conception is that within Class V, fathers are particularly notable for their nonparticipation in vaccination. In accounting for this, we suggest that the Class V father, in addition to participating in his class-characteristic social isolation, tends to have a traditionalized, hypermasculine self-image of toughness, and consequent disdain for preventive health care. Another expression of this concept was seen in Chapter 5, where it was found that the Class V fathers have the lowest score on the Father Participation Index. It appears that the Class V father is the most "different" family member in the most "different" social class.

8 Overview

The foregoing chapters have presented a good deal of information about contemporary infant care, health care, and family roles in a medium-sized urban community. While the community has its unique features and is located in a particular geographic region, we believe that many of the empirical findings could be duplicated, within broad limits, in other parts of the United States. Taking the study as a valid picture of certain aspects of contemporary society, we will develop an overview in this final chapter that embraces many salient topics and findings of the study. This chapter will also strike new ground by raising questions that build upon the data presentation and analysis of the earlier chapters. It will consider the interrelationship of components of the study which were previously dealt with perforce one by one.

This chapter is also concerned with social change. Chapter 1 showed that the main topics in this study refer to phenomena that are caught up in processes of change. The design and reporting of a household survey, conducted at one point in time, seems to belie this fact; such a survey seems to paint a static picture. Here we shall pick up the thread of social change and place the static picture into a more dynamic perspective.

This chapter is divided into three thematic sections: trends in family roles, race and social class in community context, and health services. The subject matter of each section has been dealt with previously at different points; for example, family roles were discussed in Chapter 5 in relation to the daily care of the infant, and again in Chapter 7 in connection with family health behavior. Here we will take a more consolidated view.

Trends in Family Roles

Let us recall several facts about the employment of mothers and about the participation of fathers in infant care. We found that 30 percent of the mothers were employed during their pregnancy. This figure is a composite of the 49 percent employment level for those mothers who had had no children prior to the infant reported in this study, and the 23 percent level found for mothers who already had one or more children. Following the birth of the infant, 20 percent of all the mothers were employed: 28 percent of the mothers for whom the infant was the only child, and 16 percent of the mothers who already had children. We also found that 86 percent of the fathers participated in routine

191

infant-care activities of feeding, changing diapers, or bathing. Only 14 percent failed to contribute any services in the specified categories.

These figures have strategic significance for family change. They signify pronounced deviations from the traditional concept of mother and father roles. The working wife, particularly the working mother of an infant, is taken by her employment into major responsibilities away from the household; her attention and concern are diverted from the care of her family. Under the most traditional view of the female role, it is presumed that the family will suffer if the mother's energy and attention are so diverted. There is a correlative viewpoint that the worlds of the professions, of commerce, of labor, all based upon objectivity and competition and alien to the intimate spirit of family and household, have little use for the service of married women. By the same token, the father has little to contribute by personal participation in the affairs of the household, and nowhere less than in the direct care of babies. Analogously, effort which he spends in that direction diverts him from his own "proper" concerns, namely his work and his furthering of the family's material welfare by activity in the outside world.

Our study has revealed a significant degree of departure by the mothers from the narrow confine of the traditional female role, and by the fathers from their own role tradition. What is revealed in this study and many other contemporary studies is not however simply a matter of deviation from settled norms, but a complex trend of normative change in family roles. The norms themselves are undergoing change, as well as the behavior that they regulate. The social scientist can far more easily objectify and quantify behavior than norms, particularly changing norms, yet the assessment of changing norms is an essential enterprise for the social scientist in his role as interpreter of social change. Even though processes of change are difficult to grasp and interpret, certain principles can lend a measure of comprehensibility to change.

One such principle is that societies and social behavior have a basic, inertial resistance to change. A corollary of this is that when change does occur, it is frequently masked, unacknowledged, or limited in its extent by being assimilated to preexisting, accepted patterns. To take a technological example, early automobiles were fabricated to resemble horse-drawn vehicles and were called "horseless carriages." It was thus possible for their users to feel that the new mode of transport had important similarities to what they were accustomed to. By such means the burden of psychological adjustment to novelty is cushioned.

Nevertheless, social change requires individual adjustment. Until new patterns are securely established, the individuals affected are thrown upon their personal resources. Such is obviously the case for those striking personalities who are the agents and originators of sociohistoric change. Pioneers such as Susan B. Anthony, in her work for women's suffrage, and Semmelweis, in his struggle against septic childbirth practices, pressed for reforms from the depth of their conviction and charter. In contrast, large social changes in family roles occur through widely distributed increments on the part of many independent originators who are family members. Social change of this kind is not wrought by the forceful drive of historic innovators, but personal resources come into play nonetheless.

The role of personal attitudes and meanings can be examined by reference to patterns of father participation in infant care and mother's employment outside the home. Since these patterns run counter to traditional norms and occur at the edge of significant social change, we expect that personal dispositions are significant. The patterns reveal features that would not occur if adherence to traditional norms were the main motivating element in the behavior. With these considerations in mind, let us consider the study findings, that the fathers helped more in infant care if the infant was a first infant than if it was a later infant.

While paternal involvement in infant care is probably increasing, this change is not firmly embodied in new social norms. There is no norm that requires fathers to participate more in the care of firstborn infants than of infants arriving subsequently in the family. In the absence of normative definition and pressure, we suggest that the following individual psychological factors play a part: Fathers may be more ego-involved in the firstborn infant than in later infants. The first infant establishes the family as a two-generation unit and marks the husband as a father; later infants do not confer this status upon the family. Maternal psychology also figures into the situation. Primapara mothers tend to be more uncertain of their maternal capability than multipara mothers. They seek or need help from their husbands, although with some hesitant ambivalence because meeting the challenge of total, competent mothering may lead a mother into a monopolistic, possessive bond with the infant. With a veteran's sense of competence, the multipara mother feels that the father's help is less needed in the care of a second infant; she may even reject it or divert it into other channels.

Thus, individual psychological factors stemming from both the father and mother may contribute to the father's special role in infant care. The arrival of the first infant is a unique event that constitutes a rite of passage for both parents. In terms of domestic responsibility, the transition from wife to wife-mother is greater than that from husband to husband-father. The new mother's behavior is guided by a repertoire of norms about the maternal role; however, although she learns her responsibility, the norms do not necessarily impart to her the conviction that she is personally adequate to all the infant's needs. The new father has still less of a repertoire to fall back upon. He may well feel an added responsibility for family support and he often increases his life-insurance coverage, but there are no norms that prescribe his role in direct infant care. Lacking this guidance but highly involved in family-building, he tends to participate considerably in the care of the first infant. In this labile situation, personal preferences and needs motivate behavior. New behavior is produced which expresses changing values about human relationships. Subsequently, with more children in the family, both the mother and the father settle down into the normative routine whereby the mother has a more exclusive role in infant care and the father has less involvement.

The importance of personal motivation in social change is also suggested by the pattern of employment exhibited by the mothers. Almost half the mothers in Classes I and II were employed before the baby arrived; none were subsequently employed. Among Class V mothers, only 19 percent were employed before the arrival of the baby; but following it, the percentage employed rose to 23 percent. The complete withdrawal from the labor force on the part of the Class I and II mothers can be explained by the conventional social norm about the mother's role. Similarly, that so many of the Class V mothers devoted themselves to household matters and that so few worked during pregnancy suggests that the force of conventional female-role norms was strong upon them. On the other hand, the higher level of Class I and II than of Class V employment during the pregnancy suggests that the Class I and II mothers had individual work needs, aspirations, and skills to a greater extent than the Class V mothers. Following the delivery, the picture is reversed: There was a modest increase in the proportion of Class V mothers employed, while no Class I or II mothers worked.

The behavior of the Class V mothers goes against the conventional social norm. It can best be explained by reference to the need for increased family income following the arrival of the infant. We infer that economic pressure led a number of Class V mothers to resume or to begin working; this is a form of individual motivation, though different in meaning from that which, we believe, caused many of the Class I mothers to work. The Class V mothers were apparently more attuned from the start to the traditional, nonwork role of the wife; neither pregnancy nor maternal responsibility following the delivery increased their employable skills nor their need for work as a means of personal expression or tension release. Thus the employment patterns of the Class V women and the Class I and II women can be interpreted as differential components of the general social trend toward greater female employment.

Another major family trend is what we shall call the "professionalization" of childbearing and parenthood. Our basic conception is that the decisions of couples regarding reproduction, the management of pregnancy, and the carrying out of parental responsibility are becoming increasingly intentional and increasingly knowledge-based. Under this trend, parents themselves become quasi-professionals who "practice" reproduction and parenting from a base of informed commitment. This in turn alters their relationship with established, helping professionals, away from the traditional expert-and-client mode and toward new modes.

It is instructive to think of the professionalization of childbearing and parenthood in relation to sociological concepts of profession. Sociologists have developed three distinct but interrelated answers to the question, What is a profession? In one meaning (closely in accord with the original etymological sense), a profession is a declaration of strong personal conviction for the individual so expressing himself: a dedication of self. The second meaning incorporates the first and adds the notion that a profession grounds itself on a body of cultural or scientific knowledge, and of committed practice based upon that knowledge. The third meaning builds upon the first two, adding that the members of a profession are corporately organized in relation to society. The first meaning embraces the original religious concept, profession of faith, but by extension can be applied to other goals of personal commitment. Among sociologists, Talcott Parsons has given special emphasis to the second definition in his theoretical analyses of social structure. Eliot Freidson has emphasized the third in his analysis of the medical profession and its guild-like, self-protective propensities. These three meanings reflect an analytic dissection of the phenomenon of profession, and also embody cumulative acquisitions and shifts of emphasis in meaning over several centuries of sociocultural change in our society.

Professionalized parenthood is coming now, we believe, to embrace the first meaning, that of commitment. Elements of the second meaning are expressed by the growing quest for knowledge and guidance to buttress parental commitment. Whether in the third sense of profession parents will ever constitute an interest bloc or an assertive, corporate social body remains to be seen. At the very least, the position of parents vis-à-vis traditional professionals such as teachers and physicians is being enhanced.

The concept of professionalized childbearing and parenthood is linked to changes in the reproductive aspirations of the public and in actual birthrates. In Chapter 4 we found that 38 percent of the mothers in the sample welcomed their pregnancy, while the remaining 62 percent had less positive attitudes. Our study agrees with national studies in finding that the amount of unwanted fertility is greatest among mothers of lower socioeconomic status. National studies show a decline in the number of children expected by married women; one study shows that during a six-year interval (1967-1973), the number of births expected per thousand wives declined from 2,852 to 2,262. The number of young wives expecting to bear *no* children during their marriage increased from approximately 1 percent to 4 percent, and the number expecting one child increased from approximately 5 percent to 9 percent. The crude birthrate during the same period decreased from 18 to 15.

In addition to contraception, abortion accounts for a sizable proportion of the decline in birthrates. Currently there are approximately 280 abortions for every 1,000 live births. Abortion is a more arduous procedure than the prevention of conception; it may be anticipated that as knowledge and availability of preventive techniques diffuse more widely in society, abortion will play a progressively smaller part. We suggest that abortion, precisely because it is an extreme tactic, signifies a woman's strong determination not to move forward into infant care and parental responsibility when the circumstances seem inappropriate or commitment is weak. In this sense, then, the growing availability of abortion underscores as much as contraception does the professionalization of parenthood. This is true whether abortion is so-called on demand, to accommodate the preference of the couple (or pregnant woman), or whether, as with a first trimester maternal rubella or a diagnosed defect in the embryo, there is "medical justification."

These several trends summate to the prospect of lowered reproduction rates. Along with related changes in sex roles, in family stability, and in housing, families will have fewer children. Improvements in contraceptive technique, discussed in Chapter 4, confer a greater measure of control and choice concerning reproduction. Although techniques for the restriction of conception have been practiced for centuries, their general unreliability has made pregnancy a continuous potential result of sexual intercourse. That significant segment of sexual behavior that is not oriented toward reproduction assumes more explicit importance as an independently valued activity. Beyond overt sexual behavior, the biological-cultural complex of meaning, motivation, and character present in sexual attitudes and feelings is achieving greater contemporary recognition under the rubric of "human sexuality." The isolation of reproduction as a major, manipulable element in the total complex of human sexuality also engenders a higher level of commitment to the parental role.

In Chapter 4 we discussed the dual nature of pregnancy as an experience that is in one respect a normal potential in the female life cycle, and in another respect a variant of the "sick" role. These are not radically dichotomous modes of pregnancy but they coexist only with a certain level of tension. If our hypothesis about professionalized childbearing is valid, we expect this duality to be further emphasized in the future. Commitment to childbearing and parental roles implies a high level of autonomous self-management, and a corresponding independence in the conduct of the related role activities. This position counters the reliance upon professional expertise that is implied in the traditional doctor-patient relationship. At the same time, commitment implies a strong motivation toward a successful outcome and, as a corollary, the application of those resources that maximize the probability of success. This alternative supports what has in fact become the preponderant pattern: reliance on a physician during the prenatal period and for the birth process.

In our earlier discussion of prenatal care and delivery, we stated that medical management to an increasing degree impinges upon these processes. It seems most unlikely that there will be any widespread reversal of this basic sociomedical trend. Nevertheless, we anticipate that changes within the structure of the doctor-patient relationship will allow greater scope for patient autonomy and preference. Many obstetricians and hospitals now give the mother a measure of choice concerning the degree of anesthesis to be induced during parturition. Some hospitals permit fathers to assist their wives during labor and to be present in the delivery room. These innovations find ready support in human and psychological considerations, but they can scarcely be justified by a sheerly medical rationale. Perhaps also more births will occur in homes under medical supervision, rather than in hospitals. This type of delivery at home will reflect the positive preference of the mother, not a lack of medical care or her disregard for it.

Beyond pregnancy and birth, it is to be expected that the popular interest in acquiring information on infant development and guidance on parenthood will continue, in intensified form. The two documents we singled out for attention, the government publication *Infant Care* and Dr. Spock's *Baby and Child Care*, are especially well-known, but there are many other books, pamphlets, newspaper advice columns, and radio and television productions that articulate and respond to the widespread interest. This trend is an important and distinct component within the general trend toward professionalized parenthood. The relationship of the general trend to existing specialized professional roles such as pediatricians is distinctly ambiguous. This ambiguity is suggested by such questions as what advice the pediatrician can give to the mother who seeks to know whether to breast-feed or bottle-feed the baby, how many months or years to continue breast-feeding, how many minutes to sterilize the bottles, and how quickly to respond to the baby's crying. If the professional founds his role upon the exposition and application of scientific knowledge, he will have little to say in response to such questions, for scientific knowledge does not provide definitive answers to them. Lacking a firm base in scientific knowledge, the professional in child care can nonetheless help parents, from a posture that guides rather than prescribes, to formulate their own experience in a way that bears upon the conduct of parental tasks.

We expect that the downward trend in the birthrate will be affected by a drastic reduction in the number of large families with four or more children, an increase in the number of two- and one-child families, and an increase in voluntarily childless marriages. A married couple who twenty years ago would have sought to bear five or six children is today more likely to aim for three or four; another couple who would have sought to bear three or four will in terms of current values be content with two. High fertility on the part of lower socioeconomic groups, which has for decades been a major component of the total birthrate, is on the wane; equally important, the three-child and four-child middle-class family is being supplanted by the one-child and two-child family at that class level. The change in family values does not, however, mean that families will bear children in proportion to their economic resources. Rather, we anticipate that the small family will become modal at all economic levels. Childbearing and child-rearing will become a more qualitative enterprise, professionalized on a mass basis and not specialized by economic level or social class.

We also expect that even if birthrates drop to a level that results in net population decline, much of the moderate pronatalist sentiment in our society will remain viable as a supportive supplement to the more committed sense of purpose in childbearing and child-rearing. Traditionally, couples had limited control over conception and they passively accepted the prospect of childbearing. Pronatal sentiment is woven into much public and social policy: tax advantages, employment policies, commercial advertising, and social pressure have all combined to favor family formation and a fairly high birthrate. Many of these incentives for family formation will persist even during a period of declining family size. If public policy were strongly oriented toward effecting a substantial decline in the birthrate, many disadvantages and encumbrances could be imposed upon the begetting of children. But the trend toward the professionalization of childbearing lies not in the realm of public policy but in the realm of individual and cultural values. Its thrust is not against the family as a social institution, but it is against the large family.

The findings of the study concerning family roles and activities suggest several changes which will be consequent upon the major shift in family size and values. A trend to smaller families means that first births will constitute a higher proportion of all births. Since primapara mothers are much more likely to be employed during pregnancy and to remain at work further into the pregnancy than multipara mothers, concurrent employment will become a more predominating feature of the pregnancy experience. Also, many of the role conflicts that working mothers face will persist, although there will continue to be marginal facilitations, such as somewhat greater flexibility of working hours and availability of employer- or community-provided day care. It seems unlikely, however, that public resources will be strongly committed to such support, any more than in the past. Professionalized childbearing will not lead to any significant transfer of role responsibility from the shoulders of the mother to external social supports. Our findings do, however, suggest that within the family, the father will play a larger role in infant care. When large families are predominant, the mother-infant tie becomes exclusive while the father tends to the older children or does not engage in child care at all. With the demise of the large family, we anticipate that the father as participant in infant care will become a more pronounced and consistent feature in family constellations.

Race and Social Class in Community Context

A perennial, melancholy significance is to be found in evidence that demonstrates the economic and social disadvantages that accrue to black persons and families. Although the broad pattern of black disadvantage cannot be questioned, much of the evidence comes from studies with methodological shortcomings. Many studies simply compare the life chances of an aggregate of blacks with those of an aggregate of whites, and do not compare blacks and whites in equivalent socioeconomic strata. It is well-known that blacks have lower average socioeconomic status than whites, yet controlled comparisons are the exception rather than the rule. The construction of the black-white matched comparison group in our study provides a basis for systematic comparisons across the racial line.

Our findings discerned a number of differences between black and white families on the same social-class level. The black-white differences in health care are particularly salient. Differences in the utilization of the three community hospitals emerged. However, the black families and their white counterparts tended to use the free services of the Baby Health Clinic in equal proportions. Likewise, neither the black families nor their white counterparts made much use of medical specialist services, whether for the infant or the mother. This is related to the low socioeconomic status of both racial groups, which implies less disposable income for expensive health services and a relative lack of health knowledge and health values that lead to the seeking of specialist services.

Striking racial differences appeared when we took into account the race of the physician as well as the patient. The essential findings were (a) there are very few black general physicians and no black medical specialists; (b) black patients, both mothers and infants, go to both black physicians and white physicians; and (c) no white patients use black physicians. The distribution of patients among physicians by race conforms to historic patterns of racial segregation in many American communities; these patterns are yielding gradually to ideals of equality that are also historic in our society.

Details of our findings on utilization of doctors by race testify further to the persistence of traditional racial patterns. Those black patients who use specialists necessarily go to white specialists; similarly, black students in pursuit of higher education, black businessmen in search of capital, and black political candidates for municipal or statewide office must break traditional restrictions and deal with predominantly white organizations, institutions, and communities. Examples occurred in the study sample of black families who used white family doctors instead of black family doctors. Is this an affirmative embracing of the wider society, or is it a lack of confidence on the part of these families in black doctors? Studies of race and ethnic relations show that a disadvantaged minority group frequently distrusts its own experts and leaders, as part of a pattern of self-rejection. In broader sociological terms, this may also be a part of a more general pattern of alienation of the minority group from the larger community and society. Such alienation expresses itself not only through low utilization of health services, but through low involvement in community activities, low motivation in employment and education, and in other ways.

If there is a gap between black patients and sources of health care, a gap appears likewise between the lower class and its sources of health care. There is a substantial overlap in the sample between the component of black families and the component of lower-class families. Two thirds of the black families are in Class V; black families comprise over one quarter of that class. In shifting the discussion to social class we have in mind, however, intrinsic aspects apart from race of the relationship of lower-class patients to health care institutions.

The major evidence of lacks in health care for the lower-class families appeared in the Chapter 6 discussion of the inadequate health-care constellation. This constellation indicated that Class V has more than its share of those health-care deficiencies that occurred in the total sample. Class V, the lower class, emerged repeatedly as the "most different" class in the study, but it is joined by Class IV, which is predominantly working-class, in the inadequate health-care constellation.

In accounting for the limitations and problems in health-care delivery that occur with working-class and lower-class patients, we may point to certain features in the functioning of health institutions and also to features of the working-class and lower-class subcultures. The health services most scrutinized in this study are in the nature of preventive care, for essentially normal babies and expectant women, rather than sick care. Preventive care, which occurs when one is well, is more closely linked than sick care to social class and subcultural values. Middle-class values such as scientific rationality, orientation to the future rather than the here-and-now, and confidence in the competence and goodwill of professionals tend to support the utilization of preventive services. Such values retain relevance even in the face of major illness, but in general a sick person of whatever social class is likely to make his way to some kind of professional help. Subcultural values take hold and exert a selective effect more strongly at the level of preventive or elective health care.

Patients come from all social ranks but health-care providers are, more homogeneously, middle-class persons, by virtue of their extensive formal education and occupational responsibility. Physicians in particular, who stand at the apex of the health-services system, are highly educated and affluent. Simply on the level of interpersonal communication, the lower-class or working-class patient is apt to falter in his dialogue with the upper-middle-class physician. Possibilities abound for miscommunication when the white, male obstetrician deals with the lower-class female, white or black. Another barrier of a quite different nature is posed by the fact that many health-care organizations and processes are fiercely bureaucratic. However difficult it may be for middle-class patients to traverse the application forms, the establishment of financial responsibility, the scheduling, and the waiting, it is probably still more difficult for those from the lower and working class.

Further barriers in the relationship between the lower-class or working-class patient and sources of health care lie in the situational factors of time and place. In the community we studied, the hospitals and most of the physicians' offices are located closer to middle-class residential areas than to lower-class and working-class areas. The Baby Health Clinic, heavily used by lower-class mothers, is located in an extremely inconvenient site for both public and private transportation. Also, hospital clinics and community agencies such as the Baby Health Clinic which are used mainly by lower-class and working-class patients are apt to have less flexibility in their weekly days and hours of service than are private-practice physicians, who are used predominantly by middle-class patients.

Some of these obstacles lie deep in the social structure and traditional attitudes of the community; others are more superficial and correspondingly more remediable. Health professionals who are committed to community health progress realize the central role of subcultural values in retarding progress, but have difficulty in locating points of leverage for change. The obstacles that lie in professional and institutional practice are probably in general more amenable to change than those that lie in the attitudes of patients and families. An administrator who is alert to the impact of his or her organization upon clients can at times eliminate oppressive routines with surprising ease. Intake procedures in clinics, for example, may become more detailed than is necessary for the assessment of the patient as a social and clinical being. The categories of information sought on application forms tend to expand mindlessly. Case conferences deliberate lengthily over decisions when the decision to be made is transparent in advance to all participants. Though these problems are inherent in the structure and routine of health organizations, they have significant external consequences. The detrimental consequences of overrefined practice, slowness in assessment of patient need, and complexity in provision of service fall selectively upon different client groups, being more adverse to lower-class clients.

Health Services

The interest of this study in health care is not confined to the deficits and difficulties that frequently mark the health care of socially disadvantaged families. The study has in a broader way been concerned with the articulation of the general needs for family health care and the resources for meeting those needs, within a community context that embraces a cross section of families and a variety of health-care resources. While most studies of health care are institutionally based and examine health care from the standpoint of the provider, this study has started directly from the standpoint of consumer, particularly the mother and infant within the family.

Health services at the community level are undergoing change under the impetus of powerful external forces which are gradually restructuring the health-care delivery system, the financial mechanisms for the payment of services, and health-professional education. We noted in Chapter 4 a large-scale, earlier change that is a highly significant and strategically symbolic shift in health care, namely the trend toward the use of the hospital and specialized medical services for childbirth. It substantially and directly affected health care in families and communities, though the forces that propelled the change were remote factors, such as the development of obstetrics as an organized specialty within medicine and professional realization of the greater medical protection that accrues to childbirth in hospital.

Changes of similar scope are at work currently. Federal Medicare legislation of the mid-1960s signals a direction in which health services are moving. Medicare owed nothing to biomedical innovation and nothing to the medical profession's imperative urge to establish specialties. As a means of financing health care for the elderly, Medicare may be attributed to rising public demand for medical services. Its beneficiary group is a population segment with great need for medical care and limited personal means for payment of bills. Of itself, the Medicare program did little to reshape health services or to augment the quality of health care received by the elderly, and it has been widely criticized for these lacks. But there is a distinct possibility that the health care of infants and mothers, as two discrete population segments, will in the future receive the same legislative recognition and fiscal support that Medicare now provides for the elderly. Whereas the primary rationale behind Medicare was simply the great need of the elderly for assured medical care, the rationale for federal fiscal underwriting of child and maternal health care will probably lie in the concept of sound investment to promote the health "capital" of the next generation of adults.

Looking at health care from the standpoint of consuming families inevitably magnifies the importance of consumer choice within a diversified range of health resources. We looked at how the mothers distributed themselves among the community hospitals for childbirth. We looked at the choices made for the infant's health care among various providers, and also at the mother's source of health care among a still wider array of providers. The survey of household medications revealed another significant facet of health care, substantially removed from the formal care rendered by organizations or professionals and for that very reason the more strongly reflective of health beliefs, values, and choices among the families studied.

The current ferment in health care revolves around measures to make health services more efficient, to lower costs, to make hospitals more flexible and accountable, and to develop higher levels of expertise and responsiveness among practicing professionals. Progress toward these goals will require far more scrutiny of health professionals than has occurred in the past. Equally, more attention needs to be paid to those natural behaviors that individuals and families exhibit in seeking their health care. This book takes a stride in that direction.

References

Aday, Lu Ann and Robert Eichhorn.
  1972   *The Utilization of Health Services: Indices and Correlates.* Washington, D.C.: U.S. Department of Health, Education and Welfare.
Andersen, Ronald and Odin W. Anderson.
  1967   *A Decade of Health Services.* Chicago: University of Chicago Press.
Aries, Philippe.
  1962   *Centuries of Childhood.* New York: Knopf.
Arms, Suzanne.
  1975   *Immaculate Deception: A New Look at Women and Childbirth in America.* New York: Bantam Books.
Bain, Katherine.
  1948   "The incidence of breast-feeding in hospitals in the United States." *Pediatrics* 2 (August): 313-20.
Balint, Michael.
  1960   *The Doctor, His Patient, and the Illness.* London: Pitman Medical Publishing Company.
Balint, Michael, Jone Hunt, Dick Joyce, Marshall Marinker, and Jasper Woodcock.
  1970   *Treatment or Diagnosis? A Study of Repeat Prescriptions in General Practice.* London: Tavistock Publications.
Banton, Michael.
  1967   *Race Relations.* New York: Basic Books.
Baxandall, Rosalyn.
  1975   "Who shall care for our children?" Pp. 88-102 in Jo Freeman (ed.), *Women: A Feminist Perspective.* Palo Alto, California: Mayfield.
Beecher, Henry.
  1961   "Surgery as a placebo." *Journal of American Medical Association* 176 (July 1): 1102-07.
Beels, C. Christian.
  1974   "Whatever happened to father?" *New York Times Magazine* (August 25).
Berg, Alan (with Robert J. Muscat).
  1973   *The Nutrition Factor: Its Role in National Development.* Washington, D.C.: The Brookings Institution.
Blake, Judith.
  1974   "The changing status of women in developed countries." *Scientific American* 231 (September): 136-47.
Blau, Francine D.
  1975   "Women in the labor force: an overview." Pp. 211-26 in Jo Freeman (ed.), *Women: A Feminist Perspective.* Palo Alto, California: Mayfield.

203

Boek, Walter, Alfred Yankauer, Edwin D. Lawson, and Minnie C. Wolcott.
    1958   "Medical and hospital care during pregnancy and early infancy."
            Pediatrics 22 (September): 538-47.

Bornemeier, Walter C.
    1970   "New concepts of medical education." Pp. 53-69 in Peter G.
            Condliffe and Arthur Furnia (eds.), *Reform of Medical Education.*
            Bethesda, Maryland: Fogarty International Center (National Institutes of Health).

Boston Women's Health Book Collective.
    1976   *Our Bodies, Ourselves.* 2nd ed. New York: Simon and Schuster.
            (Also 1st ed., 1973).

Bowers, John F.
    1977   *An Introduction to American Medicine.* Bethesda, Maryland:
            Fogarty International Center (National Institutes of Health).

Brenner, Charles.
    1973   *An Elementary Textbook of Psychoanalysis.* New York: International Universities Press.

Bumpass, Larry and Charles F. Westoff.
    1970   "The perfect 'contraceptive' population." *Science* 1969: 1177-82.

Caudill, William and David Plath.
    1966   "Who sleeps by whom? Parent-child involvement in urban Japanese
            families." *Psychiatry* 29: 344-66.

Caudill, William and Helen Weinstein.
    1969   "Maternal care and infant behavior in Japan and America." *Psychiatry* 32 (February): 12-43.

Caulfield, Ernest.
    1952   "Infant feeding in colonial America." *Journal of Pediatrics* 41
            (December): 673.

Coe, Rodney.
    1970   *Sociology of Medicine.* New York: McGraw-Hill.

Cohen, Gerda L.
    1964   *What's Wrong with Hospitals?* Middlesex, England: Penguin Books.

Committee on Ways and Means, U.S. House of Representatives.
    1974   *National Health Insurance Resource Book.* Washington, D.C.: U.S.
            Government Printing Office.

Davidson, William D.
    1953   "A brief history of infant feeding." *Journal of Pediatrics* 43 (July):
            74-87.

Donabedian, Avedis and Leonard S. Rosenfeld.
    1961   "Some factors influencing prenatal care." *New England Journal of
            Medicine* 258 (July 6): 1-6.

Ebert, Robert.
    1973   "The medical school." *Scientific American* 229 (September):
            139-48.

Elling, Ray H.
  1963   "The hospital support game in urban center." In E. Freidson (ed.), *The Hospital in Modern Society*. New York: Free Press of Glencoe.
Entralgo, P. Lain.
  1969   *Doctor and Patient*. London: World University Library.
Ford, Thomas.
  1964   *Health and Demography in Kentucky*. Lexington, Kentucky: University of Kentucky Press.
Frazer, J. G.
  1920   *The Golden Bough*. 3rd ed. London: MacMillan.
Freidson, Eliot.
  1970   *The Profession of Medicine*. New York: Dodd, Mead.
Freud, Sigmund.
  1962   *Civilization and Its Discontents*. New York: W. W. Norton.
Fuchs, Victor R.
  1974   *Who Shall Live?* New York: Basic Books.
Galbraith, John Kenneth.
  1973   "The economics of the American housewife." *Ms.* (August) 78-83.
Gallagher, Eugene B.
  1972   "The health enterprise in modern society." *Social Science and Medicine* 5 (October): 619-33.
  1976   "Consumerism and health care." Pp. 363-77, in Magdalena Sokolowska, Jacek Holowka, and Antonina Ostrowska (eds.), *Health, Medicine, Society*. Dordrecht-Holland: D. Reidel.
Gibbs, C. E., H. W. Martin, and M. Gutierrez.
  1974   "Patterns of reproductive health care among the poor of San Antonio, Texas." *American Journal of Public Health*, 64: 1 (January): 37-40.
Ginsburg, Benson E.
  1971   "Developmental behavioral genetics." Pp. 228-42 in Nathan Talbot, Jerome Kagan, and Leon Eisenberg (eds.), *Behavioral Science in Pediatric Medicine*. Philadelphia: W. B. Saunders.
Goode, William J.
  1971   "Family disorganization." Pp. 467-544 in Robert K. Merton and Robert Nisbet (eds.). *Contemporary Social Problems*. New York: Harcourt Brace Jovanovich.
Gough, Kathleen.
  1975   "The origin of the family." Pp. 43-63 in Jo Freeman (ed.), *Women: A Feminist Perspective*. Palo Alto, California: Mayfield.
Greene, James.
  1964   "Common-sense criteria for house calls." *Medical Economics* 41: Part 4 (October 5): 76-82.
Hannerz, Ulf.
  1969   "Roots of black manhood." *Trans-action* (October): 13-21.

Hines, Ralph.
    1972   "The health status of black Americans." Pp. 40-50 in E. Gartly Jaco (ed.), *Patients, Physicians, and Illness.* New York: Free Press of Glencoe.

Hirschman, Charles and James A. Sweet.
    1974   "Social background and breast-feeding among American mothers." *Social Biology* 21 (Spring): 39-57.

Hollingshead, August B.
    1957   *Two Factor Index of Social Position.* New Haven, Connecticut: Department of Sociology, Yale University.

Hollingshead, August and Fredrick C. Redlich.
    1958   *Social Class and Mental Illness.* New York: John Wiley & Sons.

Kahl, Joseph A. and James A. Davis.
    1955   "A comparison of indexes of socio-economic status." *American Sociological Review* 20 (June): 317-25.

Kane, Sidney H.
    1964   "The significance of prenatal care." *American Journal of Obstetrics and Gynecology* 24 (July): 66-72.

Kennedy, Stephen C.
    1967   "Prenatal care in selected low socio-economic areas of Lexington, Kentucky." Unpublished paper, Department of Community Medicine, University of Kentucky, Lexington, Kentucky.

Kiesler, Sara B.
    1977   "Post hoc justification of family size." *Sociometry* 40 (March): 59-67.

Kuznets, Simon.
    1962   *The Changing American Population.* New York: Arden House Conference.

LaDou, Joseph and James D. Likens.
    1977   *Medicine and Money: Physicians as Businessmen.* Cambridge, Massachusetts: Ballinger Publishing Company.

Lennard, Henry L., Leon J. Epstein, Arnold Bernstein, and Donald C. Ransom.
    1971   *Mystification and Drug Misuse.* New York: Harper and Row.

Lerner, Monroe and Odin W. Anderson.
    1963   *Health Progress in the United States, 1900-1960.* Chicago: University of Chicago Press.

Lieberson, Stanley.
    1958   "Ethnic groups and the practice of medicine." *American Sociological Review* 23 (October): 542-49.

Lyons, Richard D.
    1972   "Hospitals wary on charity care." *New York Times* (June 11): 36.

Maslansky, Ethel, Catherine Cowell, Ruth Carol, Sylvia N. Berman and Margaret
    1974   Grossi. "Survey of infant feeding practices." *American Journal of Public Health* 64 (August): 780-85.

McKinlay, John B.
    1972   "The sick role—illness and pregnancy." *Social Science and Medicine* 6 (October): 261-72.

Mead, Margaret and Niles Newton.
    1967   "Cultural patterning of perinatal behavior." Pp. 142-244 in Stephen Richardson and Alan Guttmacher (eds.), *Childbearing—Its Social and Psychological Aspects.* Baltimore: Williams and Wilkins.

Mechanic, David.
    1968   *Medical Sociology.* New York: Free Press of Glencoe.

Meyer, Herman F.
    1968   "Breast-feeding in the United States." *Clinical Pediatrics* 7 (December): 712-13.

Miller, Rita Seiden.
    1975   "The social construction and reconstruction of physiological events." Paper presented to Midwest Sociological Society (April). Chicago.

Minturn, Leigh and William Lambert.
    1964   *Mothers of Six Cultures.* New York: John Wiley & Sons.

Moody, Philip M. and Robert M. Gray.
    1972   "Social class, social integration, and the use of preventive health services." Pp. 250-61 in E. Gartly Jaco (ed.), *Patients, Physicians, and Illness.* New York: Free Press of Glencoe.

Moynihan, Daniel.
    1965   *The Negro Family: The Case for National Action.* Washington, D.C.: U.S. Department of Labor, Office of Policy Planning and Research.

Muller, Charlotte.
    1972   "The over-medicated society: forces in the marketplace for medical care." *Science* 176 (May 5): 488-92.

Myers, Jerome and Lee L. Bean.
    1968   *A Decade Later.* New York: John Wiley & Sons.

Myers, Jerome and Leslie Schaffer.
    1954   "Social stratification and psychiatric practice: A study of an outpatient clinic." *American Sociological Review* 19 (June): 307-10.

National Center for Health Statistics.
    1964   *Medical Care, Health Status, and Family Income.* Maryland: Health Service and Mental Health Administration.
    1966   *Hospital Discharges and Length of Stay: Short-Stay Hospitals, United States, July 1963-June 1964.* Maryland: Health Service and Mental Health Administration.
    1967   *International Comparison of Perinatal and Infant Mortality.* Maryland: Health Service and Mental Health Administration.
    1968   *Employment During Pregnancy.* Public Health Service Publication.

Newson, John and Elizabeth Newson.
   1963   *Infant Care in an Urban Community.* London: George Allen & Unwin.
Nye, F. Ivan and Lois Wladis Hoffman.
   1963   *The Employed Mother in America.* Chicago: Rand McNally.
Oleinick, Martha.
   1968   Study of child care practices and parental attitudes. Baltimore, unpublished.
Parsons, Talcott.
   1951   *The Social System.* Glencoe, Illinois: Free Press.
   1954   *Eassys in Sociological Theory.* Glencoe, Illinois: Free Press.
   1975   "The sick role and the role of the physician reconsidered." *The Milbank Memorial Fund Quarterly.* Summer 1975: 257-78.
Pediatrics Department, Chandler Medical Center.
   1977   "Mother's milk." Lexington, Kentucky.
Powles, John.
   1972   "Towards a theory of the medicine of industrial man." Centre for Social Research, University of Sussex, England, unpublished.
Pratt, Lois.
   1973   "The significance of the family in medication." *Journal of Comparative Family Studies* 4 (Spring): 13-35.
Reeder, Leo.
   1972   "The patient-client as a consumer: some observations on the changing professional-client relationship." *Journal of Health and Social Behavior* 13 (December): 406-11.
Registrar General-General Register Office.
   1960   *Classification of Occupations.* London: Her Majesty's Stationery Office.
Robertson, William.
   1961   "Breast-feeding practices: some implications of regional variations." *American Journal of Public Health* 51 (July): 1035-42.
Rosengren, William.
   1961   "Pregnancy as illness or normality." *Social Forces* 39 (March): 260-67.
Sarvis, Betty and Hyman Rodman.
   1974   *The Abortion Controversy.* 2nd ed. New York and London: Columbia University Press.
Saward, Ernest W.
   1973   "The organization of medical care." *Scientific American* 229 (September): 169-75.
Schade, George H.
   1962   *Pediatrics as a Career.* Evanston, Illinois: American Academy of Pediatrics.

Schonfield, Jacob, William M. Schmidt, and Leon Sternfeld.
    1962   "Variations in prenatal care and well-child supervision in a New England city." *Journal of Pediatrics* 61 (September): 430-37.
Slobody, Lawrence and Edward Wasserman.
    1968   *Survey of Clinical Pediatrics.* New York: McGraw-Hill.
Somers, Herman and Anne Somers.
    1961   *Doctors, Patients and Health Insurance.* Washington, D.C.: The Brookings Institution.
Spock, Benjamin.
    1961   "Should you expect your doctor to make a house call?" *Ladies Home Journal* (September): 24-28.
    1968   *Baby and Child Care.* New York: Pocket Books.
    1976   *Baby and Child Care.* New York: Pocket Books.
Stevens, Rosemary.
    1971   *American Medicine and the Public Interest.* New Haven: Yale University Press.
Sweetser, Dorrian Apple.
    1966   "The effect of industrialization on intergenerational solidarity." *Rural Sociology* 31 (June): 156-70.
Talbot, Nathan and Mary Howell.
    1971   "Social and behavioral causes and consequences of disease among children." Pp. 1-89 in Nathan Talbot, Jerome Kagan, and Leon Eisenberg (eds.), *Behavioral Science in Pediatric Medicine.* Philadelphia: W. B. Saunders.
Twaddle, Andrew C. and Richard M. Hessler.
    1977   *A Sociology of Health.* St. Louis: C. V. Mosby.
Tyroler, Herman A., Albert L. Johnson and John T. Fulton.
    1965   "Patterns of preventive health behavior in populations." *Journal of Health and Human Behavior* 6 (Fall): 128-40.
U.S. Census Bureau.
    1971   *Pocket Data Book—USA,* Washington, D.C.
U.S. Children's Bureau.
    1955   *Infant Care.* Washington, D.C.
    1963   *Infant Care.* Washington, D.C.
    1967   *Prenatal Care.* Washington, D.C.
    1972   *Infant Care.* Washington, D.C.
U.S. Department of Health, Education, and Welfare.
    1971   *Health Resources Statistics.* Washington, D.C.
    1974   *Health Resources Statistics.* Washington, D.C.
U.S. Department of Labor.
    1921   *Infant Care.* Care of Children Series, No. 2, Washington, D.C.
U.S. Public Health Service.
    1960   *Vital Statistics of the United States,* Vol. 1, National Vital Statistics Division. Washington, D.C.

U.S. Women's Bureau.
　　1972　*Maternity Benefit Provisions for Employed Women.* Bulletin 272. Washington, D.C.

Wade, Nicholas.
　　1974　"Adverse effects of a Western technology." *Science* 184: 45-48.

Walsh, John G.
　　1970　"New specialty—family practice." *Journal of the American Medical Association* 212 (May 18): 1191-95.

Wechsler, Henry.
　　1976　*Handbook of Medical Specialties.* New York: Human Sciences Press.

Weller, Jack.
　　1965　*Yesterday's People.* Lexington, Kentucky: University of Kentucky Press.

Wolfe, Samuel and Robin F. Badgley.
　　1972　"The family doctor." *The Milbank Memorial Fund Quarterly* 50 (April).

Worby, Cyril M.
　　1971　"The family life cycle: an orienting concept for the family practice specialist." *Journal of Medical Education* 46 (March): 198-203.

Yankauer, Alfred, Walter. E. Boek, Edwin D. Lawson, and Frances A. J. Ianni.
　　1958　"Social stratification and health practices in childbearing and child-rearing." *American Journal of Public Health* 48 (June): 732-41.

Yerby, Alonzo.
　　1977　"Black physicians and black communities." *American Journal of Public Health* 67 (June): 511-12.

Younger, Joan.
　　1960　"Our baby was born at home." *Ladies Home Journal* (January): 111.

Zimmerman, Jo Ann.
　　1975　"The social construction of reality in the hospital birth room." Paper presented to the Midwest Sociological Society (April). Chicago.

Index

Index

213

About the Author

Eugene B. Gallagher is a graduate of Lehigh University and received the M.A. and Ph.D. from Harvard University. Since 1962 he has been teaching at the University of Kentucky, where he is currently professor of behavioral science and sociology. In 1969-70 he was appointed visiting professor of mental health at the University of Bristol in England. In 1975-76, he was appointed visiting research professor at the Fogarty International Center, National Institutes of Health, Bethesda, Maryland. Dr. Gallagher has published articles on medical care, health economics, social psychiatry, and the applications of sociological theory to health phenomena. He is co-author (with Daniel J. Levinson) of *Patienthood in the Mental Hospital* and editor of *The Doctor-Patient Relationship in the Changing Health Scene.*